# Money and Violence

# Afrika-Studiecentrum Series



VOLUME 8

# Money and Violence

## Financial Self-Help Groups in a South African Township

*by*

Erik Bähre

BRILL

LEIDEN • BOSTON
2007

Photo front cover: Grandma Doris established a financial self-help group with her new neighbours and now it is her turn to receive the money. While the women stay for cool drink and biscuits, she considers using the money for roof alterations.

The picture was taken by the author.

This book is printed on acid-free paper.

A C.I.P. record for this book is available from the Library of Congress.

ISSN 1570-9310
ISBN-13: 978 90 04 15726 2
ISBN-10: 90 04 15726 3



PRINTED IN THE NETHERLANDS

# Contents

# Figures



# Photos

# Glossary

| | |
|---|---|
| *Abakhaya* (*um*) | 'Those of one home': Fellow migrants or 'home people' |
| *Amayeza* | Herbs |
| *Emaxhoseni* | 'The land of the Xhosa', roughly the Eastern Cape |
| Financial mutual | Collective informal financial arrangement, also known as financial self-help group |
| *Igqirha* | Diviner |
| *Igqwirha* | Witch |
| *Influx Control* | Discriminatory apartheid laws with the intention to restrict Africans in their movements, settlement and work |
| *Lobola* | Cattle given by the groom's family to the bride's family as bridewealth |
| *Stokvel* | Type of financial mutual, mostly ROSCA |
| *Spaza* | Small local informal shop that sells some food, cigarettes, etc |
| *Ubuntu* | Ideology of humanity |
| *Ubuthakati* | Witchcraft |
| *Ukutwala* | Kidnapping of the bride |
| *Umasingcwabane* | 'Let us bury each other': burial society, mostly with fund |
| *Umasiphekisane* | 'Let us cook together': burial society, mostly without fund |
| *Umasingcedane* | 'Let us help each other': burial society, mostly without fund |
| *Umgalelo* (*imi*) | From 'to pour' because money is 'poured' at meetings: ROSCA or ASCRA |
| *Umzi* (*imi*) | Homestead |

# Abbreviations

| | |
|---|---|
| ANC | African National Congress |
| ASCRA | Accumulating Savings and Credit Association |
| DPC | Development Planning Committee |
| NP | National Party |
| RDP | Reconstruction and Development Programme |
| ROSCA | Rotating Savings and Credit Association |
| SANCO | South African National Civics Organisation |
| UDM | United Democratic Movement |

# Acknowledgements

I have been in the privileged position that many people and institutions assisted me during the process of writing this book. The Amsterdam School for Social Science Research, where I did my PhD which eventually led to this book, was a pleasurable and sheltered working environment. The confidence that Abram de Swaan and Robert Ross showed in my research project was a tremendous support. Abram de Swaan particularly encouraged me to explore new avenues of thought. The importance of Robert Ross's gentle questions and suggestions, as well as his historical knowledge of the region, revealed itself mostly after our meetings during my walks back to the train station. I wish to express my gratitude to Bonno Thoden van Velzen for his continued involvement and encouragement. It was thanks to him that I did not leave out chapter three of this study.

At the Amsterdam School for Social Science Research, the many conversations that ensued during the coffee breaks and during lunches and seminars were of tremendous value. It was great to discuss research experiences, ideas, and inevitable frustrations with fellow researchers. I am grateful for the constant efforts made by Teun Bijvoet, Anneke Dammers, Annelies Dijkstra, José Komen, Miriam May, and Hans Sonneveld to maintain an inspiring environment.

The careful reading of some chapters by Birgit Meyer was of great help and encouraged me to fine-tune my arguments. The 'collective imagination' reading club initiated by Mattijs van de Port and Bonno Thoden van Velzen was an inspiring and joyous forum. Many chapters and ideas have been discussed in the 'mutual club' for which I wish to express my gratitude to Aspha Bijnaar, Abdoulaye Kane, Marcel van der Linden, Hotze Lont, Abram de Swaan, and Peer Smets. The presentations and debates at the 'Africa seminars' initiated by Peter Geschiere and Robert Ross made me aware of the specificity of my findings as well as of the similarities with other regions.

During my fieldwork in Cape Town, I was fortunate to be affiliated with the Department of Anthropology and Sociology at the University of the Western Cape. I am particularly indebted to Patrick McAllister, now at Canterbury University, New Zealand. I enjoyed our conversations about the research process and his knowledge of Xhosa society was of tremendous help. I took pleasure in the many talks with Yolisa Pikie and appreciated the way in which he combined fierce arguments with a liberating sense of humour. UMAC, particularly Sean Tait, was of tremendous help when it came to introducing me to the people of 'Indawo Yoxolo', and for their honest advice during the threatening episodes of the fieldwork.

I had the chance to teach and had plenty of time to write this thesis at the Department of Anthropology, Psychology and Social Work at the University of

Natal, Durban. During that year I had the opportunity to get to know South Africa more intimately. I wish to express my thanks to Jim Kiernan for sharing his tea and insights, particularly on trust and exclusion. It is with great pleasure that I recall the long and still ongoing conversations with Isak Niehaus on politics and power, for which I am very grateful.

I spent half a year writing at Sikko Visscher's dinner table. It made the writing easier and more fun. I wish to thank my colleagues at AMIDSt, particularly Ton Dietz for helping me to continue my research in South Africa and supporting me in the final adjustments to this book, and Puikang Chan and Marianne van Heelsbergen for their help with the layout of the manuscript.

I wish to thank Peter Zuithof for the many constructive debates on methodological issues. Giselinde Kuipers was an enormous help with her inspiring and valuable comments on numerous versions of the chapters. Our conversations on preliminary interpretations and academia in general were equally encouraging.

I am touched by the willingness of the Xhosa migrants in Cape Town, particularly in 'Indawo Yoxolo', to help me perform this study. I appreciate their courage to cross racial barriers, tolerate me, reveal details of their lives and share their inglorious thoughts and moments. In this study I have ensured that most are anonymous in order to minimise the risk of repercussions against them and because I do not wish to abuse their trust. Although anonymous, I sincerely hope that this study reveals certain aspects of their individual lives and daily concerns. Most of the people who took the time to answer my questions cannot read this book. However, in the future, it may prove to be an enjoyable way for one of their children or grandchildren to learn about their lives.

I cannot imagine how this research would have turned out if Edith Moyikwa had not assisted me and Vido Sam had not supported Edith so much. Edith's wit and loyalty, as well as her enthusiasm to reflect on her own society and life were a tremendous inspiration. I am honoured to still be able to work with her. The fieldwork experience has enriched my life tremendously and I largely owe this to her. Finally, I owe a great deal to my wife Esther Blom for her encouragement, company, and incredible support. I consider myself privileged that I was able to share my experiences, stories, and ideas with her. I feel very fortunate that we embarked on our South African adventures together, recently joined by our children Ruben and Nina. I could not have wished for a better friend. For this, and much more, I wish to thank my love.

# 1

# Introduction

## Questions

From the eighties onward, when apartheid was crumbling, more and more Africans migrated to Cape Town, South Africa. They did not leave their homes in the Eastern Cape because they liked the city like the many tourists who, not unlike the Dutch East India Company of the colonial past, enjoy its revitalising qualities. To the Xhosa migrants Cape Town was, and still is, a hostile city. People fear murder, rape, and theft. They do not know their neighbours and friends are scarce. They have no family there, either living or dead, and racist attitudes are ever present. The Xhosa migrants have only one motivation for plunging themselves into the unknown and hostile squatter camps of Cape Town and that is money.

This ethnography concerns the way in which Xhosa migrants in the townships of Cape Town collectively manage their money in financial self-help groups, also known as financial mutuals.[1] The migrants organise a myriad of groups in which the participants collectively save, borrow, lend, or use their hard-earned money to form insurances. Some mutuals consisted of only a few neighbours who met each month at a member's home, with each giving about R200 to the host member until all members had had a turn. Other mutuals were complex arrangements where members saved money together, mostly for Christmas, but also issued loans to each other. There were also many insurance arrangements involving up to a couple

---

1 These arrangements are also referred to as financial self-help organisations, rotating credit associations, rotating savings and credit associations, accumulating savings and credit associations, savings associations, as well as mutual benefit associations. As a generic term, I will refer to these arrangements as financial mutuals.

of hundred members that made sure that money was available to attend the funeral of a relative back home, or to prevent a burial in Cape Town itself. One could join a group voluntarily and the social constraint of fellow members would make sure that not all the money would be spent but would be used for the contribution to the financial mutual (cf. Ardener 1995: 7; Bijnaar 1998: 343-344; 2002: 104-110; De Swaan 1996b: 12; Rowlands 1995: 113-114).[2]

Financial mutuals were the first and often the only organisations that the migrants established. The squatter camps and new townships in Cape Town were virtually bereft of social and organised initiatives and there were no organisations to speak of in these new neighbourhoods. In Indawo Yoxolo – the main research site – it took years before the first soccer games were held. The churches were for the most part located elsewhere in the city and could therefore not play an important role in the neighbourhood. Politics were dangerous and therefore most people did not want to participate, not even at local level. Every ritual, such as funerals, initiations or ancestor worship, took place outside the city, back home in the Eastern Cape. Migrants therefore rarely organised rituals in the city. There were no alternative forms of organisation, such as participation in local politics, churches, soccer clubs, unions, or age groups. However, financial mutuals were an exception and they flourished in this social desert. The main concern of Xhosa migrants was money and it was around money that their social configurations crystallised.

In this book I approach financial mutuals as a social configuration. This allows a study of what has changed for the majority of Africans in a liberated post-apartheid South Africa, particularly regarding solidarity, trust, and consumption. Financial mutuals were particularly useful for acquiring an insight into the hopes and dreams, as well as the worries and anxieties, of poor Africans because these primarily have to do with money. After all, money was the reason for migrating to Cape Town *and* money was needed to maintain relations with kin back home. The image of migrants is often that of poor, destitute, and uprooted people. I also examine the flip side of that image and investigate what poor people do once they have some money. The migrants organised financial mutuals in order to influence the use of money, when it was used, and who could benefit from it.

For at least a century, social science has occupied itself with money and social relations. Simmel (1990 [1900]) foresaw that money, and the kind of transactions associated with money, would bring about impersonal relationships. He argued that money allows people to engage in distant and extensive exchange relations that cannot be as personal and intimate as exchange relations based on, for

---

2 The strategy to make it more difficult to spend money and easier to save has also been called the illiquidity preference (Bouman 1994a: 117; Lont 2000b; Shipton 1995: 257-259).

example, cattle or agricultural products which are not mitigated through money. This view was reflected in the approach to financial mutuals in the 1960s. Social change focused particularly on the transition from a peasant economy based on subsistence to that of a market economy. Social change, particularly that concerning the economy, was strongly embedded in modernization theory. Geertz (1962) stood at the heart of this debate and argued that financial mutuals were a 'middle rung' between the traditional and the modern world. According to Geertz and many others, financial mutuals would help people to adapt to a rational and modern society 'while at the same time minimizing the strain of transition and social transformation' (Geertz 1962: 259). Once the migrants had adapted to their modern milieu they would resort to modern financial institutions, such as banks, and financial mutuals were expected to disappear.[3] Very soon, however, studies such as the one by Meillasoux (1968) on migrants in Bamako, Mali, revealed some of the less adaptive aspects of financial mutuals. Moreover, financial mutuals do not disappear when people start using 'modern' financial institutions such as banks.

Towards the end of the 20th century social change was no longer conceptualised in terms of transition from traditional to modern, while distinctions between personal gifts and so-called 'rational' market exchange were no longer regarded as fruitful avenues of research on economic change. Current research focuses on the way in which money is locally embedded and how its meaning is socially constructed. Zelizer (1994), for example, revealed how people label money and treat money differently depending on its source, forms of expenditure, as well as the social constellation in which money operates. Bloch & Parry (1989) also argue against a distinction between gift exchange and market exchange, as well as between 'rational' and personal forms of exchange. Instead, they propose distinguishing between short-term cycles of exchange and long-term cycles of exchange. According to them, what is exchanged, whether money or other things, is irrelevant. What matters is the social constellation in which exchange occurs. Short term cycles of exchange are characterised by individual competition while long-term cycles of exchange reproduce the social order.

Research into economic change examines the constant reconfiguration of social relations and symbolic orientations under a capitalist economy. For example, Comaroff & Comaroff (1990) analysed the comparisons people make between cattle and money and the transference of a symbolic orientation towards cattle for building and maintaining social relations versus money with its completely different origin. Attention has shifted from inherent qualities of money to economic

---

[3] Ardener (1995 [1965]) focused on the origin and spread of financial mutuals across the world. See also Kerri (1976) and the discussions following his article on financial mutuals and modernization.

change that is part of globalisation and allows for new avenues of wealth, (political) prestige, social mobility, legitimacy, and identification. Economic change is set against the insecurity that is characteristic of recent globalisation (Comaroff & Comaroff 1993, 1999, 2000) or, according to Guyer (1999), of a long-term incorporation into the colonial economy. Moreover, renewed attention is directed towards financial mutuals in a transnational context, the maintenance of transnational networks, and identity (Bijnaar 2002; Kane 2001b; Van Wetering 1999).

Economic dynamics are furthermore embedded in a political analysis, either of local political systems exposed to new sources of wealth or of the economy of a (post) colonial state in Africa (Bähre 2005; Bayart 1993; Hutchinson 1996; Geschiere 1997; Wolf 1999: chapter three). Two distinct scholarly traditions can be identified concerning financial mutuals, namely one related to Europe that acknowledges politics and the state, and another one related to the developing world that surpasses these issues. Historical sociology studies the rise and demise of financial mutuals in Europe. It is, among others, concerned with collectivisation processes among workers and with how guilds, unions, and churches established mutuals that formed the foundation of the current welfare state. These European workers' mutuals disappeared due to the emergence of a social security system that, because it was part of the state, did not suffer from the kind of problems that are characteristic of collectivisation processes (some examples are De Swaan 1996a; Van der Linden & Sluijs 1996; Van der Linden 1996). Putnam's (1993) study of financial mutuals and other civic organisations in Italy has become particularly prominent. He argues that these organisations generated social capital, which in turn created the conditions for effective, responsive, and representative institutions. In sharp contrast to the studies on the state and the economy in Africa, research on European mutuals reveals more confidence in the state being able to take over, or build on, the social security provided through financial mutuals.

There is a fast growing area of research on financial mutuals in developing countries that does not take much account of political processes. If it does, for example by drawing on Putnam's (1993) idea of social capital, it paints a very harmonious picture. During the last decade, interest has been revived in the use of financial mutuals for development purposes. The contribution of financial mutuals to social security and poverty alleviation have been examined (Bouman 1978; Bouman & Hospes 1994; Adams & Fitchet 1992; Hospes 1997; Smets 2000, 2002; Lont 2000b, 2002; Lont & Hospes 2004; Kane 2001a, 2001b). The empowerment of women through financial mutuals has been given particular attention (Ardener & Burman 1995; Lont 2000a; Ross 1990). Apart from research, there has been a sharp increase in development policies and projects that aim at copying financial mutuals. Microfinance is a major development topic and 2005 was declared the United Nations Year of Microfinance. In the debates and policies on financial mutuals and microfinance for poverty alleviation, little attention is paid to conflict and political processes. This is surprising, particularly in the case of Africa, as historical, anthropological, and political studies on economic change in Africa highlight conflict and political dynamics. Political issues, particularly state formation, have also been central to the historical studies of financial mutuals in Europe.

Are financial mutuals in South Africa affected by, or part of, political processes? How are they affected by conflict, how does conflict feature within financial mutuals? Or are financial mutuals able to shield themselves from the many conflicts that are characteristic of South Africa? Are there any links between state formation – in South Africa characterised by the end of apartheid – and financial mutuals? As will become apparent in this book, conflict and politics are crucial to the functioning of financial mutuals, the way in which solidarity is shaped, the way in which people trust each other, and the way in which the money generated through financial mutuals is spent. Furthermore, it will become clear that the state also matters to these informal, often small scale, financial mutuals. Financial mutuals cannot be studied in isolation from apartheid policy, nor in isolation from post-apartheid development projects. It will become clear that an approach to financial mutuals which is depoliticised and does not take account of conflict, and which unfortunately is at the heart of the microfinance movement, is unwarranted.

For Xhosa migrants living in the 'threatening triad' of economic insecurity, violence, and volatile social relations, the conditions for entrusting money to each other in newly established financial mutuals were unfavourable. There was immense economic insecurity. Unemployment was so high that it was extremely difficult to manage a household and take care of children. There was the constant threat of physical dangers of domestic and political violence, as well as of the rapid spread of AIDS. Moreover, relationships with kin, neighbours, home-people (migrants from one area in the Eastern Cape), colleagues at work, between men and women, as well as towards Whites and Coloureds were volatile and often threatened. Often it was money, more precisely the lack of it, which complicated social relations. Notwithstanding the fact that it is quite common for migrants to establish financial mutuals in a hostile environment, it is fascinating that people who hardly know each other, who live in extremely vulnerable conditions, entrust each other with up to half their monthly salary. Financial mutuals emerged rapidly while other forms of organisations, such as churches, soccer clubs, choirs, failed to get off the ground or took much longer to become established. This raises questions such as: Why do people organise financial mutuals under such threatening circumstances? How do they manage to do so under such unfavourable conditions? This ethnography reveals how people's financial situations were constantly changing and why this made them largely dependent on others. People made strong financial claims on each other or tried their best to circumvent such claims. This book reveals how financial mutuals were at the crossroads of the manipulation of flows of money, and were therefore pivotal to the migrants' responsibilities and obligations towards others. There was never enough money since wages were low and job insecurity high, but through financial mutuals the migrants tried to influence the flows and uses of money. Financial mutuals allow us to grasp the nexus of money and social interdependencies within an extremely threatening context.

By studying financial mutuals and posing questions about the way they are organised, how participants are selected, who is trusted, and how the money is spent, it became clear how money dominated the lives and relations of Xhosa migrants living in Cape Town. Flows of money and the way such flows are influenced through social control in financial mutuals disclosed new and changing interdependencies. Financial mutuals reveal contestations, identifications, solidarities and interdependencies rooted in the particular use of money. For Xhosa migrants, financial mutuals are a new sphere of exchange, a new social arena in which the object of desire circulates among people one barely knows. Money remains hidden most of the time, which complicates the study of the nexus of money and social relations. However, in the context of financial mutuals, money temporarily comes to the fore, just like the relations that participants challenge, build, or relegate.

## Politics

This study, the choice of topic, the methodology, as well as the interpretation of financial mutuals, was possible because of the political changes that took place in South Africa since the 1980s. Apartheid had severely restricted research possibilities and had a tremendous impact on the agenda of anthropologists working in South Africa.[4] For example, anthropologists were not permitted to stay overnight in the area of their fieldwork and the government tried to control research by issuing research permits to approved projects only. It was also dangerous to discuss political issues, especially for informants. Wilson & Mafeje (1963), who wrote one of the few ethnographies on the lives of Africans in Cape Town, were confronted with the impossibility of carrying out research on political issues. At the time of their research, the two major African political organisations, the Pan African Congress (PAC) and the African National Congress (ANC), were banned.

---

[4] See Gordon & Spiegel (1993: 86-88), Hammond-Tooke (1997), James (1997: 128-129), Kuper (1995), and Scheper-Hughes (1995: 414-415) on anthropology's predicament during apartheid.

The police had also imprisoned two journalists because they refused to disclose the sources of their information. Wilson & Mafeje (1963: 11-12) were faced with these problems and therefore explicitly decided to write an apolitical ethnography in an era of great political turmoil.

Although the explicit avoidance of political issues was problematic, it was even more difficult to neglect these implicitly and define social life through an apolitical understanding of culture as was often done by the Afrikaner *volkekunde* – best translated as 'folk studies' (Hammond-Tooke 1997; Gordon and Spiegel 1993: 86-88). Critical anthropology rejected this apolitical concept of culture that served apartheid ideology so well. At the core of critical anthropology was a political interpretation of cultural practices which, in turn, meant that cultural practices that did not have a political dimension were easily ignored. James (1999a, 1999b), for example, found that researchers were hesitant to study migrant associations during the apartheid era. Researchers were worried that their findings on migrant associations would confirm apartheid notions of culture (James 1999b, 24):

> This reluctance to investigate home-based associations was particularly strong among anthropologists, due perhaps to their awareness that there was a disturbing similarity between the definitive cultural features stressed by their forebears and the concept of ethnic uniqueness which was used to justify the depredations of apartheid.

Instead of ignoring apolitical organisations based on an awareness that anthropological studies could be used to support apartheid ideology, there was also the danger of overstating the political character of organisations. It may, for example, be the case that Comaroff's inspiring ethnography on the Zion churches of the Tshidi was influenced by the tacit political circumstances of research during apartheid. According to Comaroff, the church should be interpreted as a form of resistance against apartheid through the alteration of Christian symbols. Schoffeleers (1988) argues that the political dimension of these churches was overemphasised. In his view, Zion churches were politically conservative, while the causes of suffering were dealt with at an individual level with an emphasis on healing. The macro-political and structural causes of suffering were generally ignored.[5]

Post-apartheid anthropological research is not burdened as much with the need to adopt a position vis-à-vis the state. It has become more feasible to study organisations that do not have an explicit political agenda, such as financial mutuals, and relate these to the large-scale political transformation. Furthermore, the end of apartheid meant that foreign researchers no longer risked being branded collaborators of apartheid, and this opened up new avenues for research. Thus, the political transformation allowed a study of 'invisible' financial mutuals organised by destitute, marginal, and 'invisible' African migrants.

---

[5] See also James (1999a: 69-70; 1999b: 23-24) who found that critical anthropologists were more open to study political processes, particularly class formation.

Contrary to political processes in South Africa that tended to oversee financial mutuals, the politics of development has recently paid a lot of attention to financial mutuals. The success of the Grameen Bank in Bangladesh appears to be at the heart of a strong belief in the mobilisation of community relations for a market oriented approach to poverty.[6] Recently, the belief in community and solidarity culminated in the declaration of the Year of Microfinance, 2005: 'The Year's overarching goal is to provide greater access to credit, savings, insurance, transfer remittances and other financial services for poor and low-income households in order to move towards more secure livelihoods and prosperous futures.'[7] Financial mutuals are crucial to this approach. According to the UN as well as the World Bank, trust, solidarity, norms, and social cohesion should contribute to 'sustainable social and economic development'.[8] These elements should, of course, also ensure that the poor repay the money to the financial institutions, although this is not given a prominent place on the agenda. The poor being poor lack conventional collateral such as jobs and property that financial institutions usually demand.

The recent 'discovery' of financial mutuals by development organisations, however, is accompanied by over-simplistic ideas about community dynamics, such as trust, solidarity and managing one's money under hostile conditions. Moreover, little attention is paid to the political context in which financial mutuals are organised and whether these political circumstances are at all relevant to the way in which poor people manage their money.

This book will show how vital large-scale political transformations were, and still are, for the establishment and use of financial mutuals. It reveals how financial mutuals were migrants' attempts to hide from politics and instead hope for a better future based on strong relations, plenty of money and self-worth. This ethnography reveals how financial mutuals were islands of hope for Xhosa migrants surrounded by a sea of insecurity, unemployment, murder, rape and social conflict. Migrants de-politicised their financial mutuals and created a place where they could feel secure and trusted and where money was in their control. The study of financial mutuals thus reveals the horrors from which people tried to escape, as well as their dreams for the future.

---

6 See Rahman (1999) for a critical analysis.

7 Press Release 18 November 2004, DEV/2492 OBV/452 'UN Launches international year of microcredit 2005' online on http://www.un.org/News/Press/docs/2004/dev2492.doc.htm

8 Cited from the World Bank website 'Social Capital' dated 12 september 2005, http://web.worldbank.org/WEBSITE/EXTERNAL/TOPICS/EXTSOCIALDEVELOPMENT/EXTTSOCIALCAPITAL/0,,menuPK:401021~pagePK: 149018~piPK: 149093~theSitePK:401015,00.html

As so often when people try to improve their lives, financial mutuals were not always what they promised to be. This study goes beyond the rhetoric of solidarity, mutual help and companionship. Just as important for insight into the migrants' lives were the conflicts within financial mutuals, among neighbours, among kin, and so on. The financial mutual was not only an island of hope, but also an arena of ambivalence. The money was insufficient to help everyone all the time, and trust was often an issue. Participants, moreover, used the financial mutuals to accumulate money and this highlighted inequality and could lead to jealousy among fellow members, neighbours and kin. As migrants used financial mutuals to solve some of their economic and social problems, they simultaneously created new ones. These dynamic interdependencies of migrants, and particularly those related to financial mutuals, are at the core of this study.

## Financial mutuals in brief

'Financial mutual' is an umbrella term for a myriad of collective financial arrangements that are mostly informal. In South Africa, financial mutuals were, and still are, known locally as *umgalelo*, *stokvel*, *savings*, *gooi-gooi*, *throw-throw*, *back-to-school*, *umasingcwabane*, *umasiphekisane*, and *umasingcedane*. Although financial mutuals are very popular, their informal and 'apolitical' nature made it difficult to know much about the history and the number of participants. Some estimate that there were about 150,000 *stokvels* with an annual turnover of R1.6 billion a year, while other sources mention almost ten million people participating in 800,000 *stokvels* with an annual turnover of R2.4 billion a year. Yet more research, carried out in 1991, came up with other results: about 1,344,000 people participated in *stokvels* in the metropolitan area alone. This was just over a quarter of the African urban population and the annual turnover of their *stokvels* was estimated at just over R1 billion a year. The different findings could be due to a difference in research periods, research techniques, research area, or an unclear definition of the type of financial mutuals that were studied.[9] Moreover, people do not always want to reveal their financial situations. What did become clear, however, was that financial mutuals were very common and that many Africans entrusted a substantial part of their meagre income to financial mutuals.

### *Burial societies*

Burial societies were very popular. A funeral could easily cost R5,000 or more. For a cleaner, employed full-time in the formal sector, this is approximately six months' wages. People spent so much on funerals because they regarded it as very

---

[9] See Hashatse (1992: 36-37) and McGregor (1989: 126) on these findings.

important to be buried back home in Emaxhoseni, the land of the Xhosa, an area roughly comprised of the former homelands Ciskei and Transkei. In order to have such a large sum of money available, the migrants organised burial societies. The burial society provided money, food, goods, and mutual assistance to a deceased member, or to his or her dependants.[10]

As long as Africans lived close to home, close-living relatives and well-known neighbours could assist the bereaved and make sure that the person was buried properly. When in the second half of the 19th century large amounts of gold and diamonds were found, many Africans migrated to work as labourers and had to leave their families behind due to racial segregation laws. The migration process therefore meant that many Africans were separated from their land and families (Carter 1986: 345-347; Masuko 1995; Omer-Cooper 1994: 103; Vail 1989: 8-9). The migrants formed burial societies as a collective strategy to bring back the bodies of the deceased. The emergence of burial societies, therefore, was a result of labour migration.

There were two types of burial societies: burial societies with a fund and burial societies without a fund. This distinction led to all kinds of differences as regards size, membership criteria, method of payment and forms of assistance. The burial societies that did not have a fund were mostly referred to as *umasiphekisane* ('let's cook') or *umasingcedane* ('let's help').

The members of the *umasiphekisane* and the *umasingcedane* were always female neighbours and the activities of these burial societies were regarded as women's responsibilities, which were sometimes laid out in terms of cooking. When I asked one of the founders of a *umasiphekisane* why there were no men, she replied: 'What do men know about cooking?' which made the other women laugh. The name of the organisation reflects the focus on cooking, a skill most men did not have, or were not acknowledged to have, and which women were supposed to have, even if they could not cook.[11] When someone in the neighbourhood died, the women would collect money, such as R10, from each household and give the money to the grieving family. The women would also help to organise wakes, make tea, support the bereaved emotionally, or form a choir for the funeral ceremony.

Burial societies that did have a fund were mostly referred to as *umasingcwabane* (plural *oomasingcwabane*), which meant 'let's bury each

---

[10] In the next chapter, I show how burial societies were intertwined with the migratory process. Here I limit myself to an introduction of the types of societies that existed and how they were established. During the research I collected information on 26 different burial societies operating in Cape Town.

[11] On another occasion I was able to join an *umasiphekisane* because neighbours had heard from my research assistant that I could cook.

other'.[12] It was common for these burial societies to have a proper name that referred to ideological aspects of the organisation or the people that participated in it. An example of the former was Mbuthowamangwane, a burial society exclusively for members of the Mangwane clan. Winterberg Funeral Club derived its name from the fact that the founders were all migrants who originated from the vicinity of Winterberg in the Eastern Cape. Other proper names highlighted the ideological dimension of the organisation, such as Masibambane ('let's hold each other'), Masekoduke ('let's go home') and Lukhanyiso ('a bright place' or 'something bright').

The members of most burial societies with a fund were migrants from particular regions in the former homelands of Ciskei and Transkei. Migrants identified with fellow migrants from the same region in the Eastern Cape and called them *abakhaya* (sing. *Umkhaya*).[13] *Umkhaya* literally meant 'the one from the same house' or home-people. As will become clear in the next chapter, especially under apartheid, migrants in Cape Town had to live in hostels where they formed their own social networks and organisations around their home area. These *abakhaya* burial societies admitted men and unmarried women from that region. Married women were refused because a wife was considered to belong to the home of her husband. If she wanted to join an *abakhaya* burial society, she could only join one from her own region.

The burial societies that consisted of *abakhaya* had, for example, only members from Tsolo, a district in the former Transkei, or only from Ladyfrere, Cala, East London, Encobo, or Qobo Qobo. The definitions of who was *abakhaya* and who was not were fairly flexible. For example, Masibonisane ('let's show each other') only accepted people from the Ciskei and excluded people from the Transkei.[14] Xhosa migrants could not always choose a burial society. Many burial societies were only open to *abakhaya* or neighbours.

Burial societies were very flexible in that the members themselves could decide on the rules for joining, the fees to be paid, and the type of benefits for members and their dependents. If members expressed concern about the regulations at a meeting they could also decide to change them, for example to increase the monthly fee a little if too many beneficiaries had died. The burial societies that I encountered had an average of 550 members that contributed about R20 per month. This money was put into a bank account. Sometimes the same amount of money was collected for each particular funeral. If a member died, the burial

---

12 In rare cases this also referred to burial societies without a fund, but in most cases the term *umasingcwabane* was automatically associated with a burial society with a fund.

13 See also James (1999a, 1999b) on dancing and singing groups among female Tswana migrants.

14 The notion of *abakhaya* is discussed in greater detail in the next chapter.

society, under the guidance of a committee, arranged a coffin, the transport of the deceased to the Eastern Cape, and transport for the family members and members of the burial society. They would also give money, on average R3250, to the berieved family. They would provide similar services – although the cash contribution would be lower – if a member's dependant died. Depending on the burial society this might be a parent, a grandparent, a child, or someone else living in the household.

*Imigalelo and other ROSCAs*

The term *umgalelo* (pl. *imigalelo*) is derived from the verb *ukugalela*, which means 'to pour' because the participants, as it were, poured money at the meetings.[15] *Imigalelo* can be classified as Rotating Savings and Credit Associations or ROSCAs:

> In the ROSCA, each time that savings are pooled, they are immediately redistributed among members in rotation, until each has had his turn and the ROSCA comes to an end (Bouman 1994b: 376).

On a monthly, weekly, or daily basis, the members contributed money or presents to the kitty and gave the kitty to the first member. In some ROSCAs, the recipient also had to contribute when it was his or her own turn. Money was collected again during the next meeting and it was then the second participant's turn to receive the kitty, and so on until everybody had had a turn. If the participants were satisfied with the arrangement, they could decide to start another cycle, possibly with a few new participants or different contributions.[16]

---

15 Sometimes they were also referred to as *stokvels*. The term *stokvel*, however, seemed to be more popular in the Transvaal. In Cape Town, only a particular type of *umgalelo* is sometimes called *stokvel*, i.e. when the money is spent on the organisation of a profit making party.

16 These organisations are often referred to as *stokvel*. Some have pointed out that the term *stokvel* was derived from the 19th-century English Eastern Cape stock fairs where cattle was auctioned (Buijs & Atherfold 1995: 6; Hashatse 1992: 126; Lukhele 1990: 4). According to Thomas, the term was derived from '[a] group of men who would pool their money to buy a head of cattle at a stockfair' (Thomas 1991: 292). I did not come across historical records that supported this. It could also be that ROSCAs were an adaptation of work parties where neighbouring farmers worked on each other's fields, especially during the harvest season. Another possibility is that ROSCAs were spread in South Africa via Indian migrants with similar financial arrangements, such as the chit or bishi. But all these options are pure speculation. For more material on ROSCAs in South Africa, see Burman & Lembete (1995), Hellmann (1934), Kokoali (1986), Kuper & Kaplan (1944, 180-181), Mayer & Mayer (1974, 141), Molefe (1996), Moodley (1995), Phillips (1977 [1937], 293-294), Ross (1990), Verhoef (2001), Wilson & Mafeje (1963: 132-136).

The number of ROSCA participants varied from two to a few hundred. It was most common, however, to have a different group of ten members that met each month. Such a rotation system started at the beginning of the year with everybody having had a turn towards the end of the year, ten months later. People often started the rotation again and most ROSCAs existed for a few years with alterations to the rules and participants. However, there were also exceptions. In Langa, for example, residents founded Masakhane in the 1950s and it was still going in the 1990s (Bähre 1996: 22-24).

On average, the participants contributed R200 to a monthly ROSCA and R60 to a weekly ROSCA. There were also ROSCAs with much higher contributions, like a 'BMW 518 Stokvel' where 50 members each contributed R1,000 per fortnight. The members each received R50,000 in turn and purchased a BMW 518 (Webb 1989: 27). This ROSCA was an exception that indicates that ROSCAs were not only for the poorest of people. Most Africans, however, could hardly dream of owning a car. Some ROSCAs also exchanged goods instead of money, such as bottles of brandy or other presents.

The participants would discus who would get which turn. Some members expected to need cash at a particular time of the year and preferred a certain month. If several participants wanted the same turn, and that was often the first turn, the turn was allocated more or less according to seniority. The oldest member, who was often also the organiser, could choose.[17] Once the ROSCA had already started, it was also possible to exchange turns with the consent of the other members.

The ROSCA members mostly met at the recipient's home, and sometimes at the workplace. Large ROSCAs had to arrange a classroom or church building because not everyone would fit into the small shack of one their fellow members.[18] Some ROSCAs had very short meetings where the members rushed in and out, often handing over envelopes with the contributions from absentees. Some members felt that the meetings were a waste of time and were notorious for their absenteeism. Other ROSCAs turned their meetings into long and elaborate social events. They started with a prayer to 'open the organisation' and the women would stay afterwards to drink tea or lemonade and talk about organisational matters, gossip about neighbours, and express their worries about family issues. Contrary to what Hellman (1934) encountered in the past, the participants would not drink alcohol. The belief was that financial matters were too serious and should not be

---

17 Contrary to the findings of Buijs & Atherfold (1995: 42), women often preferred to have the first turn of the ROSCA.

18 Only one *umgalelo* had no meetings. It consisted of three members who worked for different companies. They used to meet during their lunch breaks but, due to a rescheduling of their timetables, they could not meet each other anymore. Instead of meeting, they brought the money to the recipient or let someone bring it for them.

mixed with alcohol. In the rare instances that I saw a member drinking alcohol, it was done more or less secretly because the other members objected.

Most ROSCA money was spent on consumer items, such as a refrigerator, radio, iron, television, or other 'clothing for the house', as furniture was sometimes referred to. Some also used it to pay their debts or pay for parties and initiation ceremonies.

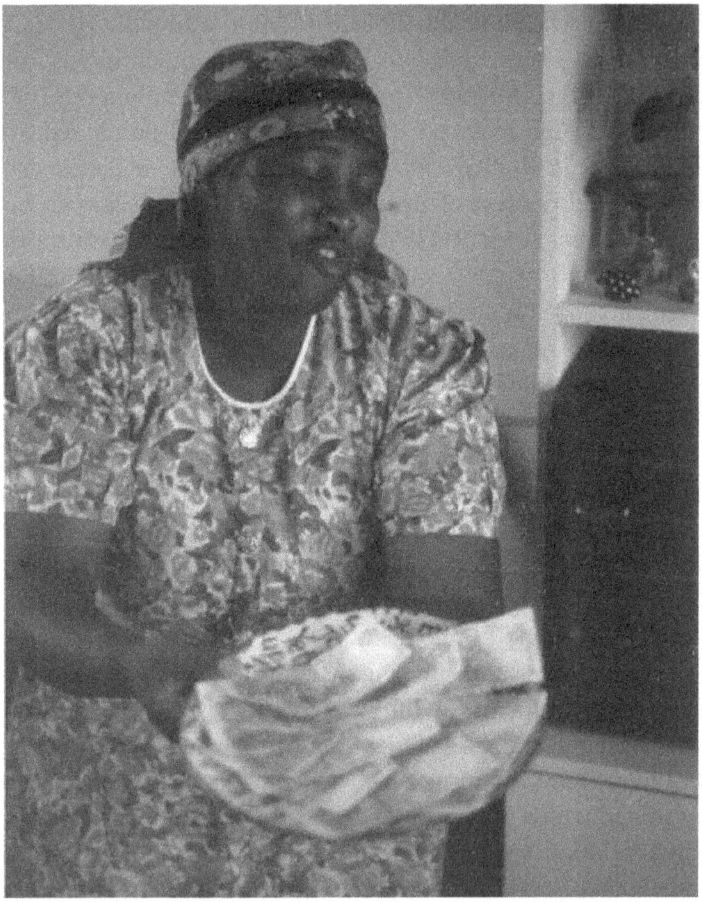

*Photo 1.1* The money collected by *umgalelo* members

*Grocery Clubs and other ASCRAs*

Christmas was the most expensive time of the year. During the summer, around December, most Xhosa migrants tried to visit their family and friends in Emaxhoseni. Migrants were worried about these visits because they might return to Cape Town to find that someone else had taken their job, and because the visit home cost money. A single trip by minibus to the Eastern Cape cost about R360. Furthermore, one could not arrive empty handed. After all, parents, brothers, sisters, extended family members, and even friends were waiting for the migrant to return with money or presents. The economic situation in most parts of the Eastern Cape, after all, was depressing. Old people and their dependants could hardly survive on a government pension of about R450 a month, which was sometimes not even paid due to corruption and mismanagement.

For the migrant and his or her family, it was embarrassing to arrive home empty handed. Presents and money were the only way one could show that the many lonely months in Cape Town had not been in vain. Most migrants, however, received only a low income as a domestic worker or unskilled labourer and were often unemployed. This contrasted sharply with the image that relatives and migrants maintained of a prosperous life in Cape Town. Many people in the Eastern Cape, of course, knew better because they themselves had migrated in the past. However, the image of a rich life in Cape Town was supported by the claims made by returning migrants. In order to live up to these expectations and to comply with some obligations, the migrants had to save money throughout the entire year.

The Accumulating Savings and Credit Associations (ASCRA, see Bouman 1994b: 376-377) helped migrants to save. Mostly neighbours and sometimes colleagues or friends formed a group and made monthly contributions. The money was deposited into a bank account and members were able to borrow money. An important difference with the ROSCA was that the ASCRA had a fund that needed to be managed. By the end of November or beginning of December, the members divided all the ASCRA money so they could afford a respectable visit to Emaxhoseni.

Most of the time, female neighbours formed an ASCRA and, to a lesser extent, female colleagues, friends, church members, or men in general. The size of the group varied from ten to forty-two members, of which the larger groups tended to be divided into smaller subgroups. The subgroups took turns borrowing money from the organisation, meaning that not everybody could borrow simultaneously.

ASCRAs usually started at the beginning of the year, in February. The meetings were mostly held on a Saturday or Sunday at the end or the beginning of each month, just after the members had received their wages. The contribution was often R50, and this was referred to as 'stage money', just like in the ROSCA. After the stage money had been collected and recorded by a secretary, people paid the interest on outstanding debts.

Once all the money had been collected, it was time for the members to borrow again. In a vast majority of ASCRAs, it was obligatory to borrow money in order to 'make the money grow faster'. Some ASCRAs forced their members to borrow at least R100 a month, while others limited the loan to ensure that members were not burdened with a debt they could not repay. In some ASCRAs, the members had to return the loan by the end of the month, while others forced the member to borrow the money for three months, or even allowed them to repay the money any time before the end of the year. In the meantime, the members had to pay interest, which was usually 20 percent per month.

The interest rate might seem high, but it was relatively low compared to other available sources of credit such as moneylenders or 'cash loan companies'. Moreover, the interest was to the benefit of the members who divided the money among themselves before the end of the year. Some members did not even contribute interest. They used the ASCRA loan to give a loan to a neighbour or colleague, who then became responsible for the interest. The neighbour or colleague had to repay the loan and the interest to the member who in turn brought it to the ASCRA. The member remained responsible for paying the ASCRA.

All but one of the ASCRAs opened a group account, such as a savings account or a thirty-two-day notice, at one of the banks in Cape Town or Bellville. The treasurer deposited the money and had to show the deposit slip at the next meeting. Once the money had been deposited, the ASCRA would not withdraw it to use for loans to members.

At the end of the year, that is at the end of November or in early December, it was time to divide the money.[19] Outstanding debts were settled or deducted from the share. Half of the ASCRAs simply divided the cash, while the other groups used the bulk of the money to shop at wholesalers such as Makro and Metro. They bought groceries together in bulk. This was not only cheaper (less transport costs and better prices), but also less time consuming, and more fun. The women were mostly very excited about what each member would receive when the groceries were divided.

## Studying townships

For the Xhosa migrants in Cape Town, it was extremely difficult to be in control of their own lives. In the apartheid days, the state severely limited their freedom and, after apartheid, violence and poverty made life difficult and a constant struggle. The liberation from apartheid has not led to a liberation from violence and destitution. For the Xhosa migrants it was still a constant struggle to gain some control over their actions, bodies, relations with others and money.

Safety issues, as well as the sharp divisions still felt in South Africa today, made it a challenge to carry out research in the townships of Cape Town. The study of relations among Xhosa migrants meant that I had to engage in volatile,

---

[19] One ASCRA was among slightly more affluent residents of Langa (Bähre 1996: 32).

constraining, and unpredictable relations myself. Although it was difficult to establish relations with Xhosa migrants in the townships, it was the only way to examine their lives in a meaningful way. The fieldwork experiences were vital for understanding the lives of Xhosa migrants in Cape Town (See also Jenkins 1994; Van de Port 1998, 1999; Thoden van Velzen & Van Wetering 1991).

Although the dangers and insecurities are undeniable there is also a tendency to exaggerate them. Drawing on his research experience in Belfast, Sluka writes:

> Fieldwork is possible even in the most dangerous contexts. Anthropologists should not select themselves out of research in such contexts on the basis of stereotypes, media images, or inadequate information concerning the dangers involved ... The dangers are often exaggerated, and in most cases they are not insurmountable (1995: 290-291).

Because of the violence in South Africa, especially in the townships, I constantly needed to address safety issues. Information on political structures, party alliances, taxi associations, and development projects was crucial. Knowledge about alliances, tensions, and reputations of people and places could be used to avoid violence as much as possible. A difficult aspect of threats and dangers was its invisibility. The anxieties, fears, and stereotypes that are so vivid and alive among many Whites did not help (see also Sluka 1990: 120). I became intimidated by the many warnings that I could not do research in the townships, as well as by comments and jokes such as 'do you have an AK-47?', when I told Whites about my research plans. Although I was frequently advised to buy a gun by those not familiar with research in the townships, I refused for several reasons. First, a weapon is valuable and one increases the risk of becoming a victim of robbery if a weapon is spotted. Second, being untrained the weapon could be used against me. Third, I might be tempted to stay in a potentially dangerous situation because of the false sense of security it provided. Fourth, it would impede the establishment of trust and might make it difficult for people to be honest to me. People sometimes told me that they had assumed that I carried a gun and were surprised that I did not have one, because 'all Whites carry a gun' when they are in the townships. The absence of a weapon was part of being a different kind of White person, and made me less threatening and more trustworthy.

Generally, Whites and Africans had different understandings as regards the risks and dangers, and how one should manage these. Whites frequently seemed to suffer from an all encompassing paranoia and anxiety brought on by an amorphous enemy. When visualised, this amorphous evil was mostly an unknown and hostile male African. Contrary to Whites, Africans tended to keep quiet about violence. If violence was discussed, it was in a 'matter of fact' way with a focus on the places and situations to be avoided. This was based on a detailed topography of places, times, and situations that were considered to be dangerous. This knowledge was much more valuable to me than the information I received from Whites. After all, the Africans lived in the townships and had to deal with violence much more frequently and were therefore much better informed about the risks.

It took time to read faces, acquire the habit of looking at people inside cars, register those around me, and learn to spot someone who was armed. I could not have done this without the constant support of my research assistant Edith Nokwanele Moyikwa. At the start of the research, a visit to the townships lasting a few hours exhausted me. This was due to the intensive looking, listening, and moving that is part of fieldwork in a volatile situation. Eventually, I got used to it and after my return to the Netherlands I had to unlearn habits that were justified in South Africa, but are regarded as signals of paranoia if one lives in a safe place, such as the Netherlands.

Green aptly describes the combination of presence and absence of dangers when carrying out research in a potentially dangerous situation:

> While it is true that with repetitiveness and familiarity people learn to accommodate themselves to terror and fear, low-intensity panic remains in the shadow of waking consciousness. One cannot live in a constant state of alertness, and so the chaos one feels becomes infused throughout the body. It surfaces frequently in dreams and chronic illness (Green 1995: 109).

It might sound banal, but it only takes a few minutes to commit a murder, and afterwards life goes on as usual. Even in a violent place like South Africa's townships, violent acts are mostly short and rarely take place when you are present. Therefore, alertness was a much more dominant condition than a short-lived fear or terror related to an immediate threat. Whenever I felt uncomfortable or ill at ease, or had just experienced a nasty fieldwork situation, I would refrain from doing any research for a day. I tried not to rationalise it away because I could not find a logical reason, except that people might pick up on my anxiety and act on it. The body language of fear and feeling uncomfortable can be read by others and may increase the risk of being victimised, while body language which shows confidence, comparability and respect towards others contributes to one's feeling of safety (cf. Williams *et al.* 1992: 350).

Because of the political dynamics and high occurrence of violence in the townships of Cape Town, I invested a lot of energy in establishing the research circumstances that minimised risks as much as possible. I could not rely on public transport, such as buses, trains, and so-called taxis, which are minibuses with fixed routes. For these reasons, it was essential for me to have a car. I did not work without my research assistant, Edith, and the furthest I walked without her was about fifty meters. To increase safety and receive information, we walked around a lot in the neighbourhood. By walking around we were able to start many fruitful conversations, exchange gossip, and engage in small talk with those we met on our way. This way, I was more visible than I would have been if I had only driven around the neighbourhood. My constant visibility helped to take away some of the suspicions that people must have had and it showed that I was a different kind of White person, because Whites generally tend to move around by car only.[20]

These safety measures inevitably restricted my participation in the lives of the Xhosa migrants. I could not reside in the township and instead lived with my girlfriend in the White upper-class suburb of Newlands and drove back and forth every day. I had planned to live with my research assistant's family in Indawo Yoxolo for some time, but their shack was quite small. I eventually bought building material for an extra room and lived there for two weeks and had planned to stay there more often for a week or so, but violence caused me to abandon these plans. Many nights, at times even every night, shooting could be heard right behind the shack and it was not unimaginable that a stray bullet would pierce a window, a metal sheet, or a piece of cardboard. Nevertheless, my two-week stay in Indawo Yoxolo had a positive effect. The neighbours considered it as another sign that I was genuinely interested in their lives. For me, it became clearer how difficult it is to be surrounded by danger all the time.

My participation at festive occasions was furthermore limited because of drunken people and, once again, the risk of violence. There is this romantic idea in anthropology that a great way to connect with people and be accepted by them is by getting drunk together. However, it was horrible to attend a graduation ceremony where men and women had been drinking beer and brandy for the past 36 hours. On another occasion, I joined some men drinking beer in a tavern. I ended up at the house of a neighbour of a friend of mine whose drunken son had fought in Angola for Poqo, the PAC's (Pan African Congress) armed wing. He felt that he had to kill me: 'One settler one bullet!', he screamed. He had an argument with his drunken mother about killing me and eventually we ended up going through heroic pictures of him and his comrades in the battlefield. Sure, we connected at some level, but it was just too dangerous to repeat. I never again drank alcohol during the research, except when it was ritually prescribed, in which case it would have been offensive not to drink a glass of brandy or beer. I also avoided the illegal drinking halls known as *shebeens*, especially in neighbourhoods where customers hardly knew each other.

I learned a bit of Xhosa through language courses and I could exchange greetings and talk on a very limited number of topics. My comprehension of the language was insufficient for a conversation, yet people often expressed their gratitude that a White man was trying to learn some Xhosa in order to greet people respectfully. It could make feelings of hostility or threats disappear, and people

---

[20] One exception was a White building contractor working in Indawo Yoxolo. He would at times bike between building sites that were only a few hundred metres apart. Eventually, and not to the surprise of the residents of Indawo Yoxolo, he was robbed and killed. Some residents believed that this was organised by some of his workers who knew that he was carrying a large sum of money to pay the salaries.

often laughed at my clumsy attempts to say something. Sometimes it is useful for an anthropologist to look foolish, especially because many migrants often struggled with their English.

The risks and dangers of fieldwork in the townships could be divided into four categories: a) being an object for politically motivated threats, b) becoming a victim of robbery, car hijacking or assault, c) becoming a victim of hatred against Whites, and d) being an 'unlucky bystander'. In order to limit these risks, I had what I would call 'social shields', or levels of protection. First, I was associated with the University of the Western Cape and people could identify me with a local, previously non-white university instead of an unknown Dutch university. Second, I was associated with a network of people that formed the political opposition to the Big Five (see Chapter 3). The opposition was well informed about the political struggles in the area and could warn me if necessary. Third, many neighbours, often involved in financial mutuals, knew me well. I made an effort to get acquainted with a lot of residents in a particular street and tell them what I was doing and who I was. I knew all the residents living in the street in which my research assistant Edith lived. This contributed to my safety and enhanced the research in general. Finally, Edith's household functioned as a safe 'harbour' where I could wait inbetween interviews or meetings, write field notes, have coffee, and hear the latest gossip. At one time in Indawo Yoxolo, the political network and the safety of the household collapsed and I temporarily had to abandon the research. I then focused more intensely on interviews and meetings in other parts of Cape Town. Only after the social relations had been somewhat restored and the immediate threat of violence was gone could I carefully build up the research activities in Indawo Yoxolo again. At other times, Edith and I had to leave a meeting because of the hostile atmosphere and aggression, as well as stay away from meetings that we felt could be dangerous.

## Outline

A constant theme throughout the book is the role of money as regards the shifting and fragile relations of Xhosa migrants. Financial mutuals should be studied as part of post-apartheid society and the question that needs to be asked is if and how financial mutuals should be considered as a reaction to, or part of, the many threats, insecurities, and anxieties of migrant life. I will, moreover, reflect on the relevance of these experiences for the analysis of social situations; how experience elucidated interdependencies among migrants, neighbours, kin, and fellow participants of financial mutuals.

*Photo 1.2* The serviced area of Indawo Yoxolo

The next two chapters examine the impact that large scale economic and political processes had on the type of relations that are fundamental to financial mutuals, namely kin, neighbourhood relations, and identification with fellow migrants (*abakhaya*). Chapter two explains the transformation of a subsistence economy into a colonial and postcolonial capitalist economy with distinct authorities over old and new sources of wealth. Under the colonial as well as apartheid economic regime, flows of money emerged that led to a reconfiguration of interdependencies, particularly of kin, neighbours, and fellow migrants. By examining these struggles for (financial) resources it becomes clear why financial mutuals emerged the way they did. Chapter three examines the presence of the post-apartheid economy in Indawo Yoxolo through an all-encompassing development project. Vast amounts of resources were distributed through a national state-driven development project that again led to a reconfiguration of local relations in which financial mutuals had to operate.[21] These two chapters make it possible to conceptualise financial mutuals within the threatening triad of violence, economic insecurity, and volatile relations.

Chapters four, five and six concern the three core dimensions of financial mutuals, namely solidarity, trust, and eventually spending the money, mostly on

[21] The objection against concepts such as 'reconfiguration' and 'transformation' to describe economic transformation is that these tend to assume that there is a particular fixed state that is followed by a process towards a new fixed state.

consuming. Chapter four highlights the dynamics of solidarity on which inclusion and exclusion are based. For financial mutuals to be established one had to cooperate with people one hardly knew. Why and how were some people excluded? Rumour and values were pivotal for exclusion, but people did not always agree with each other, or had diverging interests or ambivalent relations. What do the limits of solidarity say about identification with fellow migrants? These questions will be examined in chapter four. Chapter five examines trust among members of financial mutuals who live in a society where there are many reasons not to trust one another. Why do members trust each other and what are the limits to trust? After all, the mutuals had no legal foundation. Violence, economic insecurity and a climate of distrust made it difficult to give a lot of money to the financial mutual. Chapter six reveals the dynamics of consumption that are fundamental to the establishment of financial mutuals. Virtually all the money was used for consumption and hardly ever for housing and even less frequently for business purposes. It was puzzling that poor people spent so much money on refrigerators, stoves, cooking utensils, funerals, and initiation parties. The dynamics of keeping, receiving, and giving consumer products had an impact on the kind of relations maintained inside and outside the financial mutual. This chapter reveals why consumption uncovers a disharmonious world hidden behind the image of financial mutuals as warm, cosy, and sweet women's groups.

# 2

# The (post)colonial economy and social relations

## Introduction

In order to locate financial mutuals within society, one must consider the impact that capitalism, the apartheid state, and the post-apartheid state have had on the Xhosa economy and the constitution of social relationships. Indeed, pre-colonial Xhosa society was also subject to change and problematic relationships,[1] but the introduction of money concomitant with the arrival of colonialism and capitalism led to particularly drastic renegotiations of relations (see Beinart 1982; Hunter 1933). In an environment in which new sources of income had been generated, migration was first and foremost about cash. The demographic shift which resulted altered kin and neighbourhood relations while new and innovative relations, such as financial mutuals, emerged. The historicity of money and relationships needs to be examined first, since it shows how financial mutuals emerged.

The political economic change was one from a kin-ordered mode of production to one in which the capitalist mode of production became important. A kin-ordered mode of production meant that kinship relations were central to social labour: 'Put simply, through kinship social labor is "locked up", or "embedded", in particular relations between people. This labour can be mobilized only through access to people, such access being defined symbolically' (Wolf 1982: 91). Due to capitalist

---

1 See Wolf's central argument (1982).

expansion, the capitalist mode of production started to play a major role. Capitalists were in control of the means of production while labourers had to sell their labour power to capitalists, often at a low price (Wolf 1982: 77-78). These modes of production did not necessarily present different types of society, or evolutionary stages. Instead they should be regarded as 'constructs with which to envisage certain strategic relationships that shape the terms under which human lives are conducted' (Wolf 1982: 100)

Among the Xhosa in South Africa, three types of relations were most clearly affected by economic change, namely kin, *abakhaya*, and neighbours. First, I will briefly highlight the incorporation of the Xhosa people into the colonial and apartheid political economy. Second, the impact on relations among kin, neighbours, and *abakhaya* will become clear. How did migration change relations or lead to new ones? How could particular types of relations offer the social constraint necessary to accumulate large sums of money?

## Earning money

As early as 1777, Xhosa worked in the Cape Colony as domestic and agricultural servants, and sometimes as slaves. In return, they were paid in 'beads, brass-ware and brass plates, and sometimes in articles of clothing' (Gardner 1835: 174 cited in Cock 1980: 174). Slavery was abolished in 1834, but the many economic and political pressures forced Xhosa men and women to start or continue working as wage labourers or offered them new economic opportunities. The colonial conquest by the British army in the mid-nineteenth century forced many Xhosa off their lands and led to the foreign control of Xhosa chiefs. The occupation of land and subjugation of chiefs made it increasingly difficult for them to survive on land and livestock. The spread of lung sickness among cattle in 1855 contributed to a further collapse of the Xhosa economy and society 'killing two-thirds of the stock in some areas and virtually wiping out the herds of even cattle-rich chiefs' (Ross 1999: 51). For most, it became impossible to maintain a subsistence economy.

The rise of a millenarian prophecy in the mid 1800s revealed, as well as further intensified, the already desperate economic situation. According to a young girl named Nongqawuse, the 'end of the world' as they knew it could be stopped. She prophesised that their lives would change for the better if they destroyed the harvest and remaining cattle. Only total destruction would cause the Whites to leave, grain pits to fill up, and herds of cattle to return. Her prophecy led to the mass destruction of cattle and grain in 1857 and caused a tremendous human tragedy (Ross 1999: 51-52; see also Peires 1989). According to historical sources, between 20,000 and 40,000 Xhosa died of starvation and incidences of cannibalism have even been reported (Cock 1980: 202; Ross 1999: 52).

Natural disasters, especially the droughts of 1876 to 1878 and 1912 (Cock 1980: 203; Beinart 1982: 75-78), and rinderpest epidemics resulted in a continued destruction of the Xhosa subsistence economy. Beinart (1982) described how in Pondoland the 1912 drought and East Coast fever spread by ticks brought about the deaths of cattle on a huge scale. In roughly five years (from 1911 to 1915) the number of cattle plunged from almost 280,000 to just over 54,000. A main source of income was thus lost and the use of cattle for the establishment of conjugal and affinal relations must have been under serious threat. To prevent further spread of East Coast fever, the movement of cattle was severely restricted and cattle dipping was introduced. In 1915, a cattle dipping tax of five shilling was introduced, but regular cattle dipping was only enforced in around 1920. These measures (restricted movement and the dipping of cattle) resulted in an increase in cattle numbers, which in turn caused different problems. The increase in the number of cattle, combined with the restrictions on transport for cattle to other markets, led to a decline in the price of cattle by the end of the decade. The decreasing income levels must have been felt even more harshly due to the taxation per homestead which had already been introduced in 1895. Due to the vulnerability of agriculture, failure of cash crops, starvation of cattle, and taxation, young men decided to leave their homes and work in the mines, cities, or White-owned farms (Beinart 1982: 36, 75-78, 94, 173). In the first half of the 20th century the scale of labour migration was already massive:

> According to the 1936 Census Report, about 54 percent of the adult male population of the reserves was absent ... over half the Keiskammahoek [a district in the Ciskei] population consisted of those too old, too young, or too ill to earn wages (Bundy 1979: 225).

Whatever was left of land and cattle was further threatened by apartheid's 'betterment schemes' that started in the 1930s (Wilson & Ramphele 1994: 220). 'Betterment schemes' were a euphemism for forced villigisation: 'the movement of people into villages, the excising of old lands and the demarcation of new fields, the establishment of grazing camps, and nothing more' (McAllister 1996: 13). Particularly in the former Ciskei, I came across villages that at first glance appeared to be remote, picturesque, subsistence-based communities, but which were actually rural slums created through betterment. During a funeral in such a small and remote village, I asked a resident how old the village was, to which he replied: 'Oh, this village is very old. It was built in the early 1960s.'

Apart from the loss of land and cattle, new consumption patterns also made it more attractive to engage in wage labour. Colonial authorities purposefully attempted to incorporate Africans into the colonial economy by introducing new consumer products (Burke 1996). They regarded Africans as a potential market for goods like soap and clothing and attempted to 'civilise' them by promoting desires that were thought to have been absent during the pre-colonial past. The new consumer products could only be purchased with cash obtained through wage labour, which was to the advantage of colonial authorities in search of cheap workers (Burke 1996: 83-90).[2]

To give an example of the loss of livelihood that finally occurred, in the early 1980s in the Libode district of the Transkei more than half the population had no cattle at all, while only 10 percent owned more than ten animals (Wilson & Ramphele 1994: 72).[3] An African female wage labourer expressed the increased reliance on cash in the following way: 'We [Africans] can cope. You can put a black person in the forest and just leave water with him or her. We can manage because there is a lot we can do. But now we are chained without money' (Cock 1980: 109).

Conquest incorporated Xhosa into the colonial and postcolonial economy and simultaneously marginalised them within this economy: wages were low and working conditions were horrible. Furthermore, legislative measures introduced as early as 1828 restricted the free movement of Xhosa in order to regulate the flow of African labourers (Cock 1980: 204). Migrants in Cape Town initially lived scattered across the city's poorest areas. However, by the end of the 19th century they were forced to live away from Whites in townships on the outskirts of Cape Town (Cole 1987: 5; Ross 1999: 97-98).

Influx Control, as these policies on the restriction of African movement and labour were called, forced Africans to live in a few reserves which, in 1926, comprised no more than 13 percent of South Africa (Ross 1999: 88). The Urban Areas Act of 1923 restricted the number of Africans allowed to reside in urban areas by deporting 'those who were habitually unemployed, those who had no honest livelihood, and those who were idle, dissolute, or disorderly' (Davenport 1969 in Wilson 1972: 160). Between 1954 and 1985, Cape Town was governed by yet another policy restricting African movement, namely the Coloured Labour Preference Policy. It had to make sure that the city would be virtually unoccupied by Africans: 'The intention of the Department of Native Affairs was to phase Africans out of the Western Cape … and incorporate Coloureds by giving them labour preference' (Goldin 1987: 87).

The implementation of the racist labour policies depended to some extent on the demand for labourers. From 1968 to 1974, an increased demand for labour led to a loosening of the enforcement of these policies. During the economic recession,

---

2 It seems that Burke overemphasises the power of colonial authorities in the transference of taste. In addition to force, one can imagine that, similarly as has been described among the maroons in Suriname (Thoden van Velzen & Van Wetering 1991: 24) new consumer products were eagerly embraced.

3 Based on Hendricks' 'preliminary notes on land and livestock in Libode'. N = 12,854. Research in 1974 in the Transkei revealed that 'almost half the households surveyed owned no cattle at all' (Leeuwenberg 1977: 2 in Bundy 1979: 229). The survey took place among 757 households.

repression was enforced more severely (Cole 1987: 9). Labour policy was, however, not always carried out according to an economic rationale. For example, in the 1960s, the government had decided that the number of Africans in the Western Cape had to be reduced by 5 percent per year. White farmers were upset and feared a shortage of skilled farm labourers. Their protests were put aside and the number of Africans was reduced, notwithstanding their economic necessity (Wilson 1972: 19-20).

Against the background of the enforcement of legally embedded discrimination, migrant labour became pivotal for survival: 'In 1929, 46.6 percent of the taxes paid by residents in Pondoland were collected outside the home district of the payer, showing that at least that percentage of males over 18 years were away from home' (Hunter 1979: 108). In the Ciskei and the Transkei, households continued to depend on remittances from migrant labourers. For example, in 1982, in households with less than an annual income of R1,500, two thirds of the income came from such remittances (Wilson & Ramphele 1994: 62-63). War, taxation, slavery, the introduction of new consumer products, political domination, 'betterment schemes', in combination with natural disasters such as droughts and cattle diseases, have made it inevitable, and desirable, to have money in contemporary South Africa.

Together with the mines, the cities were believed to be *the* places to go to in search of money. Data on the composition of the urban population are notoriously unreliable and frequently contradictory. One of the causes is that many Africans defied apartheid legislation and lived in the city illegally. Therefore, they had good reason to hide from a population census.[4] Government authorities also modified the numerical representation of Africans in Cape Town for administrative purposes. It followed that those who did not officially exist did not need public services and, therefore, the urban African population was intentionally underestimated (Lee 1999: 60). Bearing these precautions in mind, the available data indicate that the African population in Cape Town grew, despite apartheid legis-

---

4 An example of these problems can be found in Wilson & Ramphele's book (1994: 92). They compared unemployment among Africans in Durban and Cape Town. In Durban's townships, depending on the definition of unemployment, between 16 and 29 percent of Africans were unemployed. In Cape Town, this was a remarkably low 6 to 9 percent. At the time of the survey in 1982-3 the pass laws were still enforced in Cape Town, while they were not enforced in Durban. This, according to Wilson & Ramphele, explains the lower level of unemployment in Cape Town. They argue that the restrictive pass laws discouraged Africans to move to Cape Town. It could also be, however, that the pass laws inhibited African migrants from telling the truth about their illegal employment status and therefore create the false impression that unemployment in Cape Town was low.

lative efforts to prevent this.[5] Because of the desperate economic situation, many Africans continuously tried to find employment outside the homeland at the risk of being caught, detained, fined, and sent back to the Bantustans.

For African women, it was even more difficult to live in the city than for African men. The Bantu Urban Areas Act of 1964 ruled that women had to receive permission to join their husband in the city. Furthermore, if a 'section 10 woman' – a woman permitted to live in the city under section 10 of this act – were to marry a 'homeland man', the apartheid state would force her to leave the city and join her husband in 'his homeland'. In the house of assembly in 1969, Froneman, who later became the Deputy Minister, defended the discrimination of women by arguing that one 'must not be burdened with superfluous appendages such as wives, children and dependants who could not provide service' (Cock 1980: 245). In 1911, in Greater Cape Town there were almost four African men for every African woman, and this number had decreased to two African men for every woman by 1951 (Wilson & Mafeje 1963: 5).[6] Most women lived in the city illegally, could not work legally, and often had no place to stay and depended heavily on their husbands. Consequently, the status of women in the city was much more insecure than that of men (see, among others, Oliver-Evans 1993: 70-81; Ramphele 1989).

In 1986, the Abolition of Influx Control Act put an end to numerous apartheid laws that restricted the movement and labour of Africans. The inability to enforce the pass laws and, finally, the abolition of these laws in 1986, made it easier for African men and women to search for a job in the city (see Robertson 1990). This led to a distinct transformation in the urban demographic landscape.

---

5 According to Monica Wilson & Archie Mafeje (1963: 2), in 1911 only roughly 1,500 Africans (1.5 percent of the urban population) lived in Cape Town. This figure increased to just over 30,000 (8 percent) by 1946 and, according to Francis Wilson (1972: 70) 55,000 Africans were living in Cape Town by 1971. The number of pass law contraventions provides another indication of levels of urbanisation and the attempts by the state to control African migrants. The number of pass law contraventions in South Africa rose from just under 50,000 in 1921 to more than 600,000 in 1970 (Wilson 1972: 232). And '[I]n greater Cape Town ... between 1962 and 1967 the number of people convicted rose by over 80 [percent] from 8,434 to 15,367' (Wilson 1972: 164).

6 Lee (1999: 67) shows how, in Langa, the female population decreased between 1965 and 1970 due to the council's policy to make Langa a township for male bachelor migrants. As a consequence of this policy, the male to female population ratio rose as high as 6.3:1 in 1970. Ramphele (1989: 399) found that in the mid 1980s the male to female ratio among hostel dwellers was 2:1. In the Transkei, the ratio had fallen from 73 men per 100 women in 1946 to 66 men per 100 women in 1974. The decline in the number of men and women in the age group 25-29 years was even stronger: from 36.1 to 28.9 men per 100 women (Clark & Ngovese 1975 in Bundy 1979: 229-230).

The African urban population increased rapidly after the abolishment of apartheid, thus contributing to the already existing housing problems.[7] Population growth combined with a housing shortage meant that the poverty in which most Africans lived slowly became visible to the Whites living in Cape Town. During the apartheid era, townships were, to most Whites, places one only saw from far off while driving along the highway. For example, Langa, the oldest township in Cape Town that still exists today, could only be seen in the distance when driving along the N2 highway. A few hundred metres of grassland used to separate the highway from the township. Another attempt by the apartheid government to conceal the poverty was to place the better houses on the side lining the highway, while the worst housing conditions remained in the interior areas and invisible to Whites passing by in their cars. In an attempt to camouflage the presence of Africans even further, the power station in Langa was, and still is, called Athlone Power Station, after the adjacent Coloured area, Athlone. In recent years, the townships have become more visible. In 1995, one could see how Africans used the grass fields between the townships and the highway to build their makeshift dwellings, made of corrugated iron, wood, cardboard, plastic, or other affordable building materials. Given this particular history it is quite ironic that, in 2005, a large-scale housing project started along this same N2 highway that connects the international airport to the city. A strip of shacks is to be demolished and replaced by flats which will obstruct the view that tourists arriving for the 2010 soccer World Cup would otherwise have of the poor housing conditions.

Influx Control discriminated against women in particular and forced many women to stay in the Bantustan and rely on the remittances sent by their husbands. Remittances, however, were frequently irregular, insufficient, or not forthcoming at all (cf. James 1999a: 77; Moodie 1988: 251). After Influx Control was abolished, many women left the Bantustans. While urban female-headed households had been relatively few in number due to apartheid policies, they started to increase due to the arrival of many migrant women.[8] A conjugal familial unit – a husband and wife living together, perhaps with children – was less prevalent, and

---

7 Ramphele has calculated that the average bed occupancy – people sharing one bed – in the single sex hostels in three African townships of Cape Town (Nyanga, Guguletu, and Langa) in the mid 1980s was 2.8. In the hostels of Nyanga on average, every four residents had to share one bed among each other (Ramphele 1989: 396).

8 'Forty percent of the children had lived apart from their fathers for 48 percent of their lives', reports Reynolds (1989: 35) on children living in the squatter camp Crossroads in Cape Town in the 1980s. In Crossroads it was relatively easy to live with fathers compared with the male bachelor hostels, which made it likely that children spent even less time overall with their fathers.

the absence of husbands meant that many children were illegitimate according to civil or customary law (Burman & Lembete 1995: 28, 46; Longmore 1959).

The above does not provide a complete picture of the impact of the changing political economy and the introduction of money. My aim, however, has only been to delineate the general process of colonial conquest and capitalist economy (especially the introduction of money, wage labour, taxation, new consumer items, war, apartheid legislation), and the impact of natural disasters (drought, lung disease among cattle, East Coast fever). The political and economic changes had a tremendous impact on the livelihoods of the Xhosa, sources of income, household relations, and conceptions of the world. They also led to financial mutuals that were at the crossroads of three very important types of relationships (kin, *abakhaya*, and neighbours) and money.

## Changing kinship authorities

Pressure on land, the demise of cattle, and an increasing reliance on migrant labour put all kinds of pressures on people who depended on each other. Young men, women, and children could earn an income and gained certain freedoms.[9] These new sources of income helped them to escape certain inequalities, but simultaneously led to new forms of oppression. Similar to Wolf's (1999) interpretation of the gift giving institution of the potlatch among the North American Kwakiutl, new income generating activities and drastic political changes gave previously marginal people the opportunity to acquire status and challenge dependencies.

A major change was that homesteads (*imizi*) became smaller due to land shortage, which in turn was brought about by foreign conquest (Beinart 1982: 98). In the 1930s there were people who still remembered that homesteads used to consist of up to twenty married men with their wives and children, while in the 1930s a homestead had the characteristics of a nuclear family (Hunter 1933: 273). The introduction of the plough had made large homesteads with its many female labourers less essential for economic survival. When a Xhosa chief was confronted with a plough he expressed the changing relationship between labour and technological innovation as '[t]his thing that the white people have brought into the country is as good as ten wives' (Hunter 1979: 202).

The way in which hut tax and dipping tax were levied also stimulated homesteads to become smaller. Hut tax was levied on the number of huts – with each wife occupying a hut – within a homestead and the head of the homestead was responsible for paying this tax. It put him in a precarious situation. Although he

[9] See, among others, Comaroff & Comaroff (1990) on South Africa, Geschiere (1983) on Cameroon, and Hutchinson (1996) on Sudan.

had to pay the tax, also for the wives of his sons, it was difficult for him to lay claim to his sons' wages. The tax made it financially more attractive for the headman to let his sons establish their own homesteads and let them pay their own taxes. From 1913-1915, the administration enforced an additional 'dipping tax' on cattle treated against East Coast fever. The dipping tax depended on the number of adult men living in the homestead and homesteads with few male members paid less tax (Beinart 1982: 98).

In addition to reasons of tax, homesteads also became smaller because men left in search of jobs. People's reliance on kin relations therefore steadily decreased, in a trend aggravated by forced resettlement. Instead of being able to rely on kin, Xhosa households were increasingly confronted with, and dependent on, neighbours who were not related to them (Hunter 1979: 60; McAllister 1985: 130). Among other initiatives, neighbours established co-operative work arrangements, such as the ploughing company where they assisted each other during the agricultural cycle (McAllister 2000). The dependency on neighbours was also reflected in ritual practices:

> The increase in [ritual] beer drinking, probably gradually from about the 1920s onwards, coincided with, reflected and provided normative or ideological support for the changing nature of rural production, in which neighbourhood and a sense of community replaced kinship as the major organising principle. Neighbourliness did not arise as a new social principle, but became more important as the kinship system weakened (McAllister 1997: 306).

There are contradictions in the literature on the consequences of these changes for relations established by marriage. Before cash income played a major role, marriage took place through the transference of bridewealth (*ukulobola*). According to Hunter (1933: 263) most marriages were not arranged, and if they were arranged it was with the consent of the lovers. However Hunter, and others, also described the practice of *ukutwala*, which was the kidnapping of the bride with her parents' consent but not necessarily with the bride's consent (Hunter 1979: 189; Laubscher 1959: 266; Moodie 1988: 239).[10] An older woman in Cape Town told me that she had been lured into marriage with a bicycle that she received for her birthday. She was very pleased with this marvellous gift and went for a bicycle ride with her brothers. It was a big shock for her when she ended up in a nearby village where she was forced to marry a complete stranger.

Parental control over conjugal relations was also reflected in the control over marriage cattle. Hunter described how each daughter was allocated to a son. This practice was called *ukushaka*, which means 'to link' or 'to put together'. The *lobola* that was received when a daughter married was allotted to this specific son. This meant that the marriage of a man greatly depended on the marriage of his

---

[10] See also Hammond-Tooke (1962: 100-102) on consentient and forced marriage.

sister and the allotment by his parents (Hunter 1979: 122-123). However, Kuper argued that in the period from 1880-1930 the Xhosa were an exception in the region because they did not practise allotment (Kuper 1982: 36). But even if *ukushaka* was not commonly practised, *lobola* did enhance parental control over young men and women. Moreover, cattle were a constitutive element of the establishment of parental rights over children: *lobola* incorporated the wife's children into the father's patrilineage.

The advantage of bridewealth payments was that it connected the wife's parents to their daughter's in-laws and gave them the authority to intervene in marital disputes:

> 'Well, if you are not *lobola*, what do you do when your husband mistreats you, since you have no home (*ikhaya*) to run to?' Any home that has benefited from a woman's *ikhazi* is bound to give her support and protection, and women frequently take advantage of this right by running back to their own people (Hunter 1933: 263).

Women often had good reasons to run away from their affines. Their new homes were strange and many felt that the practice of *ukuhlonipa*, or avoidance, was degrading to them, even if they agreed with it from a moral point of view.[11] A wife had to show respect by avoiding words, names, and letters that related to her husband's clan. She was given a new name which, if the woman was unlucky, was not flattering. She had to behave respectfully towards her husband's relatives by walking slowly, talking softly, often by sitting on a mat on the floor instead of on a chair, and through strict dress codes.

Because of virilocal residency, a married woman was, and still is, an outsider within her husband's homestead. As a relative stranger, a woman was felt to be dangerous (Hammond-Tooke 1962: 113; Hunter 1933: 267). Consequently, her affinal relations were particularly vulnerable to witchcraft. Many of the witchcraft allegations concerned the relation between a woman and her husband's brother's son and, according to Wilson, especially between a woman and her mother-in-law (Hammond-Tooke 1970: 30-31; Wilson 1952: 173 in Hammond-Tooke 1970: 30).

Wage labour provided new forms of economic power and marginalised the use of cattle for the establishing of kin relations. As young people earned cash, parental authority over them was undermined and elderly men had less to say about their marriage. Young people did not depend on their fathers or a chief for marriage cattle and instead bought their own. Consequently, elders complained

---

[11] For a detailed description of *ukuhlonipa* among the Xhosa in 1979, see Kuckertz (1997). A shortcoming of his structural analysis is that the author fails to note the contestations around this practice. For many of the women I spoke with, the practice of *ukuhlonipa* was an important reason not to get married. See also Mager (1999: 178-179) for a critical examination of *ukuhlonipa* among the Xhosa in the period 1945-1959.

that they were no longer respected. Although wage labour led to the financial independence of young men, their prolonged absence during labour migration also made men more hesitant to set up their own homesteads (*umzi*) and, as an alternative, left their wives with their parents (Beinart 1982: 96-103; Hunter 1933: 270; 1979: 59-60: 177). The *lobola* payments in cattle were replaced by *lobola* payments in money that was still spoken of as cattle. Marriage negotiations still made use of vocabulary steeped in cattle terms and the monetary value of particular beasts was negotiated (cf. Comaroff & Comaroff 1990: 209).

At this stage, parents had some control over the marriage of their children, but because marriages rarely took place parental control over their children's choice of partners started to weaken.[12] For example, in the 1930s in East London, over half the children were illegitimate, both according to civil and customary law (Hunter 1933: 273). Hunter attributed these findings to the high costs of children in a money economy, while children in a subsistence economy contributed through labour. The illegitimacy of children could also be due to the weakening paternal control over children due to declining flows of cattle that established or confirmed conjugal relations between spouses and consanguineal relations with children.

The demise of *lobola*, as well as the increased physical distance between the homestead of the wife's parents and that of her affines, made it difficult for a woman to involve her parents in a dispute. As a husband was often away working as migrant labourer, married women were frequently left under the control of his parents or brothers. Civil marriage might also have contributed to the marginalised position of women since it meant that marriages could take place without parental involvement and this may have made it very difficult for parents to intervene in disputes that their daughter might have with her husband and her in-laws.

At the same time, financial autonomy also gave women new freedom to choose a partner and decide to marry. In general, women told me, they were reluctant to marry because it would subject them to affines. A boyfriend was regarded as a better option because he could be left much easier. This, of course, had consequences for relationships between fathers and children (Bähre 2002b). As Bank found among the Xhosa in East London: '[F]atherhood is conceptualised in very materialistic terms – the image of a 'good father' is a man who can support his family financially' (Bank 1997: 175).[13] Unemployment, the decline of marriage

---

12 It might be that, similarly to the Nuer, cattle bought with money that was earned through labour migration was less vulnerable to claims from the extended family than cattle that had a 'social origin' (marriage and inheritance) (Hutchinson 1996: 26, 89-90). See also Geschiere's (1983: 629) observation that, notwithstanding drastic economic changes among the Maka in Cameroon, the elders were, at least formally, pivotal in the negotiation of bridewealth.

13 See also Sharp & Spiegel (1985) who compare the erosion of kinship and neighbourhood relations in two villages.

and *lobola*, their fears of independent women, and the man's inability to control his wife's sexual behaviour during his absence made it difficult for men to assert fatherhood. Women frequently had the sole responsibility over their children. Thus, the distribution of income between a husband and wife, or girlfriend and boyfriend, became increasingly contested (Bähre 2002b).

A migrant man often had to leave his wife in the care of his brother (see also Wilson & Mafeje 1963: 84). This arrangement was prone to tensions because many migrants feared that, during their absence, their brother would sleep with their wives. Tensions between brothers also increased if a younger brother had to hand over his income to his father, which would later be inherited by the oldest brother (Wilson & Mafeje 1963: 84). However, as far as I could see during my research, many parents were so poor that nothing substantial could be inherited. Nevertheless, the fear of one sibling 'stealing' the inheritance, even if it was not there, was vivid.

The tensions with – and often the absence of – brothers and fathers meant that migrant men had to rely more on others:

> The effect of these conflicts [between full brothers] appears to be that a man feels more free with his home-boys than with his brothers or parallel cousins; there are fewer strings attached to co-operation with them. Between sisters, and brothers and sisters, there are no similar rivalries, and relationships between them are easy in the changing, as in the tribal, society (Wilson & Mafeje 1963: 84).

Niehaus' (1994: 118) research among residents of the Qwaqwa district revealed that, 'in Southern Africa, it is rather siblings who stay together while conjugal pairs are dispersed'. Spouses were often away as migrant labourers and many relations had broken up, which meant that support among siblings became more important but also more prone to conflict.

## Migrant men of one home

While kinship dependencies changed, or even broke down, new social networks emerged. Not in the least, brutal apartheid legislation led to new relations by dividing Africans into two categories.[14] One category of Africans was allowed to stay permanently in the city, while other Africans were under strict control of the labour bureau and were only allowed in for the duration of their employment (Lee 1999: 16-18). African 'migrants' were only allowed to live in overcrowded male hostels and had to leave their families back home. Wilson & Ramphele (1994: 128) provided the following description of living conditions in the 1980s:

---

[14] Section 10 of The Natives (Urban Areas) Consolidation Act No. 25 of 1945 was particularly important.

> There are many men in South Africa whose address is not some street number identifying a house, nor even a room number to locate where he might stay in a boarding house, but a bed number to identify where he may be found in a maze of concrete bunks which accommodate perhaps 90 men in a single room.

The apartheid administration strengthened the regrouping of Africans. Africans who came from one area, which made them identify each other as *abakhaya* (singl. *umkhaya*) or 'those of one home', were forced to live in one room in a specifically designated barrack. Each room had its own official registration number and people from one particular area, such as the Umtata district in the former Transkei, were forced to share one room. The residents would often paint the area code of the licence plate, such as CCY for Umtata, on the door to indicate their place of origin (Wilson & Mafeje 1963: 50). In line with the logic of indirect rule, each room had to elect a convenor (*isibonda*) who was recognised by the local township authorities. The convenor was responsible for managing disputes within the room and could be called upon for disciplinary evictions (Ramphele 1989: 396-397).[15] Many Xhosa migrants also lived illegally in the city in overcrowded squatter camps where they were subjected to police harassment (see for example Cole 1987). Nevertheless, the clustering of 'those of one home' (*abakhaya*) in one room must have had an important effect on their organisations.

Pressures from family and friends back home also strengthened these *abkahaya* identifications. For those who stayed behind in Emaxhoseni, literally 'the land of the Xhosa', there was always the fear that the migrant worker would fail to return with the desperately needed cash: 'The special nightmare of Xhosa peasant families ... is *ukutshipha*, absconding – the vanishing of a man in town, leaving his kin at home without money remittances and without news of him' (Mayer & Mayer 1974: 179). For a migrant worker's wife, it was virtually impossible to

---

[15] In their influential book *Townsmen or Tribesmen*, Philip & Iona Mayer (1974) fail to take apartheid legislation and rule into consideration in their analysis of the difference between 'townsmen' and 'tribesmen', 'read' and 'school' people. They fail to mention the legal position of the convenor (*isibonda*) and ignore the legal distinction between residents and migrants under Section 10, although it must have been an important dimension of processes of identification and social organisation. In a discussion of their work, Bank wrote that 'The *abaqaba* ['red', 'traditional'] migrants completely rejected these urban social institutions and set out to 'encapsulate' themselves in close-knit, social networks based on their links with *amakhaya* (homemates) in town' (Bank 1999: 397). However, this 'rejection' of urban social institutions took place within the context of apartheid legislation that forced Africans out of the cities, or designated them to live in specific rooms in the barracks based on their place of origin. In his fierce critique of the work of the Mayers, Magubane (1973: 1713) wrote: 'The "urban/tribal" antithesis must not be studied separately from its social context, but rather in its economic, technological and political setting'.

make a successful claim to her husband's wage. Therefore, whenever a migrant left, his neighbours and village elders stressed the importance of remittances at public beer drinking rituals. The speakers reminded the migrant that he depended on them and was leaving in order to build the homestead in a material, religious, social, and moral sense (McAllister 1980: 208). A migrant was told to constrain himself financially and abstain from relations with 'town women' who would '"eat" his money and induce him to forget about his wife and home' (McAllister 1980: 211). In such a context, 'eating' referred simultaneously to the use of the migrant's money and sex with the migrant. The pressure that was exerted at public beer drinking rituals contributed to the identification of fellow migrants with their areas.

Men from one particular area of 'the land of the Xhosa' (*Emaxhoseni*) often shared one overcrowded room in one of the barracks. They ate together, cooked together, and made monthly contributions in order to buy groceries together (Mayer & Mayer 1974: 101-104; Wilson & Mafeje 1963: 49). Mayer & Mayer (1974) described how *abakhaya* in East London established a close-knit community. New migrants were initially taken care of by their fellow *abakhaya*, with whom they could reside in the hostels. They purchased food together and unemployed *abakhaya* could join in the communal meals in return for the performance of domestic tasks.[16] In the event of illness and disease, the *abakhaya* would also help each other: 'Each group of Red amakhaya (sic) ... forms a community of its own' (Mayer & Mayer 1974: 99). Living and eating together in groups of home-people established some level of social control. The social control of *abakhaya* kept migrants in line with the expectations of migrant labour, namely to save money for the homestead without spending it on women and alcohol in the city. This gave rise to the many financial mutuals that these *abakhaya*, living together in one hostel, organised.

The migrants' men close-knit networks constrained them from illicit behaviour, at least to some degree (Mayer & Mayer 1974; Wilson & Mafeje 1963: 47; see also Delius 1993: 130).[17] A migrant man said about the social control among *abakhaya* in Cape Town: 'Living in a flat [not among *abakhaya*] induces people to

---

16 Trustworthy elders in the hostel block were asked to safeguard money for their fellow *abakhaya* to prevent them from spending it. The money was kept in a goatskin purse called *ufelemntwini*, which means 'die for a person'. The elder would have to be killed before the purse could be taken from him (McAllister & Deliwe 1994: 51 in Bank 1999: 401). It could be, however, that the safeguarding of money by one elder was not a very common practice (personal communication McAllister).

17 The extent of social control among *abakhaya* should not be exaggerated. For example, it has been estimated that in around 1970, notwithstanding social control, migrants in Cape Town spent about a quarter of their income on hard liquor (Wilson 1972: 180).

spend too much money… I am not a bee, I cannot eat honey while still making it' (Wilson & Mafeje 1963: 39). Inappropriate behaviour could easily reach the ears of kin in Emaxhoseni due to gossiping *abakhaya*.

The inadequate reinforcement of apartheid laws on migration, the abolishment of many laws on migration in 1986, and the first democratic elections in 1994 caused migration and residence patterns to transform. Many built their shacks in illegal settlements, or rented a shack, or space, in the backyard of someone's brick house in a formal and serviced township. In 1998, for about R200 a month (but occasionally for twice as much), the migrant could rent a small shack and use electricity, water, and sanitation facilities of the main house. Subsequently, the co-residence and organisation of *abakhaya* had largely ceased to exist. Apart from one barrack in the township Guguletu, I did not encounter *abakhaya* living, eating, or cooking together the way Wilson & Mafeje (1963) and the Mayers (1974) had encountered in the past. The confinements of the hostels under apartheid caused *abakhaya* and neighbourhood relations to overlap, but the democratisation process meant that neighbours were not necessarily *abakhaya*, and that *abakhaya* increasingly lived scattered throughout different parts of Cape Town. This, in turn, caused a decreased interest in migrants to organise among *abakhaya*. The national Reconstruction and Development Programme (RDP) of the post-apartheid government also dispersed *abakhaya*. The RDP provided the poor with a housing subsidy that was allocated according to seniority: Those who lived the longest in an informal settlement had the first right to a housing subsidy. This made it difficult for migrants to influence where they lived and made it unlikely that they would have *abakhaya* as neighbours.

At the end of apartheid, *abakhaya* relations became less important for the organisation of financial mutuals. *Abakhaya* relations no longer coincided with neighbourhood relations and therefore the vital social constraint mechanisms among *abakhaya* diminished.[18] During my research I came across only one ROSCA and only a few burial societies organised by *abakhaya*. These *abakhaya* burial societies were relatively old (thirty years old or more), and were mostly located in the older established townships. These *abakhaya* burial societies were open to newly arrived *abakhaya* migrants but they were not always willing to travel to meetings held in another part of the city. If these relatively new migrants

---

[18] This also explains why there were still some burial societies with a fund among non-neighbours. If a member failed to contribute, the burial society could simply reject his or her claim. In contrast with Cape Town, women migrants in Johannesburg still organised dancing groups (*kiba*) with fellow home-people (James 1999a, 1999b). The reason for this discrepancy between Cape Town and Johannesburg could be the involvement of money in financial mutuals, which made social constraint necessary. The absence of social constraint would have fewer consequences for the participants of the dancing groups.

established burial societies they often did so in their urban neighbourhood. These burial societies typically had no fund and members would pool money whenever a member, or his or her dependant, had died.

Although migrants no longer used *abakhaya* relations for the establishment of financial mutuals, migrants still identified strongly with *abakhaya*. *Abakhaya* identifications were grounded in several, not necessarily exclusive, categories. One was the district or region they came from, often the magisterial district (see also Wilson & Mafeje 1963: 47). *Abakhaya* burial societies were often based on magisterial districts. *Abakhaya* could also mean people who went to the same town to buy groceries. A migrant from Ciskei, who was a member of an *abakhaya* burial society, said: 'First, *abakhaya* are the people from the same village. Second, they are people from the same district where you stay. These are the people who shop in the same town. Also, the whole Ciskei are *abakhaya*.' A teenage girl, who had been listening to our conversation while lying on the bed, added: 'Now the whole Eastern Cape are *abakhaya*. The Ciskei and Transkei don't even exist anymore.' Another woman argued that Ciskeians amongst each other were *abakhaya* because there were so few Ciskeians in Cape Town and so many Transkeians: 'Yes, we do neglect Transkeians, but they are from behind the [Kei] river and they are therefore not *abakhaya*.'[19] If migrants were further away from home, more people were regarded as *abakhaya* (see also Wilson & Mafeje 1963: 47-49): 'If I were overseas [in Europe] and met someone from Jo'burg, he would also be *umkhaya*.'

Many casual conversations revolved around people establishing whether they knew someone from his or her area of origin. Discussions often developed around these mutual acquaintances. For example, Mimi and my research assistant Edith introduced themselves at Mimi's *umgalelo* meeting. Both asked where they lived in Cape Town, to which clan they belonged, what their family situation was, and where they came from. After some time, Edith delightedly told me that she had shared a home area with Mimi. For some years, Edith had lived with her brother in a particular town in the Qobo Qobo district where she also attended secondary school. Edith had just found out that Mimi's brother lived in exactly the same town. Both were very pleased that they found a place in Emaxhoseni (the place where both their brothers lived) through which they could relate to each other. Conversations in which people elaborated on where they used to live and go to school and whom they knew occurred all the time.

Virtually all Africans, even many of those who were born in Cape Town, would have felt it an insult to be considered Capetonians. Instead, they identified with a particular region in Emaxhoseni, although some had visited this area only once or twice in their lives, or not at all. If one wanted to point out that someone

---

[19] See also McNamara (1980: 317-319) on the separate interaction of Transkei and Ciskei migrants.

misbehaved, a rhetorical 'where do you come from?' made the point. The insulting answer implied by this question was 'you come from nowhere'. You have no home and behave without a show of respect to others. Clearly, Cape Town was not recognised as a new home.

The many moves that people had made in the course of their lives from place to place made *abakhaya* identifications personal and flexible. Instead of having one town or region of origin, there were often many places to which people felt they belonged. This started in early childhood. Under Influx Control, many children were forced to leave the city and were sent home (Mayer & Mayer 1974: 271), but it was also often the case that children grew up in Emaxhoseni after the abolition of apartheid laws (for example see Jones 1993: 57). Children frequently moved between different households, depending on whether a household had sufficient money to take care of the child, whether parents felt that the money they sent was spent on the child, and whether they felt that the child was not being ill treated (Spiegel 1987: 120-127). Many parents could not take care of their child because they had to work. Crèches, if available at all, were too expensive, far away, poorly facilitated, or had no qualified staff. Parents also wanted to protect their children against the dangers of Cape Town. They worried that their child would join a gang or become a victim of violence. The Mayers' (1974: 271) findings on attitudes to rearing children in town still apply almost forty years later: '"Town is no fit place for a child". Rearing children there was supposed to mean a loss of parental control, with disastrous consequences for the child's morality, especially in the fields of sex, work, and crime.'

Maqashu and his wife, for example, sent one child old enough to attend school to relatives in the Eastern Cape. They also had a toddler, but he was easier to take care of and could temporarily be left with neighbours. Maqashu worked as a security officer and brought home about R800 a month. The family struggled to get by. Maqashu's wife told us (Edith and me) that they had been unemployed for about six years. They survived because they were able to get food on credit from a local shop. They repaid the debt to the shop owner at a rate of R250 per month. Another R100 was spent on public transport in order for Maqashu to commute to work. The relatives in the Eastern Cape also needed money to buy food and clothing, and pay for school fees for their child. Every month the parents had to send R250 through postal order, which left them with only R200. Although the financial problems of this family were severe – they were also regarded by neighbours as poor – they could not have the child with them and stop sending money. Maqashu's wife had to look for a job and she felt that Cape Town was a terrible place for children to grow up. This is only one example of how important relations with people in Emaxhoseni were. Children often grew up with different relatives in different towns where they attended different schools.

Upon their return to Cape Town, these moves and memories determined who was *umkhaya*. The moves between Cape Town and Emaxhoseni were also visible in the composition of the age pyramid of Africans in Cape Town, based on the 1996 census. Less than 5 percent of the African population was between ten and fifteen years old, while the age category of fifteen to nineteen years represented about seven percent of the urban African population. This increase is accounted for by the trend by which young people of that age left Emaxhoseni in order to find employment in Cape Town.[20]

Government institutions under apartheid regulated labour through labour bureaus, which limited the migrant's opportunity to introduce an *umkhaya* to his employer (Wilson & Mafeje 1963: 51). According to a small sample that concerned employment from the mid 1980s to the early 1990s, about two-thirds of the migrants said they had found employment through the labour bureaus. Only 19 percent found a job by word of mouth. Once apartheid and its labour bureaus were abolished, more people found a job by word of mouth (Oliver-Evans 1993: 39). The abolishment of apartheid could have led to an increase in the mobilisation of *abakhaya* in the migrant's quest for employment. If I asked whether *abakhaya* helped each other find employment in Cape Town, this was mostly confirmed (see Wilson & Mafeje 1963: 51). However, when I asked them for an example – for instance whether they had found a job for an *umkhaya*, got a job through *umkhaya* relations, or knew of someone who got a job through *umkhaya* relations – they could not provide any. High unemployment made it very difficult to find a job for anyone and if people knew about a job, they preferred to introduce a relative, a neighbour, or a member of the church. The contrast between ideology (finding a job for *abakhaya*) and practice (the inability to provide *abakhaya* with jobs) was also due to *abakhaya* living in different areas of Cape Town, meaning that they were rarely neighbours.

However, *abakhaya* did try to help each other a bit, for example by passing on messages and money during visits back home. Sometimes they were left in charge

---

[20] Based on a 10 percent sample of the Cape Metropolitan Area component of the Population Census conducted by SA Stats in October 1996 (CMC 2001). The authors mistakenly presented the small 0-4 age group as 'characteristic of a population with a decreasing fertility rate' or undercounting. In 1991, in the Ciskei the African population between ten and fifteen years old was 13.8 percent and the African population between fifteen and twenty years old 12.9 percent (SAS 1997: table 1.19). Such comparisons are problematic and the figures should only be regarded as a rough measure that indicates that a declining fertility rate was not the cause of the CMC findings. About the illegal squatter camp of Crossroads in the 1980s Reynolds (1989: 35) writes: 'In all, the children spent more than half of each of their lives in Cape Town… [T]hey had spent one-tenth away from their mothers and one-third away from their fathers.' See also numerous contributions in Burman & Reynolds (1986).

of a child on the same taxi home, a task occasionally assigned to the driver as well. *Abakhaya* were more likely to attend a festivity or funeral of an *umkhaya*. Although the social support migrants gave to *abakhaya* was limited, people did try to help each other and cherished the relationships with people who knew their home, school, or relatives.

Common relations (such as family members, ancestry, shared acquaintances) and places (such as magisterial districts, shopping centres, and rivers) were important to migrants who had to survive Cape Town's threatening triad. The hostility of Cape Town contributed to the identification among *abakhaya*. The city was a dangerous place where migrants could not feel at home. During apartheid, many illegal migrants tried to find a job in South Africa's industrial areas and took the risk of police detention, torture, and deportation to the Bantustans. Their illegal settlements could be bulldozed at any time and, especially during the state of emergency, the powers of the state and the police were incredible. The police did not address crime in the African settlements, which made them even more vulnerable. After apartheid, police were often absent as well or, if they were on hand, people were afraid that they were co-operating with criminal groups. In the Western Cape Province, the average murder rate in 1997 was eighty murders per 100,000 (SAIRR in Cape Times 1998). In the African townships, such as Guguletu and Langa, the murder rate was even higher, up to 120 to 150 murders per 100,000 in the early 1990s (Bähre 1996: 85; Ramphele 1991: 267). In the Western Cape in 1999, eighty-one murders and 160 rapes per 100,000 people were reported (SAPS 2000). Many rapes, however, were not reported due to lack of confidence in the judiciary system and fear of public stigmatisation. A survey of 4,000 women in Johannesburg revealed that one in three had been raped the past year (BBC 1999).[21]

At present, the occurrence of rape and murder in Cape Town is likely to be the highest in the world. Although the role of the police has changed in post-apartheid South Africa, the risk of poor, semi-literate migrants becoming victims of one or more of these crimes is tremendous, and actually unavoidable. For this reason alone Cape Town was not regarded as a home. No-one wanted to give up hope and simply accept that this was the place they were going to live permanently. The hostility of the city contributed to the identification with *abakhaya* and stressed the relationships with home in Emaxhoseni.

The fact that Xhosa took the hostility of the city seriously was evident in the preparations taken when they left the Eastern Cape. Those who were about to

---

[21] The NGO CIET Africa carried out the survey. The Western Cape, the province in which this research took place, has the highest number of rapes reported in South Africa. In 1997 there were 170.5 rapes and attempted rapes reported per 100,000 people, which is an increase since 1994 by 24 percent (SAIRR 1998: 28-29, 44; Cape Times 1998; SAPS 1998).

leave invoked the ancestors for assurance of their co-operation and assistance. They also had a special medicine, called 'medicine for war' (*ubulawu*), which provided protection. McAllister (1980: 215) notes that 'ubulawu (sic) ensures good luck, the favour of one's employer and protection from accidents, assaults and other misfortunes that might befall one at work'. The shiny and slippery sap of a particular aloe was used. This aloe was called *intelezi*, which meant 'good fortune in escaping danger', while *ubutelezi* meant slipperiness. As this name indicates, it helped a migrant to escape danger and slip out of difficult situations. Previously, *intelezi* was used to treat the army prior to battle but the new battle had become labour migration to Cape Town (McAllister 1980: 214-215).

The interdependencies between migrants and their families at home were strengthened by the hostility of the city, the dangers of the migratory process, and the importance of ancestry located in the area of origin. It was a terrible ordeal to live in the city or to be initiated and buried in such a hostile place. Upon arrival in Cape Town migrants rarely organised the beer drinking ritual that would introduce their new place to both the neighbours and the ancestors, who in return would provide protection. By neglecting this ritual, they risked losing ancestral protection. Only once did I notice a migrant brewing beer and inviting his neighbours to this ritual. It was not a great success, however, because many neighbours felt that they had not been invited properly. They spread a rumour that the neighbour did not want them to attend in order to limit the costs of the ritual.

At times, migrants told me about the large luxurious homes that they were building in Emaxhoseni. They conveyed images of large square brick houses with corrugated iron roofs and beautiful furniture – as opposed to the traditional round huts made of grass and clay with a thatched roof. These were portrayed as real homes and, therefore, it was useless to invest in a shack in Cape Town. Nofurniture, for example, used the R1,360 from her *umgalelo* (ASCRA) for her home in the Umtata district in the former Transkei. She had lived in Cape Town for ten years but preferred to invest her money in a four room house and nice furniture in Emaxhoseni. The place was empty and her children, who stayed with relatives in the same compound, took care of the place but did not live there. She still wanted to go back home: 'I will be buried there.' She had not introduced her shack in Cape Town to the ancestors through a beer drinking ritual. She wanted to finish her home in Emaxhoseni before buying furniture for her place in Cape Town. Obviously, the beer drinking ritual was never going to take place, and Umtata would always be her home, even if it was only as an ancestor.

To sum up, in the 1990s the identification of *abakhaya* was still important but did not govern migrants' lives like it did in the 1960s. It is possible that, during apartheid, migrants overemphasised what they were able to do for *abakhaya* in order to conceal their inability to help people. Nevertheless, significant changes did take place. The breakdown of apartheid meant that *abakhaya* were no longer neighbours, which made it less likely that *abakhaya* relations would be used as support networks. *Abakhaya* did try to help each other out, but opportunities were limited. Furthermore, under apartheid the intersection of *abakhaya* with neighbourhood relations provided a social constraint that was vital for financial mutuals. When apartheid ended, this form of regulation ceased to exist and relations in the city became more diverse. This, in turn, caused a decrease in the relevance of *abakhaya* relations for financial mutuals.

Although *abakhaya* were often no longer neighbours and had loosened the ties of mutual co-operation, *abakhaya* identifications were still pivotal to the migratory experience. The analysis of *abakhaya* identifications reveals how important home was for the migrants in Cape Town. The identification with home had religious significance, especially concerning relationships with the ancestors. It also had an economic dimension, because the identification with home revealed the economic and social interdependencies between migrants and their kin in Emaxhoseni. The hostility of Cape Town, moreover, made it even less attractive to set up a permanent life there. Labour migration, also after apartheid, was a treacherous and insecure experience in itself. Xhosa migrants were willing to endure it because they hoped to make some money, but not because they liked Cape Town.

## Female neighbours

Under apartheid, the few African women in the city were usually there illegally, could not get employment, and depended on their men's income and shelter. This dependency made women very vulnerable, especially as unmarried women competed with wives or other unmarried women over men with a job and lodging (Ramphele 1989).[22] Due to the apartheid legislation, men were initially central to the migratory process of women (James 1999b: 48-58). Women migrated in order to join their men – for social and economic reasons – or in order to earn money for their dependants. As James (1999b: 49-50) wrote on women who moved from the Northern Province to the Johannesburg and Pretoria area:

> All these women, whether married or not, relied on individual, usually male, family members, related either by blood or by marriage, to bring them to town and to connect them into broader networks after arrival. It was because female migration from the Northern Province was not undertaken by groups of people … that they were tied, at least at the start of their migrant careers, to husbands or male kin and to the home-based networks to which they belonged.

---

22 See Mager (1999) for a detailed examination of women's position in the Ciskei from the mid 1940s to the end of the 1950s. For the sexual dimension of the migratory process in the Rand, see Bonner (1990; 1995) and in the South African mines see Moodie (1988; 1994).

After some time, James (1999b: 62-63; 1999a) described, these women did not want to depend only on the home-boy networks of the men, and instead established their own groups based on home relationships. By establishing *kiba* groups, migrant women setup their own identification with 'those of one home' (James 1999b: 62-63; 1999).

The organisations that Xhosa women established, however, were quite different from those established by Sotho women described by James (1999b). Moreover, female Xhosa migrants initially joined their husbands' burial societies in Cape Town and did not start to establish distinct female *abakhaya* burial societies. Unlike the Sotho women who organised activities based on their identification with people from home, Xhosa women in Cape Town did not do so. The difference between Sotho and Xhosa women could be due to the social constraint that was necessary for the formation of financial mutuals. In the Sotho women's *kiba* groups, social constraint was less important because there was no money involved. Xhosa women did not organise financial mutuals with *abakhaya* because these relations did not offer social constraint, while neighbours did.

When the apartheid laws were no longer enforced, women were increasingly able to migrate to Cape Town.[23] Unlike the illegal migrants during apartheid, they were able to set up their homes independently from men. The women's neighbours were only incidentally *abakhaya* and social constraint and trust had to be sought within the neighbourhood and not among *abakhaya*.

Although neighbourhood relations were very important for the organisation of financial mutuals, they have received little scholarly attention in South Africa. In South Africa, critical social scientists were particularly interested in political struggles, as well as the uses and abuses of 'community' for policy purposes, as in the case of Thornton & Ramphele (1988: 29). The pre-occupation with political struggles focused on 'community', but 'neighbourhood' was implicitly considered apolitical and, therefore, not worthy of much attention.

'Neighbourhood' as an analytical category is undervalued, despite the fact that it is very important to the Xhosa, also from a political point of view. During apartheid, for example, neighbours established street committees, organised rent boycotts, consumer boycotts, stay-aways, and tried to take over functions from local government (Seekings 1992: 217-222; Van Kessel 2000). Notwithstanding this role of neighbourhoods, these initiatives were easily drawn into the debates on 'community'.

A distinction needs to be made between 'neighbourhood' and 'community'. Neighbours were people with whom one interacted on a daily basis, while the

---

[23] Although women moved to Cape Town in order to look for a job, in 1996 half of the African women in Cape Town were unemployed. A third of the African men were unemployed, while 5 percent of White males were unemployed (CMC 2001).

community encompassed a much larger group of people whom one generally did not know, except as local leaders and other prominent figures. Generally, those living in the same street were identified as neighbours. However, some streets were very long or had a sharp curve so that residents of one street were not necessarily neighbours. Still other streets were very short, like a dead-end street, and therefore the residents of that street regarded themselves more easily as neighbours of residents in the adjacent street.

The neighbours' children played with each other and formed a vital link between neighbours. They were sent for messages, bought eggs, bread, cigarettes, or alcohol at the spaza shop (local store) down the street. Children were an important source of information for their parents who asked them about the latest gossip in the street. Occasionally, there were birthday parties to which all the children of the neighbourhood were invited. Their mothers would come along to dish out cake, biscuits, and lemonade and would give presents to the beautifully dressed birthday child. Neighbours also asked one another for favours. It was common to ask a neighbour for some money, such as R10 for a taxi or paraffin for cooking. This was considered a loan, but both neighbours often knew that it would not be returned. One could perhaps return the favour whenever the neighbour needed some help. Neighbours also kept an eye on each other's children or homes. Some even gave their door key to a neighbour who would then let visitors or a child into the house. Moreover, neighbours tried to help one another find jobs, much more than *abakhaya* did.

Neighbours were well informed about the lives of those living next door. Corrugated iron and cardboard were far from soundproof and the small houses were very close to one another. Sometimes neighbours literally could overhear what their next-door neighbours were saying while they were inside their houses. Moreover, the confined space meant that many quarrels took place outside for everybody to observe. Neighbours visited each other, gossiped, and drank tea or chicory coffee, but only rarely stayed for a meal. If people visited their neighbours at around dinnertime, it forced the neighbour to offer them some food. It would have been very impolite of the host not to offer anything, but also very painful if he or she had hardly anything to give. There were jokes about the strategies people devised to avoid sharing food. One suggestion was that it was best to start eating one's meat immediately, or instead hide it under the potatoes, just in case a visitor would arrive. Another option, I was told jokingly, was to offer a visitor one's spoon: 'Here's my spoon. Come and share a meal with me.' The hope was that a visitor would decline the offer of using the same spoon. Some visitors had the reputation for abusing hospitality. They would 'accidentally' arrive when neighbours were eating. When the visitor was offered food, he or she would say: 'No, I'm not so hungry, just some meat is fine.' Mostly, however, neighbours tried to avoid causing embarrassment by adapting eating times or visits. I never encountered anybody eating, except at my research assistant's place, and during funerals and festivities. This was quite telling if one takes into consideration that people lived in a one-roomed or two-roomed house and had little opportunities to hide while eating.

Neighbourhood identifications showed a flexibility that resembled *abakhaya* identifications. When I asked Edith to indicate on a map who her neighbours were she marked a large section covering about 110 plots, with a rough estimate of about 400 residents. She felt, however, that the selection was to some extent arbitrary because other people, who lived further away but with whom she had contact, were also her neighbours. Another woman told me that someone who lived almost on the other side of the settlement, about five to ten minutes walk away, was also her neighbour. They used to be close neighbours in the past and, after they had moved apart, they continued to consider each other neighbours. The identification of neighbours was thus based on a combination of social and physical proximity.

Because neighbourhood identifications were fairly flexible, they formed a practical basis for organising groups together and there were never too many or too few neighbours to form a financial mutual. Neighbours established all kinds of financial mutuals together, except for the fairly large burial societies with a fund. They were a convenient group of people to work with, and moreover, joint activities, such as collecting money for a funeral or forming a financial mutual, helped to define the neighbourhood. Thus, financial mutuals were not only based on neighbourhood relations, but also identified people as neighbours. Financial mutuals were especially useful for recent migrants, since these helped them to get acquainted with their new area.

Burials particularly helped to define a neighbourhood. The collection of money determined who were considered neighbours. The collection engaged people in reciprocal relations that were regarded as constitutive of neighbourly relations. In other words, being neighbours was realised by doing neighbourly activities. Noxolo, who was involved in such a collection among new neighbours, told me that the person whose door she could see from her own place were her neighbours. If she saw the entrance to their place, she could see who was walking in and out and what everybody was doing, which made them her neighbours. There were about a dozen shacks that one could see across the street from her whom she identified as neighbours. The residents on her side of the street were also Noxolo's neighbours, although she could not see their doors. Right behind Noxolo's shack was an open field. Noxolo could look across the field and the adjacent street into the residents' houses, so they were therefore also her neighbours. Noxolo, furthermore, was not the only one to collect money for the funeral since women in streets further away also collected money and were considered neighbours of the deceased as well.

In 1997, residents of a street in Indawo Yoxolo established a burial society without a fund in order to get to know each other. One of the central figures in this burial society was Mr Qina. He showed me a handwritten pamphlet that he had composed in Xhosa together with his neighbour and which was distributed in the neighbourhood:

> *Residents,*
> All who stay at this street are being asked to be present at a meeting which will be held at Mqwathi's place on the day of 22 October 1997 on Wednesday 7 pm.
> It is about getting together on the days of dark clouds.
> We will appreciate your presence,
> Thank you

Out of respect for the dead, one should avoid a clear reference to death. People were afraid of death and therefore referred to it as 'the days of dark clouds' or 'when something happens'. Mr Qina was quick to take the paper out of my hand. He was afraid that the meeting might be seen as a political meeting. As will become clear in the next chapter, there were many political tensions in the area that could damage such initiatives. Mr Qina kept the pamphlet in order to prove that he was not interested in political issues and had simply tried to organise a burial society among neighbours.

That evening about forty people, mostly women, gathered on Mr Mqwathi's plot. The meeting started when Mr Qina stood up and took off his hat out of respect. He gave a speech in which he made clear how humble his attempts were to organise a burial society: 'We are from different areas, and in some areas we should do something. Some would contribute money, but that's not what we call a burial society. It is not a burial society; it is just an idea for people in the street only … It is just for the street.' One man immediately supported him: 'People enjoy life when they are still alive and forget about it when things happen. It is a good idea because a person is never thrown away.' Other men made supportive statements such as, 'we are going to get to know each other', or 'we are all here and we don't know each other, because we only get to know each other if there are problems'. One woman had received the pamphlet but did not really know what the meeting was about because she could not read. She lived one street further and left after she was told that she could not join because she did not reside in their street.

Because Mr Qina had taken the initiative, he was elected chairperson. They also needed a vice-chairperson, a secretary, a vice-secretary and four other board members. These functions were far from popular and the members were elected by appointment. For example, Mr Cophele stood up and said: 'I elect Mr Moya.' Mr Moya, however, was not pleased to be elected and got up to say: 'I don't want to be elected. I work and I don't have the time.' Mr Qina, however made clear that: 'If we can take that excuse we all have excuses. So please, just understand that everyone has an excuse but we don't want to make this meeting an excuse.' Mr

Moya ended up being elected anyway, just like Mr Jonase who also protested: 'I am sorry, but I am very busy. I go to church and have a lot of responsibilities.' But his protest was not accepted either and another man said 'people, accept when you are elected, because if we make one excuse, we take all excuses. We don't take volunteers, as this is very important. We all have our problems.' Later Mr Jonase again tried to make the position available to others: 'I ask people to elect other people along the line and let other people do what they are doing. Everyone should have a chance, otherwise I will loosen myself from the ties.' However, his efforts were in vain and nobody was eager to take his place.

People became impatient and hungry as it was getting past eight o'clock. They decided to collect R20 after each death and cover only those who 'stay under one roof'. Kin in the Eastern Cape themselves were not covered and the burial society did not contribute to travelling costs for attending funerals in the Eastern Cape. Before everyone left, the committee members stood up and introduced themselves by their name and plot number. This revealed how the neighbours hardly knew each other and that the burial society created neighbourly relations. After a prayer, everyone rushed home to cook dinner.

Financial mutuals helped to establish neighbourly relations especially among new residents in new areas. Although feelings of solidarity and mutual support were important, one should not neglect the social tensions that could exist among neighbours. Later, in the same street where this burial society was established, I heard from two neighbours of an extreme case in which a child was punished. The child had stolen a few audiocassettes from his neighbour, who then complained by saying that, according to her, the child was not worth anything: if it was up to her, the child would be killed. After this, a group of neighbouring men had kicked and beaten the child to death. Because one of the men was aligned to a group of powerful and violent people in the area, the parents were too scared to do anything about it and the murder was not reported to the police.

The concept of community, with its political history in South Africa, led to an underestimation of neighbourhood relationships and emphasised political life too much. Migrants became new neighbours who knew little about each other, which was in strong contrast with the situation in longer established neighbourhoods in Cape Town and the Eastern Cape. Especially in Emaxhoseni, neighbours played a central role in rituals, such as circumcision and beer drinking rituals. In neighbourhoods which had been established longer ago, people collected money for a common goal more often. During my fieldwork, this was done only once in Indawo Yoxolo, but, unfortunately, the collectors, who were associated with the powerful political group of the Big Five, took most of the money. Although Indawo Yoxolo was a new place, the neighbourhood was already playing a major role because, within months, neighbours were organising financial mutuals. Women organised financial mutuals in the neighbourhood which, in contrast with the experience of migrant men in the past, no longer coincided with *abakhaya* relations.

## Conclusion

Three kinds of social relations were central to financial mutuals: kinship, *abakhaya*, and neighbours. These relations were not static, but changed considerably over time. In this respect, the dramatic impact of colonialism and capitalism on the Xhosa economy can hardly be underestimated. It not only led to changes in the political economy, such as the introduction of wage labour, money, taxation, and the availability of new consumer items, but also to political changes, such as those brought on by war, apartheid legislation, and natural disasters that undermined the subsistence economy, including drought, lung disease among cattle, and East Coast fever. A society with a kin-ordered mode of production changed into a society in which the capitalist mode of production became dominant.

The consequence of this economic change was the transformation of social relations. The elders' position was challenged due to the decrease in customary marriages. Young men and unmarried women had greater autonomy due to the money they earned themselves. Dependencies between husbands and wives were fraught with new tensions due to no longer adhering to *lobola* and the prolonged absence of migrant men. Children increasingly became a financial burden, competition between full brothers changed, and new demands were made on newly available money. Furthermore, compounds became smaller and people were often forced to resettle in the Bantustans. Such changes meant that reliance on neighbours increased and that neighbours, both in urban and rural areas, were less likely to be kin.

In order to support themselves and their families, many Xhosa tried to find work in urban and industrial centres outside of the Bantustans. Cape Town was governed by the Coloured Labour Preference Policy, which resulted in a minority African population and a further marginalization of Africans in the city. The migratory process led to the establishment of a new type of relations among the Xhosa migrants, namely those based on the identification of *abakhaya*, i.e. 'those of one home'. In order to understand why migrants went to cities such as Cape Town, one has to be sensitive to what 'home' meant to migrants. The male migrants – under apartheid it was even more difficult for women to migrate – identified with each other due to a shared notion of origin, which coincided with responsibilities towards home, such as building the homestead and a commitment towards the ancestors. The threatening experiences of migration made home even more important, and in post-apartheid South Africa as well, the threatening triad of violence, economic insecurity, and volatile relations did not make migrants feel at home in the city. Instead, it encouraged migrants to emphasise and possibly romanticise the home they left in the Eastern Cape.

Apartheid policy forced male migrants – often accompanied by 'illegal women' – from the same home to live together in one room. *Abakhaya* would live together, eat together, cook together, and exercise some social constraint over one another. These *abakhaya*/neighbours offered the social cohesion and constraints that were needed to form financial mutuals. Financial mutuals, at least to some extent, ensured that migrants did not abscond during their stay in the city but returned home with gifts and presents for their kin. They also made sure that, after death, the migrant's body was returned home for a proper burial.

The breakdown of the apartheid laws loosened *abakhaya* relations. Although *abakhaya* identifications were still important, they did not lead to the establishment of financial mutuals anymore. Instead, neighbourhood relations became increasingly important as a type of social relation that was independent of kin and *abakhaya*. Consanguinity no longer meant physical proximity. This was because the migration of women to Cape Town coincided with the further separation of *abakhaya* relations and neighbourhood relations. The end of apartheid brought with it a change in urban demographics from mainly single men living in barracks to households, often headed by females, in newly established neighbourhoods. The neighbourhood was central to the organisation of the migrants' social life, including the care of children and various forms of mutual care. The social constraints that neighbours offered gave women more possibilities to organise their money in financial mutuals.

The structural changes in the three types of relations (kinship, *abakhaya*, and neighbour) were accompanied by new structural tensions between people who depended on each other. Financial mutuals played an important role in the making and breaking of these tensions because they influenced the allocation of money within the wider kinship network and because they helped to establish personal bonds between neighbours. This is one of the major attractions of the study of financial mutuals. Financial mutuals were central to the establishment, as well as people's understanding, of *abakhaya* and neighbourhood relations in the city. Moreover, the study of financial mutuals revealed how, by allocating money, migrants tried to establish, maintain, or challenge kin relations.

# 3

# The economy of development and social relations

## Introduction

When I briefly visited Indawo Yoxolo for the first time in 1995, it was a small informal settlement squeezed between a large Coloured township to the south, and a railroad track and an African township to the north. A few dozen shacks were scattered between the bushes, a muddy path served as a road, the bushes were used as toilets, and there was no electricity or water. In order to obtain water, those living in Indawo Yoxolo had to ask the residents of the township next door, who were not too pleased with their new neighbours. There was only one kindergarten, accommodated in a pink shipping container and run by a few residents of Indawo Yoxolo. Although the kindergarten allowed women to drop their children off on their way to work, the mothers and staff had many complaints. There was nothing with which to entertain the children, and the children just sat on the floor for most of the day. People also complained about the government's promise to provide lunch since no food was provided.

Adjacent to these shacks, construction workers were clearing bushes and levelling the ground with heavy machinery. Indawo Yoxolo was part of the national Reconstruction and Development Programme (RDP), an effort by the ANC government to try to overcome some of the inequalities and poverty left behind by apartheid. They intended to develop the illegal squatter settlement of Indawo Yoxolo into a formal township complete with electricity, toilets, water, streets, streetlights, schools, public telephones, bus stops, taxi-ranks, sports fields, and plots for poor people to live on.

Indawo Yoxolo presented the opportunity to examine how financial mutuals were established from scratch, as Xhosa migrants had just moved to the place. The aim of this chapter is twofold. First, it provides an account of Xhosa migrants living in a post-apartheid township, namely, the living conditions with which people had to contend on a daily basis and the wider socio-political context in which financial mutuals are embedded. Second, it reveals the presence of the post-apartheid state, a presence most strongly felt in the realm of development. Police protection was virtually nonexistent in the area, leaving people to fend for themselves, at times with horrific consequences. At the time of my research, local government was weak, understaffed, and only marginally functional. There were a few schools, but even these were caught up in the development process. As will become apparent in this chapter, the post-apartheid state was in an almost exclusive manner active through the development projects. This had consequences for the local political processes in Indawo Yoxolo as well as for the way in which financial mutuals were organised.

## The development dream

Optimism for the post-apartheid future was very high. With the release of Mandela in 1990 and the first democratic elections in April 1994, many, including those outside South Africa, hoped for a drastic change for the better. As the Comaroffs wrote: 'In South-Africa, after all, the end of apartheid held out to indulge that *everyone* would be set free to speculate and accumulate, to consume, and to indulge repressed desires. But, for many, the millennial moment has passed without palpable payback' (Comaroff & Comaroff 1999: 284). Many, of course, realised that the ANC could not overcome the legacy of apartheid within a few years, but nevertheless people expected that the political changes would lead to redistribution. In addition, many Whites initially feared that Africans would steal their property. For example, someone recalled how, in the Eighties, African women had marched to Cape Town's previously White suburb of Lansdown. These African women were walking through the streets of Lansdown and expressing their dreams about those houses with gardens – sometimes also with swimming pools – that they were going to claim once apartheid was over. These dreams about the future were so real that some women were said to get into a fight because they both intended to claim the same house once apartheid was over.

Inequalities had to be abolished by redistributing resources and establishing development projects.[1] Central to the post-apartheid era was the national Reconstruction and Development Programme (RDP) (ANC 1994). Poverty stricken Africans and, to a lesser extent Coloureds had to get improved communal facilities, such as sanitation, roads, better policing, and health care. More jobs had to be created and schools had to be improved through, for example, a national 'school-feeding programme' which had to ensure that children received at least one decent meal a day. The government installed a special temporary RDP minister without portfolio, Mr Naidoo. After a couple of years, the numerous RDP projects were to be integrated into the portfolios of the other ministers.

One of the most prominent features of the RDP was the housing grant for the poor. From 1994 to 1999, one million low-cost houses were going to be built. According to income, housing subsidies of up to R15,000 were made available.[2] It was only possible to apply for a full subsidy if one earned less than R800 per month. This subsidy was not distributed directly in cash to the applicant. Private sector building companies and, in some instances, NGOs could be contracted to build roads, plots, electricity connections, sewage systems, toilets, and other facilities. If applicants were eligible for a grant they were allowed to occupy and own a plot in the neighbourhood developed by the RDP. Throughout South Africa, the variety of the structures and facilities varied greatly, depending on the costs involved and the priorities that were set. The main emphasis, however, was on public services and underground infrastructure, such as water supply, sewage pipes, electricity wires, streetlights, and roads.

Because the vast majority of the population was denied the right to vote during apartheid, the ANC incorporated an active approach towards democratisation into its development plans (ANC 1994: 119-135). Under apartheid, the ANC associated development with government rule, racial segregation, and apartheid ideology. However, in the post-apartheid era, the ANC 'soon found itself adopting the

---

1 See Nauta (2001) for a study of land reform in the Eastern Cape.

2 Source: Masakhane (1995: 4). The structure of the subsidy had an awkward effect on the housing situation of the applicants. Those who received a full subsidy chose a plot with an 'RDP house', as the tiny, concrete one-roomed houses with a corrugated iron roof, one door, and two windows, and a sink were called. Those whose income was too high for a full subsidy would not have enough money for such an RDP house on their plot and instead they built a shack. Many others hoped that they could save enough money in the future to add to the remains of the subsidy in order to build a two-roomed, or maybe even a three-roomed house. This meant that some of the poorest, and those without much hope of improvements in their financial situation, would live in the better looking, but not necessarily better built, RDP houses. Those who were financially slightly better off, or expected to be in the future, lived in a shack.

"pragmatic" language of 'reconstruction and development" (Crush 1995: xii in Li 1999: 296). The RDP document stated:

> Our people, with their aspirations and collective determination, are our most important resource. The RDP is focused on our people's most immediate needs, and it relies, in turn, on their energies to drive the process of meeting these needs ... Development is not about the delivery of goods to a passive citizenry. It is about active involvement and growing empowerment. In taking this approach we are building on the many forums, peace structures and negotiations that our people are involved in throughout the land (ANC 1994: 5).

In Cape Town, the Development Planning Committee (DPC) largely carried out the RDP development. Within five years it wanted to develop and upgrade 34,500 sites and improve the housing situation of more than 35,000 poor families. People from twenty-one informal settlements, eight areas of backyard shack dwellers, and residents of three hostels were supposed to benefit from this project, which was also accessible to another 6,200 Coloured families who were on waiting lists for housing (DPC 1994: 8).

During my fieldwork in 1995, one could almost feel the energy that the political changes brought. Although many felt that some people's expectations far exceeded the possibilities of economic improvement, they also felt that economic improvement was going to take place, even if it would take another generation. By 1997, the mood had changed. Particularly better educated young Africans and White so-called 'liberals' (the term had become derogative by then) expressed their resentment. Many Africans felt that, although they had contributed to the struggle, they did not share sufficiently in the benefits, or that the ANC elite had abandoned the deprived masses. Although not to the same extent, destitute African migrants were also disappointed when they did not experience much economic improvement. Due to the costs of these public services and facilities, there was often little or no subsidy left to build a house for the applicant. Therefore, most houses measured only a few square metres and consisted of one room only, which led to many complaints about matchbox houses. Moreover, by the beginning of 1998, only a fifth of the planned houses had been built (Mail & Guardian 1998a: 4). The development process resembled a cargo cult in which goods would arrive if one performed the proper rituals. In this case, these secular rituals were built around democratisation, community participation, and empowerment. The case study of Indawo Yoxolo shows how development actually took place, how resources were channelled, and what the local responses to development were.

## Development policy

By the time I returned to Indawo Yoxolo, in 1997, many of the development projects were finished and the place had changed drastically. The pink container was still housing a kindergarten, and the shacks I saw in 1995 were still there, although later I found that some of the people had gone and new people had arrived. Apart from that, the place was unrecognisable. One no longer reached Indawo Yoxolo by turning off the paved road that led to the adjacent Coloured townships, driving over the curb, and following a muddy path into the bushes. Instead there was a paved road from which streets branched off in a herringbone pattern. The bushes were gone and along the streets were neatly ordered plots. Each plot had its own private electricity connection, toilet, and water tap. Schools and sports fields were under construction, there were curbs, and two public telephones (which were out of order most of the time). Moreover, there were plans to build taxi ranks, a public library, bus stops, and other public facilities.[3]

The plots clearly distinguished the somewhat more established residents from the very new residents. Those who had moved there some time ago, for example half a year or longer, had put a little fence around their plots, had planted vegetables or shrubs that were trying to survive in the sand, or had built a shack at the rear of their little boxy government houses. The newer streets toward the east of Indawo Yoxolo still had some vacant plots. The residents had not yet built an extra room onto their RDP houses and the ground was bereft of vegetation. Still further to the east, the construction workers continued to dig and install electricity, sewage, and water pipes, as well as survey plots and roads. The squatter camp that I visited in 1995 still existed and had become a relatively small section of Indawo Yoxolo. Because of the absence of paved roads, curbs, and demarcated plots, it contrasted greatly with the rest of Indawo Yoxolo. The residents of this squatter area were still waiting for the housing grant that would allow them to move to their demarcated plot.

Almost all the residents of Indawo Yoxolo were from Emaxhoseni. For example, Lennox's home was near Umtata, the capital of the former Transkei. In the mid 1980s, Lennox had moved to an informal settlement near Nyanga in Cape Town where water, sanitation, and electricity, were absent, except for a few dirty and badly maintained communal facilities. When I met Lennox for the first time in

---

3 When I visited Indawo Yoxolo in 2005 and 2006, it had again transformed drastically. It had become very crowded, more flats had been built and new residents had put their shacks on existing plots. In some instances, a plot that was designed for one dwelling had three shacks on it. By now, Indawo Yoxolo also had a police station which was situated in a shipping container which was less vulnerable to vandalism than a brick building. The police would leave in the evening and lock the container.

October 1997, he had moved to Indawo Yoxolo only a few months before. Lennox still visited Paula Park and participated in a financial mutual with his previous neighbours. The residents of Indawo Yoxolo were all (at least officially) from numerous illegal squatter camps and backyard shacks of Cape Town that had grown because of urbanisation and the housing shortage.

The RDP policy had significant political consequences. The RDP had to be implemented by local community representative bodies that gathered in a so-called RDP forum. All local political organisations and community-based organisations were supposed to be represented in a local RDP forum. Each RDP forum was asked to establish development priorities according to a number of themes that were set out by the RDP document.[4] The development projects had to be discussed with government structures, private enterprises, and community representatives before they could be implemented. Development had to take place through community participation and people's involvement in democratic processes, instead of via a top-down approach in which policymakers would decide what was best for people. Since the late 1980s, due to disappointing experiences with structural adjustment lending, the end of the Cold War, and the dominance of neo-liberal thought, more and more importance was attached to democracy (Leftwitch 1994: 366).

In Cape Town in 1991, political organisations, grassroots organisations and government bodies had established the Development Planning Policy Committee, consisting of different political parties, government institutions and community-based organisations.[5] Later it was renamed the DPC (Development Planning Committee) and it became part of the RDP in 1993-94.[6]

The DPC also focused on community involvement in development, just like the RDP did. The DPC's commitment to community participation was laid down in three of the nine objectives stated in the formulating phase. For example, the first objective was: 'To establish a coalition of community, public sector and private

---

4 These themes were Public Works, Arts and Culture, Tourism and Environment, Public Transport, Education, Housing, Sport, Social Security, Safety, Health, Religion and Youth.

5 The forum consisted of the African National Congress (ANC), Cape Provincial Administration (CPA), South African National Civics Organisation (SANCO), Western Cape Regional Services Council (WCRSC), Western Cape United Squatters Association (WeCUSA), Cape Town City Council (CCC), Western Cape Civics Association (WCCA), Ikapa Town Council, Umzamo Development Project, Crossroads Town Council and at a later stage, the Pan African Congress (PAC) (DPC 1994: 1).

6 The RDP money was insufficient to execute the development projects and, therefore, the DPC had secured extra funds from the Provincial Administration of the Western Cape and the Cape Metropolitan Council. This made it possible to raise the RDP subsidy for housing from R15,000 to a maximum of R17,250 for each plot and have more money for infrastructure and community facilities (DPC 1996a).

sector stakeholders in order to undertake the foundational strategic planning and policy-making for the project, and to agree on the Terms of Reference' (DPC 1994: 4).

Instead of an RDP forum, the DPC had its Project Committee. The Project Committee consisted of representatives of numerous community-based organisations who had to determine the implementation and management of the projects. They had to inform and consult the community about the DPC plans and, most notably, decide on the rules and procedures for the allocation of sites and the implementation of the allocation process (DPC 1994: 14). Families who had lived the longest in a particular area were allowed to move to the new plots first. Special priority was given to people older than twenty-one who lived with dependents (DPC 1996d: 1).

## The project committee

The Project Committee in Indawo Yoxolo was very powerful. The members of the committee functioned as intermediaries between the community, the DPC structure, and private construction companies. They controlled the list of applicants and decided how the rules were applied. It was very difficult to know how long the squatters had lived in a particular area, and that gave the Project Committee the space to prioritise applications. Furthermore, the Project Committee had a large influence on the recruitment of local labourers who were needed to build Indawo Yoxolo. It was a requirement that at least half of the labourers were residents of a particular area and it was up to the Project Committee to assist in their recruitment. High unemployment and widespread deprivation made the Project Committee very powerful.[7] Figure 3.1 shows an overview of the political situation in Indawo Yoxolo as I found it in September 1997.

The DPC Project Committee was made up of representatives of residents of the areas that were eligible for a plot in Indawo Yoxolo. Unfortunately, I could not determine exactly which members of the project committee came from which settlement. It was clear, however, that their main stronghold was in the old, unserviced Indawo Yoxolo that I had encountered in 1995, and that they had less support among the residents of the serviced Indawo Yoxolo who had already received their plots. The residents of the unserviced area and the surrounding squatter camps depended more on the Project Committee than others because they were still waiting for a housing subsidy. Opponents of the Project Committee

---

7 The development of Indawo Yoxolo with its focus on community participation can be understood as a project of rule. See, among others, Bähre (2001), Escobar (1991), Ferguson (1990), Schroeder (1999), Scott (1998).

referred to them as the 'Old Committee' because they favoured a new committee. They also called them the 'Big Five'. The Big Five refers to the five powerful animals of South Africa's game parks: leopard, lion, elephant, rhino, and buffalo. The adoption of the name Big Five for the Project Committee emphasized the power and danger of this group. Moreover, the name Big Five reminds one of the big man paradigm.[8]

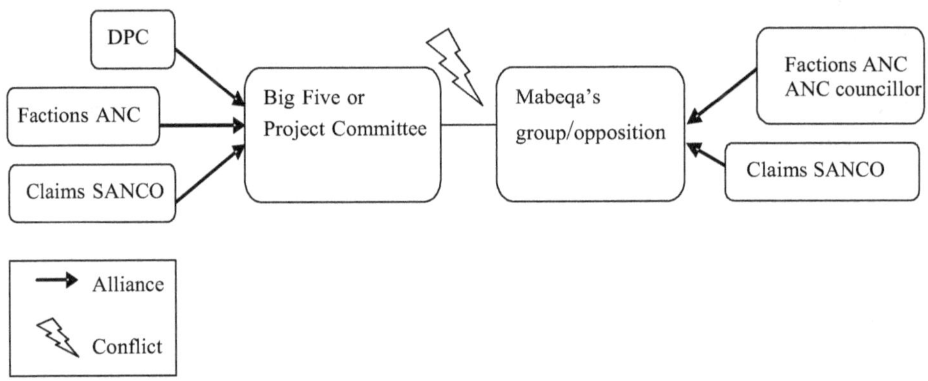


*Figure 3.1* September 1997

The following is a brief description of the Big Five (Bula, Zantsi, Nqase, Posa, and Mtontsi) and their status, as well as the rumours around these political figures. As I already mentioned in the introduction, it was impossible for me to get close to the Big Five. They were too dangerous and it was best to avoid them as much as possible. I once had a brief conversation with Nqase. He was known as 'the gun' of the Big Five and he was considered stupid enough to kill and get caught and was involved in all kinds of dirty business, outside of Indawo Yoxolo as well. He was not reputed to be the brain of the organisation, but it was common knowledge that he was willing to murder people. Nqase was a big man and around forty years old, possibly younger. He was always nicely dressed, had a small, trendy mobile phone, and one could see his gun bulging from underneath his jacket or sweater. Our encounter was a very uncomfortable experience. I was playing soccer with two kids in front of Edith's place while teenagers were playing street theatre. The teenagers were preparing a sinister scene in which the young men forced themselves on a girl as if they were raping her. The bystanders shouted instructions and showed their approval or disapproval of the acting performances. Nqase chatted with Edith and my girlfriend Esther and I interrupted my soccer to join

[8] See Thoden van Velzen (1973: 602) for a critical analysis of the big men paradigm.

them. We shook hands, talked a bit about the weather, made some jokes, laughed a bit, and after that he strolled away. To an outsider it must have looked like one of those ordinary conversations neighbours have all the time. But I knew that he had recently killed Gilbert Mabeqa, the man who had introduced me into Indawo Yoxolo and who was one of the key figures that opposed the Big Five. Nqase, of course, was also aware that I knew about his murder, and Nqase also knew that he and the other Big Five members had threatened to kill Edith, as well. Nevertheless we managed to pretend to have a friendly and open conversation about the weather.

Zantsi was reputedly the most powerful and smartest of the Big Five. I was told by a Big Five opponent in Indawo Yoxolo that whenever the Big Five resorted to violence, he was 'accidentally' away for a visit to his home in the Transkei. Due to my endeavours to stay away from the Big Five, I had actually never seen him, except for once in the distance when he and some others drove to the Indawo Yoxolo squatter camp in two cars. Bula, the third member of the Big Five, was from Gxuwa (Butterworth), the same place Gilbert Mabeqa came from. His reputation was also that of a powerful man who threatened and blackmailed people. The remaining two members of the Big Five, Posa and Mtontsi, were not as powerful. Mtontsi was a small, badly dressed man who, despite his young age, missed a considerable number of teeth. He worked frequently for the construction companies and was often drunk. Posa was hardly ever seen or heard from and, therefore, I would often forget about him being a member of the Big Five.

The Big Five controlled the DPC projects, as well as all the other initiatives in the area. This included the building of schools, the appointment of teachers, the distribution of RDP plots to applicants, and even the plans to build speed bumps to slow down traffic. They supported school teachers who took children's lunches, forcing them to buy sweets and chicken feet from the women – also Big Five supporters – who had their little food stalls on the school grounds. The Big Five were also responsible for finding local labourers to work for contractors, such as Donald & Gromit and A&W Construction. Moreover, they co-operated with certain factions of the ANC and, at times, also with other political parties (National Party and United Democratic Movement). Their most important power base, however, was as the DPC Project Committee.

Their control over the distribution of resources made the Big Five very powerful. As Barth wrote on leadership among the Swat Pathans: 'Only through his control of this resource [land] can he attract the clients with which to inflate his political ego' (Barth 1959: 7). The Big Five should be regarded as a Mafia-style organisation and leadership rather than as patrons or leaders of a system of collective clientelism.[9] The Big Five used violence and intimidation to maintain and exploit their position. They also demanded bribes before a plot was allocated to an applicant. Moreover, they promised to make Indawo Yoxolo a better place in return for their support, as one would expect from patrons. They did not, however, host parties or give money to people at public events, such as funerals. Although the Big Five provided jobs and gave some people political support, they did not present themselves as, nor were they considered to be, guardians of the welfare of the community. Their Mafia-style rule was based on intimidation, murder, and corruption, as well as control over the resources of the development projects.

## The opposition

Politics in Indawo Yoxolo changed when more people left the informal settlements in order to move to their plots in Indawo Yoxolo. Those who already had a plot were less dependent on the Big Five. They had already been on the housing list that the Big Five controlled and had received their housing grants. The Big Five were still able to intimidate these people and gave, or at least promised to give, some people jobs. However, they were no longer able to threaten to withhold housing subsidies.

Some of those who already received plots organised opposition to the Big Five. This opposition had no official name. They sometimes called themselves the 'new committee' because they considered themselves to be the legitimate successors to the 'old committee'. The composition of the residents in Indawo Yoxolo had changed since the Big Five were in power and, therefore, the 'old committee' had to relinquish its position. The opposition wanted to elect new community leaders who represented all residents. Their most prominent leader was Gilbert Mabeqa, a former ANC 'comrade' who had moved with his wife and teenage daughter from Guguletu to a plot in Indawo Yoxolo. I call this the opposition to the Big Five Mabeqa's group because of Gilbert Mabeqa's central position. The supporters of Mabeqa's group lived in the serviced Indawo Yoxolo. Mabeqa, Gxyiza, Constance, Michael, and my research assistant Edith were among the most active people opposed to the corrupt and violent Big Five.

Mabeqa's group was, just like the Big Five, related to the ANC or, at least, certain factions of the ANC within the local and provincial governments. They had

---

9 Instead of relationships between individuals (patronage), collective clientelism is characterised by less personal relationships than a group of leaders have with the residents of a community (Burgwal 1995: 27-28, 144). See Van der Linden (1997) on the way in which housing projects in Pakistan are thwarted because of patronage relations.

unclear relations with the South African National Civic Organisation (SANCO), the civic body that succeeded the UDF. They claimed to be the legitimate SANCO committee in Indawo Yoxolo, but the Big Five made the same claim. The most important political stronghold of Mabeqa's group was Councillor Gqoli. Mr Gqoli had been the only candidate at the local government elections in May 1996, for ward X of the Central Substructure.[10] Ward X consisted of three nearby informal squatter camps, of which Indawo Yoxolo was one.

The part of Indawo Yoxolo with paved streets, plots, and facilities was part of ward Z, which also included adjacent serviced townships. The developed part of Indawo Yoxolo did not fall under Councillor Gqoli's ward but under the councillors of Z, who were unknown to the residents of Indawo Yoxolo. Because the councillors of ward Z were unknown, and because Indawo Yoxolo was divided between two wards (the developed part of ward X and the squatter camp of ward Z), Mabeqa's group attempted to promote Councillor Gqoli as the legitimate representative of ward X *and* Z.

Councillor Gqoli co-operated with Mabeqa's group because he was concerned about the violence in Indawo Yoxolol but also because the RDP structure undermined local government. The legacy of apartheid had left local government in shambles. Local government had few resources, was understaffed, and had to change from an apartheid-style institution to a democratic one. In the meantime, however, local government benefited fairly little from the resources that the state provided for development. These resources were distributed via the distinct RDP organisations. The Project Committee's control over the development project undermined Councillor Gqoli's position in the local government. The Big Five did not acknowledge Councillor Gqoli as the legitimate councillor. Instead, they supported other councillors from the illegal squatter camps where they had previously lived.

### *Future dwelling*

Mabeqa's group tried to undermine the Big Five by challenging its relations with development offices, government institutions, and political parties. This was because the success of the Big Five was largely due to the support they received from these people and organisations.

The private sector company Future Dwelling had a central co-ordinating role within the DPC development projects. It managed the relations with the private sector, subcontractors, government institutions, and provided the Big Five with

---

[10] The local government elections in the Western Cape Province and Kwazulu Natal (the only provinces where an ANC victory was uncertain) were postponed for six months. In the Western Cape there was a political battle over electoral borders because the way the borders were drawn had important consequences for the election results and tax revenues.

resources. Future Dwelling knew about the complaints against the Big Five. In 1996, the bribes for plots were discussed at a workshop involving participants of the RDP projects. The DPC Bulletin, which was freely distributed in the areas where the projects took place, reported: 'The workshop decided unanimously that no payment is required in order to be considered for a site' (DPC 1996b: 2). In the following issue of the DPC Bulletin, corruption was mentioned again: 'There is *no charge* for being nominated a beneficiary in a DPC Project' (DPC 1996c: 2; original italics).

Notwithstanding the DPC's workshops and newsletters, corruption continued. I heard of applicants who paid the Big Five up to R1,200 in order to be put on the subsidy applicants' waiting list. Not everybody, however, was able, or willing, to pay these sums of money. People who did not pay had to stay in the unserviced squatter area of Indawo Yoxolo. The Big Five would only allow them to live on a plot after they had paid a bribe. In September 1997, the Big Five shot at an opponent who did not pay them a bribe. This man took me to his shack and told me that the night before a Big Five member shot through his window while he was asleep.

Future Dwelling was in close contact with the Project Committee and depended largely on the information that the Project Committee gave them. In October 1997, Future Dwelling threatened to evict residents of the squatter area in Indawo Yoxolo. These squatters had already been allocated a plot in the serviced Indawo Yoxolo but refused to move to their new place. Future Dwelling wanted them to move the squatters away because the land was needed to build additional plots, roads, sewerage systems, and so on. Future Dwelling threatened to evict the squatters and their homes with bulldozers if they did not move quickly. They argued that if people failed to occupy their plots, they would not be entitled to a serviced plot in Indawo Yoxolo, either because they were not entitled to an RDP subsidy, or because they had only recently moved to the squatter settlement of Indawo Yoxolo. Those who had moved to the squatter settlement after the development projects had started were not entitled to a plot either. Either way, they had to be evicted from their homes, by force if necessary.

Future Dwelling did not make any noticeable attempts to find out why the residents of the squatter settlement refused to move to their plots. That same month, seven residents tried to stop their evictions and had a meeting at the local council of which Indawo Yoxolo was a part. Fortunately, I was allowed to attend the meeting. Councillor Gqoli, Mabeqa, and Gxyiza were also present at the meeting, but Future Dwelling had ignored the invitation. The fear of retaliations was great among the seven residents. They told the councillors how the Big Five had threatened them and had demanded bribes before they were allowed to occupy their new plots. It was not that they did not want to live in the serviced area, but that they could not leave the squatter settlement safely. They explained that the Big

Five had shot one of the complainants and accused the fieldworker of Future Dwelling, Mguye, of siding with the Big Five and supporting Future Dwelling's eviction plans. They insisted on a new Project Committee that excluded Big Five members and included some of Mabeqa's people. The seven residents felt very uncomfortable about putting forward their complaints against the Big Five and Future Dwelling; the Big Five might have taken further action to intimidate them. Councillor Gqoli arranged to call the police to take a statement from those residents who had been brave enough to come forward.

*The school*

The Big Five also controlled the development of a library and schools, which were also part of the DPC. Leed Construction was going to build the library and had to employ local residents. The community liaison officer of Leed Construction was Mrs Ntshona (*iindaba yoxolo* 1998), who was also known to be a Big Five supporter. As a community liaison officer, she had an income and could offer residents of Indawo Yoxolo desperately needed jobs, possibly in return for bribes or political support.

By the end of 1997, some of the schools were still being built and people hoped they would be opened after the new school year starting at the end of January 1998. In 1997, there was only a kindergarten in a pink container and a primary school housed in a container and a prefabricated classroom. The primary school was in a terrible state because almost all the furniture and some windows were broken, and there was not enough space. All this made it unsuitable for teaching. The principal of this school was loyal to the Big Five. The parents accused him of stealing food from the 'school-feeding programme', a national presidential project and also a segment of the RDP. Every couple of days, a pick up truck arrived with bread and 12.5 litre buckets of peanut butter and jam. The parents said that the principal stole the buckets and sold them to his friends for only R25 each. Consequently, many children had been deprived of their lunches.

Another problem concerned the annual school fees. To be enrolled at the school, the parents had to pay R10 for each child at the beginning of the year. The teachers were supposed to give the parents a receipt and children were only permitted to take year-end exams if they could show this receipt. About thirty mothers claimed that they had paid the R10 but were not given a receipt. They had been completely unaware of this procedure, and heard about it only when their children were excluded from the exams until they had paid another R10. The parents were very angry and accused the principal and some teachers of stealing their money.

Early on a Friday morning in October 1997, the parents held a spontaneous meeting with the principal. When I arrived in Indawo Yoxolo that particular morning, the parents, including Edith, were already at the school. They had not announced the meeting in advance because the principal and the teachers would have hidden from the parents if they had been warned. This time, however, the principal was practically taken hostage by approximately twenty women and three men. The principal knew that attempts to escape would be dangerous and he was forced to listen to the parents' complaints. When we entered the classroom, the principal was nervously and quietly sitting behind one of the few desks that were scattered around. Nqase, one of the Big Five members, had heard about the meeting and also arrived. Unlike the other people, Nqase did not have any children living in Indawo Yoxolo and, therefore, had no legitimate reason to be in attendance. He was obviously there to protect the principal and he made sure people could see his gun.

The parents disagreed about what they should do with the principal. Some women argued that the principal had to be killed because he stole food and sold it to his friends, he stole school fees, he was never at school, and he had refused to meet the parents. Some parents, however, felt that such a punishment would be too harsh. They wanted to bring the principal to the police and report him to the Department of Education. The parents in favour of killing the principal convincingly argued that the police and Department of Education would do nothing. They felt that they had to solve the problem themselves. The principal and Nqase kept quiet during this discussion and the atmosphere was tense. The parents were excited that they were finally able to confront the principal with their frustrations. They screamed out allegations and complaints and this intimidated the principal and raised anger levels. Edith and I left the meeting because of the tense atmosphere. Later that morning we returned to see if the meeting was still taking place. When we entered the classroom, the situation had changed dramatically. Only a few women were left and everyone was quiet, and Nqase and the principal were still there. Nobody said a word and Nqase left soon after we had entered the classroom. One of the parents told us that Nqase had threatened to kill anyone who challenged him or the principal. Most of the parents had left feeling angry and powerless and only a few dared to stay longer, feeling just as angry and powerless. No further actions were taken against the principal, and Nqase protected him successfully.

A few weeks later, in early December 1997, the parents met with the school inspectors at the local constituency office. Some of the parents were Big Five supporters, among them was Ma Ntshona (who worked as the community liaison officer for Leed Construction), who attended despite the fact that she did not have any children in Indawo Yoxolo. Other parents, like Mabeqa and Edith, were going to oppose the Big Five. Mabeqa and Edith asked the inspectors and parents if I could attend the meeting, but I was not allowed. I had to wait in the car and Edith told me about the meeting afterwards.

The problems mainly concerned the new primary and secondary schools that were being built with RDP money. The schools were scheduled to be opened at the beginning of 1998, but there were not yet enough teachers. The officials from the Department of Education wanted to appoint teachers already contracted by the department. They wanted to appoint additional teachers only if there was insufficient staff. The parents who supported and who opposed the Big Five all felt this was unacceptable. They refused to have outsiders hired and insisted that the Department of Education appoint residents from Indawo Yoxolo. They felt that, because of the high level of unemployment, all the teaching positions had to be filled by locals and not by residents from other townships.

There was also disagreement between the Big Five supporters and Mabeqa's group. Mabeqa's group expressed a fear that the Big Five, as usual, were about to take control of the hiring of additional teachers. They told the representatives of the Department of Education about the Big Five's corruption, intimidation, and violence, and their fear that only loyal people would be given teaching positions. The department's officials did not seem to be too concerned and did not take any action.

To my great surprise, Edith later told me that a Big Five member had approached her. He asked her if she would like a teaching job at the school. She did not have the formal qualifications but was among the best-educated in Indawo Yoxolo because she had graduated from secondary school. Edith declined the offer, although it was very tempting. The Big Five had probably hoped to incorporate some of its opponents, but Edith told me she did not want to have anything to do with them.

### *ANC*

By the end of 1997, the political situation had changed. In October 1997, the ANC of the Western Cape Province established a Commission of Inquiry into the allegations of corruption and violence by the Big Five. Some of the complaints against the Big Five had reached the provincial body of the ANC and they could no longer be ignored.[11] The Commission of Inquiry interviewed twenty-seven residents of Indawo Yoxolo, who testified about the intimidation, violence, and corruption. The residents informed the Commission about the bribes of up to R700 that they were forced to pay Big Five members in exchange for plots to which they were already entitled. They reported that the Big Five seized plots from legitimate owners and sold them to people who did not qualify for an RDP grant. They complained about the violence of the Big Five. One plaintiff stated that he had been beaten with the

---

11 The information on the proceedings and results of the Commission of Inquiry is from the Commission's confidential report to the ANC, which was passed on to me by an NGO.

butt of a firearm and that another man had been shot. The man who was shot had not seen who had fired the gun, but had heard from one of the Big Five members that it was they who were responsible. Another man testified that one of the Big Five members had threatened him at gunpoint.

The Commission of Inquiry furthermore noted that one of the Big Five had attempted to steal money from the German embassy. The embassy had promised to donate R15,000 to upgrade one of the schools in Indawo Yoxolo. When the teachers collected the cheque at the embassy, they received R12,800. Two Big Five members found out about the donation, allegedly through the principal, and demanded that the cheque be handed over. The teachers were scared and surrendered the cheque immediately, after which they informed the embassy, which then blocked the cheque. The Big Five were therefore unable to cash the cheque and Nqase forced some teachers to return to the embassy and say that the cheque should be unblocked. They were told to say that there had been some confusion and that they still wanted to cash the cheque. The embassy, however, was suspicious and did not issue another cheque until the teachers had written a project proposal. The teachers, as well as the Big Five, left it at that and no further attempts were made to get money from the embassy.

The Commission of Inquiry gave the Big Five members the opportunity to respond to the allegations. The Big Five members blamed Councillor Gqoli for the problems in Indawo Yoxolo. They were unhappy with the fact that he openly supported Mabeqa's faction and felt that he had no right to interfere in Indawo Yoxolo. They responded to the allegations of bribery by saying that they had collected a small amount of money from residents (R50 per household) to cover their administrative expenses. It was 'for Tipp-ex and petrol', as someone put it. They denied that they had been selling houses. According to the Big Five, some did not want their plots and preferred money instead, so accordingly they had only tried to help people to sell their plots and to keep an eye open for prospective buyers.

The Commission of Inquiry drafted a report advising the ANC of the Western Cape Province on further actions. The Commission concluded that 'comrades' were frequently accused of crimes without being guilty of misbehaviour. They stated, however, that it was probably true that the Big Five had been selling plots, as this was known to happen in many informal settlements in the Western Cape, such as Crossroads. The twenty-seven testimonies gave the Commission sufficient evidence that four comrades were involved in the illegal selling of plots in Indawo Yoxolo, even in the period during which the Commission of Inquiry was already in session.

The Commission furthermore concluded that the scarce availability of resources contributed to the conflicts. Indawo Yoxolo had been incorporated into a greater RDP structure, but really wanted a separate RDP structure altogether. They had noticed that some felt that Indawo Yoxolo was neglected and was not receiving its share because the adjacent African township was being favoured. According to the Commission, the ward councillor and ANC member Mr Gqoli had failed to recognise the tensions between Indawo Yoxolo and the adjacent African township and should not have interfered. Thus, Mr Gqoli sided with the opponents of the Project Committee (the Big Five), and heightened the divisions in Indawo Yoxolo. Another factor which, according to the Commission of Inquiry, contributed to the conflict was that the DPC had started to hand out money at meetings as an incentive to attend. The Project Committee had also tried to monopolize meetings by distributing money among their own supporters while sending other visitors away.

The Commission of Inquiry recommended the ANC of the Western Cape take action against some of the Big Five. In the twenty-seven testimonies, two of the Big Five in particular were accused of the selling of sites to people who were not on the application list for RDP housing, the illegal selling of plots, the 'selling' of an occupied house, and furthermore theft, harassment and intimidation at gunpoint. It was recommended that these two be expelled from the ANC for six months. Another Big Five member, Mtontsi, was to be given a stern reprimand. Among other things, he was accused of harassment, of administering beatings with a firearm, and of the illegal sale of houses. The most severe recommendation concerned Zantsi, who was to be permanently expelled from the ANC. Zantsi had, according to the twenty-seven testimonies, bribed people, illegally sold their plots, and attempted to kill one of the complainants. The Commission did not investigate the allegations against Zantsi and these allegations were in fact not the reason for their recommendation. Instead, they wanted to expel him because of his lack of party loyalty:

> Reason for this stern action [expelling Zantsi from the ANC] are [sic] that he has really acted in a devious manner, like leading a march to the ANC office and organizing the radio to come thus ridiculing and bringing the name of the organization in disrepute. Also there are strong rumours and information which we have investigated and found to be true of him inciting a mass meeting in Indawo Yoxolo for people to join the NP or Holomisa (UDM) (Commission of Inquiry, 22 October 1997).

Because some of the Big Five held key positions within SANCO, the Commission of Inquiry proposed that SANCO be informed about the problems in Indawo Yoxolo. They furthermore noted that the participation of these 'comrades' in the RDP had to be re-evaluated and that people who wished to take legal action should be encouraged to do so. The Commission of Inquiry did not report the crimes to the police. The ANC of the Western Cape enforced the Commission's recommendations. However, after one year, Zantsi was re-admitted to the ANC, despite the fact that he was supposed to be expelled for life. It was not so much the criminal activities of the Big Five that concerned the ANC: they needed a loyal

Project Committee in order to establish control over the area. One of the recommendations of the Commission was that a proper ANC branch be established in Indawo Yoxolo, which had been absent up to then. Thus, the ANC provided political security to the Big Five in return for their political loyalty, and that security is one of the parameters of the big men paradigm.

Thoden van Velzen (1973: 596) has suggested that – in the analysis of power relations – it is important to incorporate 'those who are neither big men nor followers' but relatively independent of big men and relatively powerless. Mabeqa's group and the twenty-seven complainants were neither big men nor followers and tried to challenge the political security of the Big Five. The ANC recorded the allegations but, after mild punishment, continued to support the Big Five. The ANC wanted other political parties to be kept out of Indawo Yoxolo, an ANC branch in the area, a stop to relations between the Big Five and SANCO, the removal of the councillor from the area and the Big Five's proof of loyalty to the party. Although Mabeqa's group and the twenty-seven victims of the Big Five's terrorisation were able to express their discontent towards the ANC – just like they had protested against the school principal and the Department of Education – such protests did not undermine the Big Five's power.

*Challenging Future Dwelling*

Although people were intimidated by the Big Five and realised that it was dangerous to challenge them, they had asked for a meeting with Future Dwelling. In November 1997, Mabeqa, Michael, Gqiza, Edith, the local SANCO leaders, two Gwayta town councillors, and a few other residents of Indawo Yoxolo had a meeting with the director of Future Dwelling, Hendrik, and one of the other employees. Everyone was aware of the ANC's Commission of Inquiry into the Big Five, but the residents from Indawo Yoxolo were under the impression that the inquiry was still taking place as its results and procedures were not yet, and never, made public. Therefore, at the time of this meeting, they were uninformed of its outcome.

They met at Future Dwelling's office, which was not far from Indawo Yoxolo. There were no Big Five supporters and it was, therefore, no problem for me to attend. Because of the tense atmosphere, Hendrik was not in a position to ask about my role in the proceedings, although he was probably not terribly thrilled about my presence. I detected that Hendrik was, in any case, visibly unhappy about the meeting, but he could not avoid such a large turnout of angry people. The residents informed him about the problems they had been experiencing with the DPC Project Committee, i.e. the Big Five and Mguye, the Future Dwelling liaison officer who was responsible for the contacts with the Project Committee. They repeated the allegations they had expressed earlier at the Gwayta Town Council meeting, namely that the liaison officer of Future Dwelling had sided with the Big

Five and was also involved in corruption. Instead of challenging the corruption and violence in Indawo Yoxolo, they protested that Future Dwelling actually supported the Big Five.

The residents felt that that the Big Five were never properly elected and did not represent the new residents of Indawo Yoxolo. They told the director that Future Dwelling was not the only organisation that chose to ignore the problems: Mr Mbuyi, from the Department of Education, also persistently ignored Mabeqa's group and continued to work with the Big Five.

The response of the employee of Future Dwelling present at the meeting, was that Future Dwelling was waiting for the results of a large-scale ANC investigation into housing and the RDP in the Cape Metropolitan Area. This investigation was separate from the Commission of Inquiry's investigation of the Big Five. The director added:

> Things have changed in Indawo Yoxolo since we started. All political groups have to be included which represent the whole community. It has to be an inclusive community committee and should be elected. Then we have an accredited RDP forum in Indawo Yoxolo. It must include the entire community.

In attempting to explain the impossibility of establishing a committee that would comprise Mabeqa's group *and* the Big Five, the residents described the levels of violence and intimidation. 'How can you expect us to co-operate with people who threatened us and tried to kill one of us?' they asked the director. He, however, kept repeating his 'formula' that the Project Committee had to be inclusive and completely ignored the objections that were raised.

As for the Future Dwelling's liaison officer accused of corruption, the director was not willing to take any disciplinary action: 'One cannot change people's jobs based on some rumours' was his response. However, he did promise that the Liaison Officer would henceforth work in another township and that another liaison officer would replace him. It was later rumoured, however, that the particular liaison officer initially accused of corruption had continued to keep control over the situation in Indawo Yoxolo through the new liaison officer who, residents complained, relied heavily on his predecessor's advice. He also continued to work with the Big Five and completely ignored Mabeqa's group. This ongoing support of the Big Five led to rumours that Future Dwelling, including its director, was also involved in the corruption. There were also speculations about the ANC's involvement because it became apparent that the large-scale investigation into housing and RDP issues in the Cape Metropolitan Area was never going to come to conclusion.

Some regarded the slow pace of the investigation process as a deliberate attempt by the ANC to conceal its involvement in corruption. No remarks alluding to corruption were made about the National Party (NP), however, despite the fact that they were the largest political party in the Western Cape Province and in the Cape Metropolitan Area.

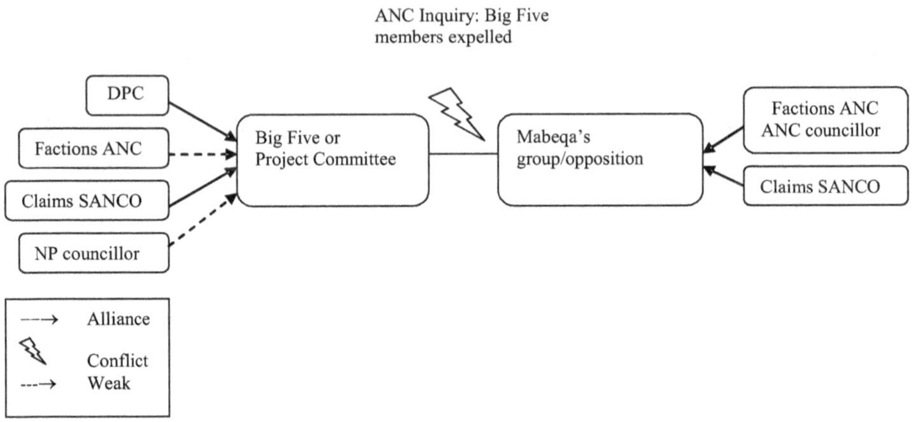


*Figure 3.2* October 1997

Future Dwelling's approach to the conflict seemed to have been politically motivated and, as figure 3.2 clarifies, it meant that the Big Five could remain in power. Future Dwelling co-operated with the Big Five because they were the most powerful group in Indawo Yoxolo and thus most likely to carry out the development projects successfully. Although Future Dwelling used the rhetoric of inclusive community representation, their primary concern was simply to get the job done. The Big Five's willingness to use violence worked greatly to their advantage because it made them more powerful in Indawo Yoxolo. Future Dwelling thus provided the Big Five with the support that made them powerful men (cf. Thoden van Velzen 1973). It gave the Big Five control over the distribution of resources, ignored their crimes, and provided political security by ignoring opponents. The opponents' main challenge was to influence the distribution of resources and to undermine the Big Five's political security.

*Reconfiguration of the political field*

From January 1998 onwards, the Big Five made attempts to co-operate with the National Party. Their position as big men was still secure because Future Dwelling kept them on the DPC Policy Committee. But the Commission of Inquiry had led to tensions between the Big Five and the ANC. Moreover, the national and provincial political landscape had changed and this appeared to influence local political alliances. These changes become clear if one considers the first democratic elections.

The 1994 elections resulted in a tremendous victory for the ANC. It secured the majority for the national government and had only narrowly missed a two-third majority that would have allowed it to draft the new constitution without the co-operation of other political parties. The ANC had a majority in all the provinces except KwaZulu Natal and the Western Cape. In KwaZulu Natal, Buthelezi's Inkatha Freedom Party (IFP) became the largest political party. In the Western Cape, the National Party was dominant and, being supported largely by Whites and Coloureds, thwarted an ANC victory. The ANC co-operated together with the NP and the IFP in the Government of National Unity with ANC leader Nelson Mandela as president and the NP leader De Klerk as vice-president. The Government of National Unity emphasised that transition had to be peaceful, that the new South Africa was inclusive, and that minorities would also have a voice. In the Western Cape Province, the NP majority and the ANC minority had also formed a similar government of unity.

Two years later, in June 1996, the NP left the Government of National Unity. It felt side-tracked by the ANC and argued that democracy would benefit from a strong opposition party. Strategically, it also seemed better for the NP to become an opposition party in preparation for the upcoming national elections.[12] The break between the ANC and the NP in the national government was followed by a similar move in the Western Cape. The ANC indicated that it could no longer co-operate with the NP and argued that it had been completely powerless within the provincial government. There was no unity and the NP was said to consistently ignore the issues that the ANC put on the agenda. With the next elections in mind, the ANC preferred to take up the role of opposition party, withdrew from the ministerial posts in the provincial government, and opposed the NP from the benches of the provincial parliament. On 20 January 1998, the NP voted in the new provincial ministry, which consisted only of White and Coloured men and excluded the ANC. At a national level, the ANC could manage without the political support of the weakened NP, and at a provincial level the NP was able to perform better without the ANC. Among others, Barth (1959: 16) and Scott (1985: 134) have discussed the dynamics of such a political process, namely that if a party in power strives to acquire a smaller majority, or be part of a smaller coalition, or of no coalition at all, the power can then be held by a smaller faction.

---

12 One of the consequences was that the post of Minister of Finance, which had been occupied by the NP, became available to the ANC. The new Minister of Finance (Trevor Manuel) introduced GEAR (Growth, Employment and Redistribution). GEAR put more emphasis on a macro-economic restructuring of the economy, creation of jobs, and government responsibility than the RDP did. Later increasing attention was also paid to Black Economic Empowerment (BEE).

Those who were aware of this political change – many could not be bothered with politics – felt that in the Western Cape the NP was now completely in charge of all government activities in the province. The ANC had stepped out of the government and, therefore, some felt that they had become unable to provide development initiatives for Africans. The Big Five were affected by the withdrawal of the ANC from the provincial government, as they were continuously in need of political security and needed control over the flow of resources to Indawo Yoxolo. As a result, the Big Five attempted to co-operate with the NP in the adjacent Coloured township Mountain View. It was conjectured that the NP would be able to secure the Big Five's position as controllers over development. For its part, Mountain View's NP was eager to embrace the community leaders of Indawo Yoxolo. African support would bolster the party's image and could attract more votes in the upcoming provincial elections. Although the Big Five rubbed shoulders with the NP because some had been expelled from the ANC, they did not completely alienate themselves from the ANC either. Rather, they carefully explored the relationship with the NP while keeping an eye on the ANC. Ideological concerns did not appear to be a consideration for the political alliances being forged.

Generally, the residents of Indawo Yoxolo restrained themselves from commenting on the political changes. Nobody seemed to like the NP, and many were disappointed in the ANC because the RDP 'houses' were not really houses, poverty was still prevalent, and the ANC had generally failed to fulfil its promises. Some wondered how the ANC could provide money and services to Africans once they had left the provincial government. Some even suggested that it was better to join the NP. An ANC 'comrade' in Indawo Yoxolo told me: 'It is better to be oppressed by Whites than by your own people.' In general, people expressed their disappointment about politics and did not bother to discuss political issues, much in the same way that they had tried to avoid politics during the apartheid days.

The Big Five must, at least to some extent, have felt threatened by the changes that were taking place. Perhaps it was pure coincidence, but three weeks after the new provincial government was installed, Nqase killed Gilbert Mabeqa. Mabeqa and Michael were walking around in Indawo Yoxolo on a Friday in the early evening when Nqase and Bula approached them. Nqase shot Mabeqa twice, once in the back and once in the back of his head. Then Bula shot Nqase in his leg and Michael ran for his life. Nqase's leg wound was later used as an alibi in a court case as to claim that Nqase killed Mabeqa out of self-defence. After some time, however, Nqase was found guilty for the murder of Mabeqa and consequently served a short prison sentence.

Edith told me the next day that one of the Big Five supporters had visited her that morning to inform her of Mabeqa's murder and also tell her that she was on the hit list as well. Later that day, Bula, who was also a Big Five member, visited

Edith and proudly notified her that they had taken care of Mabeqa. He advised her to leave Indawo Yoxolo because she was going to be the next one to die. Within a few days, all the known political opponents of the Big Five fled to Councillor Gqoli and went into hiding. Only Edith and Gxyiza remained in Indawo Yoxolo. Gxyiza felt he could not abandon his wife and children and said: 'I am too old to run away. If they want me they can come and get me.' Later that week, when Edith was walking to catch a taxi, she was threatened again by one of the Big Five: 'We will do everything, yes everything, to get what we want.' But he added that they were going to wait a while before they would kill again. They were waiting for their opponents to come out of their hiding places. It was, after all, much easier to kill someone in Indawo Yoxolo than elsewhere in the Cape Flats.

Edith felt increasingly intimidated and the situation was horrifying. All of Mabeqa's political allies had fled and the Big Five were brimming with confidence and were more powerful than ever before. Although some opponents had appealed to the police for security measures, nothing came of it. As usual, there were never any police officers in Indawo Yoxolo. Everybody, including myself, asked Edith to leave Indawo Yoxolo, at least for a while. Edith's husband was not supportive of her departure. Being unemployed at the time, one can imagine that he worried about food. He did, however, allow her to stay with his sister in Gwayta, but Edith herself did not feel safe at her sister-in-law's place, which was only about a twenty minute walk from Indawo Yoxolo. As is very common, there were also tensions between Edith and her sister-in-law. Her sister-in-law admitted that she had intended to poison Edith only a few weeks earlier, around Christmas. But because everyone was sharing plates, the sister-in-law did not succeed; she had been too afraid she would poison the wrong person, possibly her own brother.

Against her husband's wishes, Edith went into hiding. A few days later, I accompanied her to her place in Indawo Yoxolo so she could see how her child was doing and to fetch some clothing. While I was reading the newspaper in front of the shack, Edith and her husband started to argue and her husband pulled Edith into the shack and tried to lock her in. Edith protested loudly and attempted to force the door back open. Her husband, however, had hidden a screwdriver beneath his trousers lying on the bed, which he took and stabbed Edith in the hand. Edith screamed and her husband continued his attempts to keep her in the shack. Edith struggled to break away, but he held her arm, trying to pull her back inside, while I, hearing the commotion, dropped my newspaper and started to pull her other arm to help her get away. Her husband finally let go and Edith and I went to the Groote Schuur hospital for medical treatment. We then went to the police in Mountain View but they proved to be very uncooperative. We were left waiting for hours on end. Some of the African women who had been waiting there for a few days finally left and decided not to report the assaults they had suffered. One of the women told me that her husband had shot at her, but had luckily missed. As usual, the police did not take the allegations of domestic violence seriously and they did not show any interest in the larger political context of the violence that took place in Indawo Yoxolo. Many officers were unidentifiable because they did not wear their badges. After we had waited for half a day, I approached one of them and insisted on knowing his name and rank. He told me his name and rank and anxiously asked me: 'Why do you want to know this? Are you going to take it any further?' I asked him if he knew what else I could do. Within five minutes, the statements were finalised and a police car was ready to accompany Edith to Indawo Yoxolo so she could get some clothing. Sometimes it helps to be White.

On the surface, everything seemed to be back to normal in Indawo Yoxolo. I was astonished to see how little visible impact the murder of the leader of the opposition to the Big Five had had on most people. A prominent resident was killed, but that only took a few minutes and only a few people had to flee Indawo Yoxolo. I was surprised that life went on as usual, although the political consequences of this murder were significant. Most residents were too scared and intimidated to talk about what had happened and this denial of violence seemed to be a successful way of coping with daily life.

Within a few days it had become impossible to do any research in Indawo Yoxolo. The Big Five were in complete control and every vestige of safety had disappeared. Those I trusted and who were concerned about my safety had been chased away by the Big Five, and even Edith did not want to return to Indawo Yoxolo and had found another place to live. In the weeks that followed, I only did research outside of Indawo Yoxolo since some residents attended financial mutuals meetings in other areas of Cape Town. Moreover, I was aware that I should not restrict the research to Indawo Yoxolo or neglect relations with people and institutions in other parts of Cape Town. I focused particularly on financial mutuals in Khayelitsha and Philippi, where many residents were also recent migrants to Cape Town.

These events revealed the consequences of a participant observation approach in conflict situations. The only way to perform my research was to rely on a few people and establish trustworthy relations with them. Without such relations, I could achieve no insight into these conflicts, their causes, and consequences. Nevertheless, the possibilities to do research were also restricted because of the limited freedom I had to move around, and the inability to talk freely with all who were involved in this conflict. People's lives were under threat, and a court case was pending. In such a situation, one cannot expect people to reveal all their actions, motivations, and opinions.

A few weeks later, Edith and I restarted the research. In the meantime, the brother of one of the Big Five members had presented residents of Indawo Yoxolo with a contract. It would allow a construction company to use the remains of their subsidies to build small one-roomed houses on their plots. Many people wanted to keep the remains of their subsidies because they wanted to join an NGO called Victoria Mxenge. This NGO had a housing scheme that enabled the participants to save extra money and cut costs by doing the building work themselves. This scheme would also enable them to build bigger homes. However, fear of the Big Five compelled people to sign the contract anyway. No-one received a copy of the contract, nor did they dare complain about the terrible 'houses' that were built.

Mr Mabeqa's murder led to a court case being brought against Nqase. In addition to the murder charge, the police had found two boxes of illegal firearms at Nqase's place and there were further charges related to the murders of one or more people in the nearby township of Crossroads. Despite a total of five cases being brought against him, he was still released on bail. Just a few days after the murder, he was strolling around Indawo Yoxolo, chatting to everyone on the streets. When I finished my fieldwork in December 1998 he had still not been convicted, but I heard from Mabeqa's wife that he was finally imprisoned in 1999, more than a year after the murder. By the end of the same year, however, he was back on the streets of Indawo Yoxolo.

The Big Five were now more powerful than ever and continued their work as the DPC Project Committee. However, Nqase must have been afraid to walk around freely. He often wore a white substance smeared on his face. A widespread interpretation was that he had visited a diviner or herbalist and had received the substance for protection. Overall, however, the murder of Mabeqa confirmed the power of the Big Five over the development projects and the people in Indawo Yoxolo. The national and provincial political changes, as well as the ANC's Commission of Inquiry were threats to the Big Five. The strategic murder of Mr Mabeqa had a successful outcome that reinstated their position of power in times of temporary political insecurity.

*The wake*

Up to the day of the funeral, every evening at seven o'clock there was a wake at Mabeqa's mother's place in the nearby township Guguletu. Usually wakes were held at the home of the deceased, but for safety reasons the wakes had to be relocated to Guguletu. The wakes were well attended, by at least a hundred people. The routine at the wakes was that someone, mostly a man, walked forward and gave a speech that highlighted his relationship with the deceased and the unavoidability of death. After the speech – and sometimes during the speech if an elaborate speaker went on for too long – the choir started to perform a well-known gospel song and many people sang along. It was difficult for Edith to translate what happened during the wakes due to her emotional involvement, but she managed to communicate some things to me. I felt uncomfortable writing in my notebook during the wakes so I made notes once they were over. Church brothers, reverends, neighbours, family members, and friends gave speeches, and all avoided references to the cause of death or its political context. Instead, they highlighted the fact that death was unavoidable: it was God's decision to present bitter things to people.

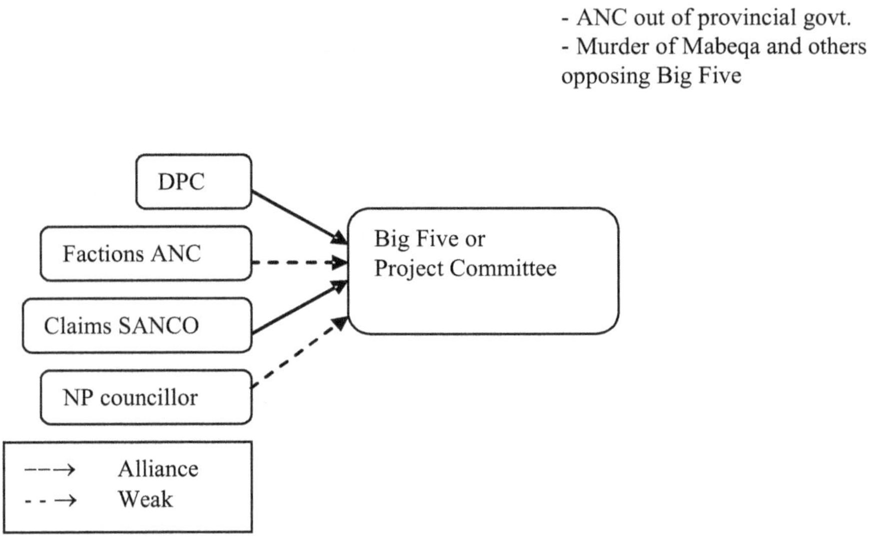


*Figure 3.3* January/February 1998

Only once did the political context of Mabeqa's death become explicit. One of the people present was regarded as a Big Five supporter. Many were shocked that he was there and felt that he had come to spy for the Big Five: 'He wants to find out who Mabeqa's supporters are.' The already tense atmosphere heightened when he stepped forward to give a speech. He said: 'One word, one heart, one heart, one word', in order to emphasize the unity of the bereaved. The crowd started mumbling and people became nervous. The man continued: 'As some of us have to go back to Indawo Yoxolo after this service …', but the rest of his sentence was drowned out by the ensuing noise. The secretary of Mabeqa's group, Constance, had started ululating and dozens of other women joined her. The noise was so loud that it was useless for the speaker to continue. Some of the people were angry with the ululating women and said: 'Let him speak first!' The man was shocked and confused and left the stage. The choir started a gospel number in an attempt to diffuse the tense atmosphere and to shout down the ululating women. This was fairly successful, as the women stopped to join in with the choir.

In the meantime, the man who had left the stage was detained by young men on the sidewalk. They encircled him and increasingly more men joined in. What followed was a fierce debate about what they should do with him. The atmosphere was tense and charged and everyone was excited and eager to see some action. When I asked Edith: 'What will they do with him?', she laughed and made a cutting movement with her finger across the front of her neck. She rolled her eyes and let her tongue hang out of her mouth, mimicking a murder. Some felt that the man should have had the opportunity to speak first and then be killed. Others, however, felt he had to be killed straight away and that he should not have the opportunity to defend himself. I immediately left and phoned Councillor Gqoli on his mobile phone, perhaps the only man who might be able to diffuse the scene. He duly arrived and the captive was allowed to go.

The speaker's words appeared to be an attempt to reconcile the Big Five and Mabeqa's group, but he had failed completely when the ululating women shouted him down. In the 'battle of the voices', it was eventually the choir that, at least to some extent, was able to stop the acceleration of emotions. In a way, the contest of voices resembled a voting system, like one sometimes sees on television shows or in the British parliament. The 'battle of voices' that was dominated by women was in favour of peace, after which the young men captured the Big Five supporter and then let him go after having intimidated him. Although Mabeqa's group were severely under threat, they did not retaliate by murdering the Big Five supporter.

Mabeqa was buried in Gcuwa (Butterworth) in the Eastern Cape, the same town that Bula came from. Bula's family did not attend the funeral. They were probably afraid or embarrassed. Mabeqa's wife, Nopumsile, could not understand why they did not come. She felt that they should have. After all, they could not be held responsible for their son's deeds and for the problems in Cape Town. The main worry of Nopumsile, who sought refuge with her mother-in-law, was Mabeqa's clothing. The police were in the possession of Mabeqa's personal belongings and she was afraid that the Big Five might use them for witchcraft purposes. She said that Mabeqa could not rest until his clothing was returned. Mabeqa's mother shared Nopumsile's worries. She had recurring nightmares in which she saw her son's face and in which he told her that he wanted his clothes back. Although they tried several times, the police refused to give back Mabeqa's clothes and watch.

The clothes were also Mabeqa's neighbour's concern. She dreamt about them twice. In her dream, she entered Mabeqa's house and saw that everything was broken. The doors of Mabeqa's wardrobe, which together with the bed and cupboard, was the only piece of furniture they possessed, were open. She said it was a terrible dream. We told her that Mabeqa's clothes were missing and she was convinced that this explained her dreams. She said it was very likely that Nqase took them from the police to a witch (*igqwirha*) in order to inflict more pain on people. Nqase was seen with white substance on his face for protection. Sometimes, a diviner (*igqirha*) could also be a witch (*igqwirha*), and the white substance on Nqase's face was proof that he had already visited a witch.

## A new opposition

In the following months, the Big Five and their supporters killed three more residents of Indawo Yoxolo. One was a known opponent of the Big Five, and another was the younger brother of an opponent. They shot the latter through the corrugated iron wall of his shack because they mistook him for his older brother. A Big Five supporter also kicked a twelve-year-old child to death, as I already mentioned in chapter two. Michael, who witnessed the murder of Mabeqa, was also shot at. His story was confusing and seemed inconsistent. He told me that he was taken by surprise late at night when people entered his shack. He claimed they were police officers sent by the Big Five, and that they first shot him in the hand, and then in the stomach and leg. He said he was unarmed, but because he was first shot in his hand it seemed logical to me that he had either held a weapon or was reaching for one. Half-a-year after the shooting he was still a crippled shadow of the strong and confident man he used to be.

The murder of Mabeqa and the destruction of the opposition to the Big Five led to more political changes in Indawo Yoxolo. 'Shooter' – a telling nickname – claimed to be related to SANCO. Before Mabeqa's death, it appeared that he also opposed the Big Five, although he was not a prominent figure. Rumour had it that he had switched sides and joined the Big Five. Sometimes for weeks in a row, residents saw Shooter walking around at three o'clock at night. Every couple of minutes he fired a shot in the air, waking and terrifying the people in the vicinity. Due to the bad state of the shacks and RDP houses, it was quite possible that one of his many bullets would eventually pierce through a wall, window, or roof and injure someone.

Shooter joined the leader of the Big Five, Zantsi, and they established a SANCO interim committee for Indawo Yoxolo. The SANCO interim committee had planned elections for 6 September. They were held during a meeting at a public area in Indawo Yoxolo. Although this was a public place, it was regarded as a space controlled by the Big Five because they usually held their meetings there. Because of this location, and the central role of Zantsi and Shooter in its organisation, the meeting was attended mainly by Big Five supporters and curious bystanders. Most residents of Indawo Yoxolo, however, were uninterested or too scared to oppose Shooter and Zantsi. At this 'election', Shooter and Zantsi elected themselves. Shooter became the chairperson and Zantsi a board member.

Shortly after the elections, a long-lasting dispute over housing grants and the allocation of plots started between Shooter and Zantsi. Some residents still lived in the squatter settlement and had yet to move to their new plots. Future Dwelling continued threats to evict them but had not yet taken any action. However, due to the unwillingness or inability to bribe the Big Five, they were forced to stay in the squatter settlement. The Big Five and Shooter, who also had his own supporters, were fighting about the exact number of residents on that particular site. This conflict caused a rift between Shooter and Zantsi. According to Zantsi, there were 312 households on the site in question that qualified for a plot. Shooter argued that there were 424 households, because this was the number of people officially registered on the DPC's housing list, a list controlled by the Big Five. Zantsi, however, had made an actual count with members of the city council's Housing Committee after a meeting on 8 October. They had counted 312 households. Shooter questioned this count because a councillor who was known to be loyal to Zantsi had chaired the meeting and organised the count. The discrepancy of nearly a hundred households fed allegations of corruption against the Big Five. They were rumoured to have registered people who did not qualify for housing subsidies and to have bribed them, or to have sold plots to people who were not even registered.

The dispute between Shooter and Zantsi was not only due to this incident. An analysis of the parameters of the big men paradigm provides a basic structural explanation for this conflict. Again, national and provincial political processes appeared to influence local political relations. In September 1997, Bantu Holomisa and Roelf Meyer established a new political party: the United Democratic Movement (UDM). Bantu Holomisa headed the Transkei under the apartheid regime and, after the 1994 elections, he became the national deputy minister of environmental affairs. He was expelled from government and the ANC, and the general opinion was that this was because he had complained of the ANC not adequately addressing the problem of corrupt party members. Roelf Meyer was a young NP politician who had played a major role in the 1992-93 negotiations that had led to the abolition of apartheid. Meyer felt increasingly dissatisfied with the NP's inability to reform and attract black voters. Together they presented the UDM as an alternative party, which was not based on race, and which, unlike the NP and the ANC, was not embedded in the history of apartheid. It was expected that their main stronghold was going to be in the Eastern Cape, because Bantu Holomisa had been the leader of the Transkei homeland.

Virtually all African migrants in Cape Town were Xhosa and came from Emaxhoseni, of which Transkei was a part. The UDM wanted to gain support in Cape Town for the 1999 elections. The opponents of the UDM expected them to attract many voters. Because of the large support that the NP had previously received, voting behaviour in this province was more crucial than in other provinces where it was clear that the ANC was going to win. After he was approached by the UDM, Shooter established a UDM branch in Indawo Yoxolo. The new political opportunities expected to emerge after the elections prompted Shooter to turn his back against the Big Five, but some still regarded him as a Big Five ally and suspected that the opposition was fake.

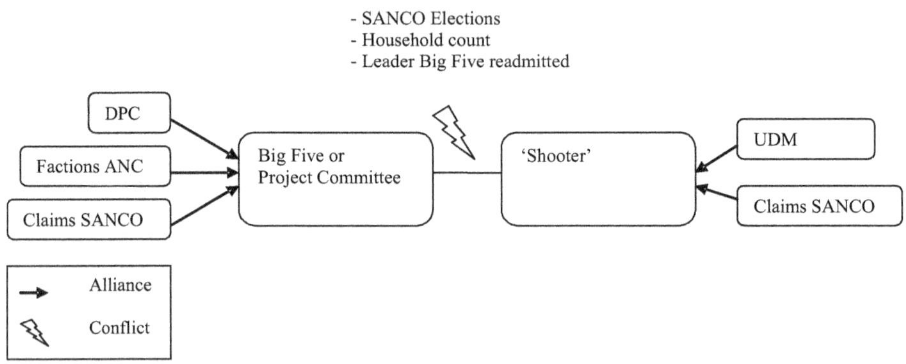


*Figure 3.4* September/October 1998

Although Zantsi had been expelled from the ANC for life as punishment for his lack of loyalty, he was re-admitted by the end of 1998. Probably with the next elections in mind, the ANC judged it wise to retain among their ranks a powerful leader in Indawo Yoxolo. Consequently, the Big Five turned its back on Mr Vogel, the local councillor for the NP in Mountain View. Although there was a court case in process against Nqase – and after my return to the Netherlands I heard of court cases against other Big Five members – the Big Five remained the most powerful political group. The ANC had won the 1999 elections for that ward and Zantsi was appointed councillor to Indawo Yoxolo.

Two opposing groups had developed once again. It seemed to be a central characteristic of politics in Indawo Yoxolo that, as soon as one opposition force was destroyed, a new political opponent emerged. The new opposition was a fence sitter, if not an ally to the Big Five. African political structures, especially in Zulu history, have been characterised as systems of fission and fusion (Gluckman 1971; Kuper 1997: 74-77; Shapera 1956). Gluckman (1971: 25-26) argues that relationships among Zulu should be understood within the context of relationships between Whites and Zulu. The temporal equilibrium of Zulu social structure could, since colonialism, only be understood by incorporating the role of Whites. Similarly to how development projects work in contemporary South Africa, colonial rule was channelled through 'tribal' chiefs who enabled control over Africans and allowed certain Africans to become powerful leaders. Shooter's fence sitting in Indawo Yoxolo seems to illustrate Gluckman's analysis of a situation where two unequal groups exist, in which membership could not be changed:[13]

> 'Where there are unequal groups and membership can not be changed... Dissident members of the superior group may become leaders of these new interest-groups within the inferior. Conversely, some members of the inferior group become interest-groups assisting the superior and standing opposed to the mass of their own group' (Gluckman 1971: 48).

Continued opposition against the Big Five was an expression of discontent by some residents of Indawo Yoxolo. The marginal residents of Indawo Yoxolo tried to challenge the political security and flow of resources. This took place through the fissions and fusions expressing the tensions and alliances between people. RDP development created a temporal equilibrium in Indawo Yoxolo, which was 'disturbed' by national and provincial political changes, and a new opposition emerged. Clearly, conflict was central to the temporal equilibrium in Indawo Yoxolo.

The changing political landscape and the murder of Mabeqa and other opponents eventually bore no consequences for the relationship between the Big Five and Future Dwelling. Future Dwelling's support of the Big Five could not be attributed to a lack of information. DPC's own Bulletin of June 1998 warned against corruption:

> *WARNING! WARNING! WARNING!*
>
> *No one should be made to pay money to be allocated a site in any DPC housing project for families with a household income of less than R1500 per month. The site and house is free and fully subsidised by the government.*
> *No community leader or unauthorised person is allowed to allocate sites/houses. There are no shortcuts! No one can pay to be nominated as a beneficiary of a house or site in the DPC.*
> *If you have any queries you can contact: The Project Facilitator. Tel. xxx Fax. xxx*

The pamphlet caused a stir in Indawo Yoxolo. It did not reveal who the project facilitator was, but people suspected Mguye because he had co-operated with the Big Five before. People were afraid that the project facilitator would inform the Big Five about their phone calls and kill them. Instead of a warning, the notice was regarded as a trap set by the Big Five in order to find out who their opponents

---

13 This is the situation that Gluckman (1971) describes which most closely resembles the political situation in Indawo Yoxolo.

were. This was an understandable fear considering Future Dwelling's attitude towards the conflict. To my knowledge, nobody dared to phone Future Dwelling.

The Big Five, however, did not like the pamphlet at all, which suggested it was not a trap. However, in such a politically charged and tense situation, it became difficult to distinguish the truth from paranoid interpretations. Eunice, a neighbour of Edith's, told me that Ma Ntshona had asked her to help distribute the pamphlets throughout the neighbourhood. Ma Ntshona was the Big Five supporter who was liaison officer for Leed Construction and a parent's representative at the school (although she had no children in Indawo Yoxolo). The Big Five discovered that Eunice had distributed the pamphlets, and she told me that some of them had paid her a visit. They informed her that the Big Five had held a meeting about this incident and were discussing what they should do with her. They were in doubt, they said. Some were in favour of shooting her, while others felt that it was more appropriate to burn her alive, but one of them had convinced them all that it was better to talk with Eunice first so she could offer a defence. Eunice feared for her life, and told them that the pamphlets came from Ma Ntshona. Because Ma Ntshona supported the Big Five, she did not think that they would object, and the Big Five did indeed decide to leave her alone. They gave Ma Ntshona a R150 fine instead. Eunice was very relieved and felt that Ma Ntshona received such a small punishment because the Big Five did not want to alienate her. Ma Ntshona knew a lot about their crimes and could easily go to the police should they turn her against them. Apart from this pamphlet, I noticed no other attempts by Future Dwelling or other DPC organisations to discontinue their support of the Big Five or prevent violence in Indawo Yoxolo.

In 2006, there were again local government elections. Zantsi was the ANC candidate but residents wondered if he was going to win as his popularity had decreased and the development project was nearing its end. It appeared that with the finalisation of the development project his power base had started to weaken. Yet it was not the police, an NGO, or political problem that threatened Zantsi. It was his girlfriend. She was getting increasingly upset that Zantsi was seeing another girlfriend and was neglecting her. As a result, she eventually called a community meeting in the beginning of November 2005 in order to ask the residents to help her solve the problems she had with Zantsi. At the meeting, because she was angry, she put forward a lot of complaints about her boyfriend. She told everyone that he was having an affair with another woman, stole an RDP house from its legitimate owners and gave it to her, and had also misappropriated funds. Allegations such as these revealed that her loyalty towards Zantsi had ended. After this meeting, the ANC suspended Zantsi and took away a van that he had misappropriated. Moreover, unlike in the previous local government elections, there was a contender. Similarly to Shooter, this opponent also used to be affiliated with the Big Five but had distanced himself from them and became a candidate for the Universal Party (UP). At least in Indawo Yoxolo, some considered this very small party to be a serious threat to the ANC's dominant position. It was expected to attract Coloured voters who felt discriminated against by the ANC. The distrust of the ANC was strengthened after it was discovered in July 2005 that the advisor to Cape Town's major, Blackman Ngoro, had written in an editorial on the Website of the Afro Rights Committee in Asia that Africans are "culturally superior" to coloureds, who, unless they underwent an "ideological transformation", would "die a drunken death".[14] Although the advisor was eventually fired, the confidence with which members of the ANC expressed such racism only fed the feelings of alienation among Coloureds. In Indawo Yoxolo, the emergence of the Universal Party created new terrain for political entrepreneurs. Some residents of Indawo Yoxolo believed, however, that if the UP councillor were to win the elections he would immediately leave the UP and join the ANC. With the marginalisation of Zantsi, due to decreasing development funds and an angry girlfriend, this became a likely scenario.

Only a few weeks before the elections, it became clear that Zantsi was still standing as local councillor for Indawo Yoxolo. The ANC had split Indawo Yoxolo into two wards and without publicly readmitting Zantsi to the ANC, Zantsi had become the ANC candidate of the western ward. His UP opponent had left the UP and had become the ANC candidate for the other eastern part of Indawo Yoxolo.[15] After the elections, Indawo Yoxolo was confronted with two ANC councillors, one for the eastern half, and one for the western half. Very soon, however, residents felt that Zantsi was the councillor for the whole of Indawo Yoxolo and rumour had it that he had intimidated and chased his opponent out of the area.

## Conclusion

The development dream was shattered, even to those who had not believed in the dream that much from the start. The plans of the ANC proved too ambitious and the utopian vision for South Africa had to be relinquished. This can partly be seen in a policy shift by the government away from development towards strengthening a market economy through Black Economic Empowerment (BEE) programs. As

---

14 Marianne Merten, Racist Website Wars in W Cape, Mail and Guardian, July 22: 2005, online on http://www.mg.co.za/articlePage.aspx?articleid=246100&area=/insight/insight__national/

15 The UP election results were very poor. In the Cape Metropolitan Area, they only received one out of the 210 council seats.

the case of Indawo Yoxolo shows, the ideology defining community and development was problematic. Conflict and violence accompanied the actual development projects. The many reports on conflict in service delivery, particularly when it concerns housing, give the impression that Indawo Yoxolo is not a unique case.[16] According to field workers of a Cape Town based NGO working in the field of conflict resolution, the conflicts in Indawo Yoxolo were also present in Crossroads and more recently in the housing developments in Joe Slovo Park near Langa. The RDP policies led to a type of authoritarian rule through its provision of political security and resources to a group of powerful local leaders. This exemplified virtually the only state presence in Indawo Yoxolo, as was the case in many other settlements where African migrants started to live.

Far from being hegemonic in nature, development gave rise to, or fuelled, existing conflicts concerning the distribution of resources. There were people who attempted to challenge the way development gave rise to a ruthless regime by a few powerful people. Their attempts to question the distribution of resources and political security had hardly any effect as they were systematically ignored (Bähre 2005). These political struggles were central to the relations defined by the migrants and no neutrals were allowed in this conflict.

The post-apartheid state was most manifest through violent development and it was in this context that migrants tried to organise their financial mutuals. Financial mutuals were attempts to create some sort of safe havens and withdraw into small social circles, even if they were only temporary. Most financial mutuals were organised among neighbours who lived very close to each other, and together they hoped to build something that allowed them to feel secure and valued. Financial mutuals were, as the next chapters will show, defence mechanisms against the political, economic, and psychological threats that people experienced, not in the least as a result of the development economy.

Needless to say, violence and conflict made it difficult for me to do research. I could not move around freely, was not able to talk with everybody, and was dependent on a few people, particularly my research assistant. In this conflict, there was no place for any neutrals, meaning that, with a substantial number of the residents of Indawo Yoxolo, I was unable to hold fruitful conversations. Violence made people suspicious and hesitant to talk about political events. However, at least I was aware of this limitation and appreciated how financial mutuals were embedded in this political-economic field. In addition to the methodological obstacle that violence caused, it was crucial to understand the interplay with social relations on which financial mutuals were built. I was able to evaluate the way in which violence and distrust had an impact on people's actions, what they were willing to say and to whom.

---

[16] See Fakir's (1999) newspaper article on community project and ideology. For an examination of the quest, as well as the problems of 'community', see Baumann (2001).

# 4

# Creating mutuals: Reluctant solidarity

## Introduction

How did Xhosa migrants who hardly knew each other and lived under abominable circumstances form financial mutuals? It was a challenge to co-operate with neighbours in the context of the threatening triad of violence, economic insecurity, and volatile relations. Most migrants did not want to be involved in local politics or civil organisations, even if such organisations could have a huge influence on their lives. They were preoccupied with the immediate problems of money and volatile relations and, therefore, people tended to organise themselves around these concerns only. The close-knit networks among Xhosa neighbours were less threatening than the 'outside world' was (see also Wacquant 1997; Reis 1998).[1] Financial mutuals that were organised by neighbours were, therefore, less vulnerable to the outside world and co-operation with neighbours felt safer.

Financial mutuals were the first organisations that migrants developed – except for the organisation of violence and development. This chapter discusses the way in which neighbours established financial mutuals with each other. As the neighbours did not want to co-operate with everybody, it was inevitable that some had

---

1 Reis used Banfield's (1958) concept of 'amoral familism' to highlight how, in a situation of insecurity and deprivation, one's relations can be extended beyond kin relations. See also Laughlin (1974) on deprivation and changing relations.

to be excluded. The process of exclusion was bound up with identification processes, i.e. 'you are one of us' or 'you are not one of us'. Social exclusion was a precarious process for neighbours who were confronted with each other on a daily basis. The processes of identification revealed why some could join, while others were not allowed to participate or were only able to participate marginally. Many financial mutuals closed in November and December. People evaluated the past year and decided if they wanted to continue, break up, or start a new group. Most of the residents of Indawo Yoxolo had left their previous settlements only months before and they now had the first opportunity to leave the financial mutuals in the old area and establish new ones in Indawo Yoxolo. What were the important factors for including or excluding potential members and what social dynamics were part of excluding particular neighbours?

## Exclusive values

In his discussion of collective insurances De Swaan (1996a: 155-157) notes that small, voluntary collective care arrangements tended to exclude people with a low status and little capital, while, at the same time, people embraced those with a high status. This also proved to be true for financial mutuals in South Africa (cf. Burman & Lembete 1995: 43). People who had little money did not organise their own financial mutuals based on lower contributions. The likely reason why those excluded did not establish their own organisations was of a social nature. After all, they were excluded mostly for moral reasons and these 'outcasts' were not likely to join hands and trust one another. Moral and social indicators were much more relevant than one's financial situation for inclusion in or exclusion from financial mutuals. Financial circumstances, in fact, were difficult for neighbours, colleagues, or *abakhaya* to judge. Unemployment and underemployment meant that a person's financial situation could fluctuate greatly within short periods. Income was also difficult to measure because people often concealed their financial situation from others. People would hide their wealth to prevent certain claims from kin, while at other times they would hide their poverty out of embarrassment. Still others did not always have a clear picture of their own financial situations. Adversity, risk, and potential claims or contributions from kin or household members meant that one's financial situation largely depended on others. To judge the financial situation of others was even more difficult, and that made it an inappropriate yardstick for exclusion. In the end, the decisive variables were moral and social. A person's financial situation did not necessarily say anything about his or her feelings of solidarity and responsibility, since a rich person could also default. A much more relevant factor as regards inclusion was how people valued particular relationships and how they gossiped about them. Based on these judgements, people were eager to identify with some and reluctant to identify with others.[2]

For Xhosa migrants, violence, economic insecurity and volatile relations made moral guidance ever more pressing. Moreover, status conversion – the conversion of economic power into status, prestige, and moral superiority – meant that moral evaluations of others were, at least partly, embedded in economic circumstances.[3] People suffering from hunger, malnutrition, disease and abuse are no longer able to behave appropriately without money. It was only by having some money that a person could live up to the standards that made others want to associate with him or her. For the Xhosa migrants, moral evaluations concerned three values in particular: 'helping each other', 'taking care of oneself', and respect. These values, the ambiguities they carry, and how they interplay within particular social configurations were at the core of separating those who were 'one of us' from people who one preferred to reject.

'To help', or *ukunceda*, was highly valued, as is clear from the names of the financial mutuals described in chapter two. At one ROSCA meeting, a member stressed the importance of helping in a song that she sang for a fellow member:

Jesus, you are a friend of the soul,
I am coming to you to help this heart,
I have no other hope, which I can build on to,
No other place to help myself.

Many desperately needed help to survive the threatening triad of violence, economic insecurity, and volatile relations. As grandma Doris said in a prayer at her ROSCA (*umgalelo*): 'Let God help us, as we come from nothing.' Even if only in small ways, people did try to help one another. Those who gave money and goods to their fellow financial mutual members expressed humility and gave speeches emphasising that 'it is only something small that I give you', or 'I know it is not much, but it comes straight from the heart'.

In addition to the role of the financial mutuals, neighbours, colleagues, and friends tried to help. Frequently, neighbours borrowed money or asked for some food and promised to pay it back. Even if people did not return the favours, this did not automatically mean that someone could never ask for help anymore. The

---

2 Lamont (1992) has analysed how even people with a lot of money, like the French and American upper-middle classes, apply moral standards for identification and exclusion. The upper-middle classes of Lamont's study invested in and worried about morals. Their opinions were at the front lines of social boundaries.

3 See Bourdieu (1984) and De Swaan (2000: 57) on status conversion. Van der Geest (1997) reveals how pivotal money was for morality and the value of relationships in Ghana.

lack of money was a constant theme running through the migrants' lives. The help that one could offer was limited and, as the entanglement of sex, blood, and money revealed, the directional flow of money had drastic consequences for the relationships one had with people. This was the great advantage of financial mutuals, namely that people could help fellow members without incurring too much expense because members had to reciprocate the help they received. Other help, such as from colleagues and neighbours, was restricted and rarely concerned more than a few rand. Only at public events, such as funerals or initiations, could competition cause people to contribute relatively large sums of money.[4] More important was the help and assistance that people received through kinship relations. Many complained about the stress of obligations and people's unwillingness to help, but it was nevertheless a last resort for shelter and food.

People also stated how important it was to take care of oneself properly. Contrary to what one might expect, accumulation could be legitimate if money was needed to take care of oneself. Many men, for example, supported their wife's or girlfriend's participation in financial mutuals. Many men knew about the financial mutuals, although they were often kept in the dark about the details and felt that it was good to accumulate money in order to buy something that was worthwhile, such as cooking utensils, furniture, or clothing. Nokwanda was a case in point. She moved from Khayelitsha to Indawo Yoxolo by the end of 1996 and participated in a ROSCA called *Masiqumane*, which, as she explained, meant 'let us cover each other's back'. The ROSCA members contributed R20 per week and additional small gifts. When I asked her what the attraction of *Masiqumane* was for her, she replied:

> Some of us are unemployed and our husbands have little money. Although we have little money we want to buy other things than only food. If you buy groceries and come back with a kettle instead, the husband will complain: "Why do you buy a kettle and no food?!" But not when you have it via the *umgalelo*. Then the husband thinks it is good and says: "Look what these women are doing!"

The other women who were present at the meeting laughed and recognised this kind of behaviour. They also used the money for things like a kettle, curtains, and so on, and their husbands were glad that they accumulated money in their ROSCA.

During a meeting of another ROSCA, a woman told us how she had tried to use the ROSCA to fool her husband. She had joined a small ROSCA and when it was her turn she used the money to buy groceries. On her way back home, she dropped her shopping bags off at her neighbour Thandi and went home to tell her husband: 'I need money from you to buy groceries, otherwise we won't have anything to eat.' He gave her money and she visited her friend Thandi, had a cup of tea, saved herself a trip to town, and returned home with the shopping bags. Instead of

---

4 See also Kiernan (1988) on Zulu Zionist churches.

spending the money, she pocketed it and used it for something else. She said that she was certain that her husband knew nothing about it, but one evening they had an argument. Her drunken husband shouted: 'Ah, you should keep quiet. I know that you do your shopping at Thandi's place.' Her husband had known it for months and the women at the meeting burst out in laughter. Later he told his wife that he had not said anything because he felt it was a good idea that his wife accumulated some money. The woman said that her husband had told her that he had been waiting for the opportunity to use it against her.

Rich people were looked up to and people wanted to identify with them rather than with poor people. Didi Burial Society, for example, had split up after a controversy over status and support. Some members had refused to pay for the funeral of a poor member while they were more than willing to pay for the funeral of a rich man's daughter. The fact that this rich man was not even a member of the burial society had fuelled the tensions. On the one hand, wealth could evoke feelings of jealousy and envy because people aspired to it. At the same time, however, many tried hard to look their best, even if they had little money. The value that was attached to accumulation could conflict with 'helping each other'. Having little money meant you had to make difficult decisions about who to help, for what goal, how to accumulate, and how to spend.

The third value was respect. Men, in particular, could talk at great length about the reciprocal nature of respect and ways to earn dignity. Violence and the undignified poverty made it ever more important to relate to others in a respectful way and be treated the same. The selection of members of financial mutuals was firmly rooted in the way one showed respect to others. Respect was related to habitus: the way a person behaved verbally and physically, how one spoke to elders, body language, and the actual shape of one's body. It was felt to be degrading and insulting to show no respect to others. Showing respect was crucial for the maintenance of proper relations, which also meant that one would comply with the hierarchies embedded within them: 'How can you expect a child to respect you if you don't show respect to the child?'

To show respect, one had to address a person properly. 'Father' or 'mother' were reserved for older people, while 'brother' or 'sister' were used for people of one's own age. The tone of voice should be soft, a handshake gentle and slow. It was even more respectful to greet by sticking out one's right hand while supporting it by holding it at the wrist with one's left hand. Bending slightly forward or bending one's knees a bit when shaking someone's hand was also part of the body language that denoted respect. Prolonged eye contact had to be avoided. If one gave or received something, especially something valuable, such as money, it was respectful to give or receive it with two hands. Proper receiving was done by letting the other person put it in the palms of one's hand, and not by taking it out of the hands of the giver. These social conventions conveyed humility, vulnerability, and respect.

For women, there were particular ways of showing respect. Married women had to follow rules of avoidance concerning their affinal ancestors (*ukuhlonipa*). Moreover, having children was crucial for a woman's respectability and status: 'If you don't have children or can't have children, they don't even treat you as a person', I was told by a woman without children. Her husband and her affines abused another woman because the couple did not have any children. Together with her belongings and children she was thrown out onto the street and had to live with residents elsewhere in the Cape Flats. It was deeply humiliating for her not to have children, and everybody talked about her. Although some felt sorry for her, she was ostracised nevertheless. In another instance, Umatoto, who wanted to join a ROSCA, was excluded because she was childless. She had pretended that her sister's children were hers, but was quickly found out, after which she was told to leave the ROSCA.

If one is extremely destitute, abused, uneducated, or an alcoholic it is virtually impossible to give respect to others and, therefore, it is impossible to be respected. In general, Africans treat beggars with great contempt. Being poor was regarded as embarrassing enough, but to ask for money while doing nothing was disrespectful and infuriated those who tried hard to get by and live decently. I vividly remember the treatment of children who were sometimes begging for money and food at the traffic lights in Indawo Yoxolo. The driver in front of me indicated to the child that he had some money for him. When the child approached him, the driver stretched out his hand and, instead of giving money, grabbed the child's hand firmly and waited for the light to turn to green. In the meantime he stepped on the accelerator and clutch to make the engine roar, pretending to prepare to drive away at a great speed while dragging the child along. Eventually, the driver let go of the child and drove away laughing, while the child's peers joined in on the laughing. Another variation was to slap the begging child's hand fiercely. I was assured that this would teach the children not to beg but show some respect. The general opinion anyway was that these children were only begging for fun so they could buy sweets and skip school.

To sum up, 'helping each other', 'taking care of oneself', and respect were crucial values that determined inclusion and exclusion. People who complied with these values were more likely to be included, while those who did not help others, did not take care of themselves properly, and behaved disrespectfully were not welcome. What complicated the processes of exclusion was that these three values could be ambiguous and in conflict with one another, especially if one had little money. 'Helping each other' centred on sharing, while 'taking care of oneself' valued accumulation. Precarious choices had to be made about whom to help, and how to take care of oneself. Furthermore, the reciprocal nature of respect meant that those who gave respect also deserved respect. But what if a person did not give respect? This presented a dilemma, namely whether to treat a person with contempt or to uphold one's standards and nevertheless treat that person respectfully.

## Poor reputations

During many conversations it became clear that it was felt that people were, at least to some extent, to blame for their own misery.[5] People demonstrated their distance from them with jokes, gossip and abuse. A process of disidentification (see De Swaan 1997) took place, which meant that feelings of hatred and revulsion dominated. These feelings and the stigmatisation that accompanied them allowed the exclusion of people. Moreover, such feelings could legitimise a person's malicious behaviour towards that person. Reputation was pivotal for the ways people perceived each other, and judged each other's behaviour:

> The small politics of everyone's everyday life is about reputations; about what it means to 'have a good name'; about being socially bankrupted; about gossip and insult and 'one-upmanship; in short, about the rules of how to play 'the social game' and how to win it' (Bailey 1971: 2-3).

The three values were embedded in the creation of reputation, and thus these values defined a social phenomenon that extended beyond the relations of those directly involved. By means of gossip, a person's reputation had more effect than his or her own immediate interactions with others as regards introducing him or her into a wider social configuration. Once a reputation was established, it was very difficult to escape it and people rarely expressed disagreement about the reputation of neighbours (cf. Elias & Scotson 1965: 6). Reputation meant that some were 'one of us', and others 'one of them'. Depending on the emotional processes of identification and disidentification, people were excluded or included from a financial mutual. This opinion was not a private one, but rather – through gossip and the politics of reputation – was subject to a social process in which people tended to agree on a person's morals, social skills, and financial abilities.

Although the neighbours in Indawo Yoxolo hardly knew one another, reputations emerged very quickly and were based on little information. Although reputation was not directly based on money, one nevertheless needed money to help others, take care of oneself, earn respect, and be respected. Without money it was impossible to adhere to these values and live a decent life. Poverty was felt to

---

[5] See also Howe (1998) on Belfast where unemployment is explained in terms of individual incapacities while more structural aspects of poverty and unemployment are not acknowledged.

be embarrassing and I found it a difficult topic to address. My own wealth, education, and future prospects contrasted sharply with theirs and that made it uncomfortable to ask questions that concerned their poverty. When I had established some trust, people eventually began to tell me about particular conflicts and worries that were related to poverty. However, it was always difficult to discuss whether people felt embarrassed, jealous, angry, or other emotional dimensions of destitution. It was uncomfortable and appeared to have a considerable disturbing effect on the person with whom I had the conversation. In response to this, it was tempting to distance myself, also in writing, through cynicism, irony, and black humour. Although such defences were at times unavoidable, as with many neighbours in Indawo Yoxolo, they had to be contained. After all, they could hinder an analysis of the situation.

The best illustration of how reputations were established within a very brief time is through an account of some of the neighbours of my research assistant, which shows the experiences and rumours on which gossip was based and how they influenced a person's reputation. It also highlights how vital money was for one's reputation and its moral effects. Many of these neighbours will also appear in the case study of the funeral.

My research assistant Edith lived in a bright green, two-roomed shack with her husband Zama and their nine-year-old child Nana. At times, other people joined the household, like Zama's brother and Edith's sister's son Thomas. Edith, Zama and the child used to live in Paula Park, an informal settlement near Guguletu. There they applied for an RDP subsidy and moved to Indawo Yoxolo in April 1997. Edith belonged to one burial society and she had just started an *umgalelo* together with three grandmothers who lived about 200 metres away from her house. In order to learn more about ROSCAs and to get to know people better, I too joined this ROSCA. Every member contributed R200 per month. Edith considered joining one of the new organisations in the neighbourhood, but in the beginning of 1998, it was not certain which initiatives would finally materialise. In early 1998, she joined an ASCRA for her children (see the next chapter on this ASCRA).

Edith's neighbour was nicknamed Magazi, after a deceitful movie character. He was known to have many girlfriends, among others the daughter of his girlfriend, and he was the minister of a small independent church that gathered in the living room of his two-roomed shack. He did not belong to any financial mutual, nor did the girlfriend with whom he lived. Magazi claimed that his church had an *umgalelo* together with other branches of the church, but some members of the congregation said that he was lying, as there were never meetings with other branches. Just like most of the neighbours, I was not particularly fond of him and could easily agree about his reputation. However, like many of his neighbours, I tried my best to hide my feelings and continued to engage in polite conversation.

To avoid insulting him by accident, I always called him brother (*bhuti*). I used to address him as father (*tata*), but I found out that he was not that old. More importantly, I felt that he had endangered my life and that of my girlfriend Esther when he drove us to his brother's funeral. He drove like a madman and we found out that he did not even have a licence. Moreover, he had left us waiting at Kentucky Fried Chicken in Queenstown – just about the best waiting place available – for about half a day before he arrived to pick us up on the way to Cape Town.

At the end of the year 2000, Magazi died in a lake in the Eastern Cape. He was baptising new members of his congregation when the current pulled him down. The woman who was being baptised was able to escape, but both Magazi and the bus driver who tried to save him drowned. At first, the congregation had cheered and was full of excitement that their minister had been taken away by God. It was only the next day, after they found the two bodies on the shore of the lake, that they started to mourn their tragic loss.

Nomfundu and her boyfriend lived next door to Magazi. At the end of 1997, Nomfundo belonged to a burial society and a savings scheme for housing organised by the NGO Victoria Mxenge. At that time (January 1998), she did not take part in a ROSCA or ASCRA, although she was very interested in doing so. She had repeatedly asked her neighbours if she could join an *umgalelo*, but the neighbours refused her and devised all kinds of excuses. I was informed that 'Numfondu is a mental case', and 'the tape in her head has broken again'. She used to talk fanatically about the world coming to an end, the number 666 which refers to the beast of the apocalypse, and the devil. She would pick up news from the radio or television and give it a surprising twist of her own. She could approach neighbours aggressively with her views and tell them about God's huge satellite dishes that were going to be used in a fight against the devil. Neighbours frequently felt insulted by her. For example, she had deposited a pile of rubble partly on her neighbour's plot. When he wanted to discuss this with her, she started to scream and swear and told him to 'fuck off'. The lack of respect towards others was an important reason for keeping her out of a financial mutual. People told me that if one lent some money to her, she would never return it. Instead 'she suddenly accepts you as a friend and keeps the money'. Neighbours complained that she would 'overeat'. She would visit neighbours around dinner time and even accepted the food that they offered her, when she should have refused it. Occasionally, she also brought visitors along. Although some felt sorry for Nomfundu, they were also irritated by her rude and demanding behaviour.

The relationship between Nomfundu and her boyfriend was often problematic and, at times, Nomfundu tried to involve the neighbours in their fights. For example, when Nomfundu's boyfriend abused her, she turned to a neighbour for shelter. Her boyfriend followed her, but the neighbour refused to let him in. He returned to their shack and destroyed everything. He broke the water pipe and flooded the place, threw food in the water, destroyed the electricity cables, broke Nomfundu's iron, and threw all her humble belongings into the water on the floor. He took R50 that Nomfundu needed to commute to her work. Nomfundu was only able to go to work the following day after borrowing some money from a neighbour. She then took a train to a friend's place, where she stayed for a while.

Around the same time Nomfundu had a fight with her next door neighbour, Magazi, who had, by that time, already made several attempts to rape her. This particular fight started about a wooden, self-made fence that marked the boundaries of the two plots. Nomfundu was already irritated that the members of Magazi's congregation walked on her plot all the time and became angry when she saw one of the church elders leaning against the fence. She told him that it was not a strong fence and that it had broken before. But Nomfundu told me that she had jokingly added that he was a man and therefore could fix any damage he might make. Magazi visited Nomfundu immediately after the church service and Nomfundu told me that she expected him to apologise. But, instead, he started beating her. Nomfundu ran out of her house and tried to lock herself inside the toilet, but Magazi kept beating her. Nomfundu went to the police but without any result. Therefore, she turned to some Big Five supporters and asked them to handle the situation. They called Magazi to a meeting and Nomfundu recalled with great satisfaction how scared he was. He almost wet his pants out of fear of being beaten, she said. They gave him a probational fine of R10,000 which he would only have to pay if Nomfundu submitted a new complaint against him. This intimidated Magazi, but did not make Nomfundu any more popular among her neighbours. Nomfundu had the reputation of being a troublemaker, a difficult person who, at times justifiably, could be rude and unpredictable.

Nomfundu would have liked to have belonged to an *umgalelo* where stamps from the supermarket chain Shoprite were saved to purchase groceries. However, she was kept out. She also wanted to join Masifunde, an ASCRA that was being organised by her neighbours at the beginning of 1998. She had heard about the initiative and kept asking her neighbours about it, but they were reluctant to include her. At one of the first meetings, which took place at Ma Dlamini's place across the street from her on the first Sunday of January 1998, Nomfundu showed up uninvited. She wanted to join, but the neighbours objected and asked whether Nomfundu was able to pay the R20 contribution. Nomfundu had no money, which was a very uncomfortable situation, but Ma Dlamini's oldest daughter quickly put a banknote in her hand. Nomfundu told the women that she did have money and therefore could join. At this meeting, Nomfundu was fined R 0.25 for talking loudly. Unlike others who were also fined, she refused to pay the 25 cents. Incidents like these, as well as Nomfundu's awkward behaviour, irritated the neighbours. However, they also knew of the destitution that Nomfundu faced, which made them pity her. The neighbours harboured ambivalent feelings towards Nomfundu, ranging from pity to irritation. Being rude and impolite to neighbours seemed to be one of Nomfundu's last resorts to get her way and defend herself against exclusion.

Makafreeman, mother of Freeman, lived a few plots further down the road. Her husband had a little welding business and made burglar bars for windows. He owned a small pick-up truck in which he delivered his merchandise. Makafreeman's husband and Edith's husband Zama belonged to the same clan. Zama once asked him for help with transporting some things. I wanted a mattress and building material to be delivered to Edith and Zama's place so I could stay there for a while. When Zama asked his clan member for help, he replied that he was more than willing to help, but just not on that particular evening. When we saw him and his pick-up truck at home that night, it looked like he had fed him an excuse. According to Zama, he was embarrassed to take money for the job from a clan member, but did not want to do it for free either. Nevertheless, Zama got on fairly well with Makafreeman's husband. There were not very many nasty rumours being circulated about them. Makafreeman also belonged to the stamp *umgalelo* with Edith that Nomfundu had wanted to join.

Next to a few empty plots stood a two-room shack which was the home of Nophuma, her husband, her husband's sister, and the sister's child. They sold cases of beer but did not run a *shebeen* (illegal bar in one's living room) because neighbours were likely to complain about the drunkards, loud music, and fights. Nophuma died in October 1997 after she fell off a station platform and was run over by a train. Her neighbours were convinced that Nophuma did not fall by accident, but had committed suicide. They speculated that her life had become impossible because of her husband's sister. I was assured that it was common knowledge that a woman never gets along with her sister-in-law.

Nophuma's husband told me that they belonged to a burial society and received some money for the funeral. The husband's sister had joined the neighbourhood ASCRA Masifunde. Nophuma was the first neighbour to die and thus it was the first time the neighbours collected money. There was a meeting called after the collection in order to see if the neighbours could establish a burial society without a fund among neighbours. Only eight women showed up and the initiative collapsed. One of the problems was that the neighbours Ma Zantsi and her friend Xoliswa had called for the meeting, but they were not liked by all. Many worried about their involvement in politics and felt that this could harm the burial society. The idea to establish a burial society was occasionally resubmitted, but the prevailing response was that there was no pressing need for it as long as nobody in the neighbourhood died.

Noxolo, her boyfriend, and her children lived next door from them in a two-room shack. From the freezer in one of her rooms she sold chicken, pork, sausages, ice cream, and sometimes she had bread and eggs. Noxolo was careful not to give too much on credit. If her neighbours had too much debt, they would buy their groceries elsewhere because they were embarrassed to see her. Edith and I visited Noxolo many times for a chat. She was pleasant and knew a lot about the neighbours because they were her customers. Some people seemed to be more visible than others, and Noxolo was one of those visible people. Noxolo belonged to an *umgalelo* with her mother and her mother's neighbour, who lived in the adjacent township. Noxolo had lived with her mother before she moved to Indawo Yoxolo and still considered her mother's neighbours, in a way, as her own neighbours. Another possible reason why she did not want to join an *umgalelo* with her neighbours was because they were also her customers, which could have complicated their relationships.

The school principal who was accused of corruption and 'taken hostage' by angry parents lived next to Noxolo. We did not talk much with him and his family and, to my knowledge, he did not belong to any financial mutual in the neighbourhood. Contrary to many other neighbours, one would never meet them on the street and have a chat. Their involvement with the Big Five and the bad relations with angry parents meant that they did not take part in any activity within the neighbourhood.

The shack next to the principal's had a bright blue colour. It was lived in by a few men who participated in a ROSCA in which the *abakhaya* members contributed R500 a month.[6] The principal's wife was not sure whether she should join Victoria Mxenge, an NGO whose members saved for housing purposes. She was suspicious of any initiative in the area and told me: 'Why do you need to go door-to-door to find members if it is such a good organisation?' In January 1998, she considered joining a R250 ROSCA with her neighbours, but felt that she could not afford it and could not trust the neighbours. She had also heard about an ASCRA, but was unfamiliar with it and doubted whether it could work. She was afraid of corruption in the ASCRA and Victoria Mxenge because of Ma Zantsi's involvement. Ma Zantsi also lived in the neighbourhood and had the same clan name as one of the Big Five members and some regarded her as the mother of this Big Five member. Ma Ntshona, the liaison officer for Deel Construction who sided with the Big Five, was also involved in Victoria Mxenge. She wanted to avoid anything political and felt intimidated by Ma Zantsi and Ma Ntshona. She would have liked to have joined an organisation but felt that she could not afford to take the risks involved.

There was little contact with the neighbours on the other side of the street and Edith complained: 'They don't even greet you. They think they belong to a higher

---

[6] I only spoke with his wife about his ROSCA, which made information slightly less reliable.

class.' Only a few people were known, like Ma Dlamini. She was the head of a three-generation female household, as she lived with her daughters Margeret and Xoliswa, and Xoliswa's young daughter. Sometimes there were also other people at their place. From the beginning of 1998, the newly established ASCRA Masifunde had its meetings at her place every Sunday afternoon. Her two daughters also belonged to this ASCRA and one of them was the chairperson.

Voyiswa and her two small children lived across the street from Ma Dlamini. She was unemployed but nevertheless wanted to organise an *umgalelo* with Nomfundu, an attempt that was unsuccessful. Voyiswa had a poor reputation, and Nomfundu, who did not have a very good reputation either, seemed to dislike her. Voyiswa had approached Edith for a R200 monthly ROSCA but Noxolo had warned her. Noxolo had once lent money to Voyiswa who had refused to give it back. Other neighbours also complained about her. She was said to sleep around and could be very rude to her neighbours. One neighbour had told me in confidence that she suspected that Voyiswa used witchcraft. Voyiswa had sent one of her children to her with a piece of paper that said: 'Could I please borrow R15 from you.' But the neighbour sent the child back empty handed. She explained to me that she had no money herself but that she was also afraid that Voyiswa would use the money for witchcraft. Notwithstanding Voyiswa's poor reputation she had managed to join a financial mutual called Masifunde; in her case, it was explained to me, neighbours found it difficult to oppose her rude behaviour without becoming rude themselves.[7]

Another neighbour had the derogative nickname Noparuru, an allusion to her speaking disability. She lived with a small child and had a teenager who visited her on and off. Her teenaged son spent most of his time with his gang members and stayed in a shelter in Woodstock, one of the Southern Suburbs near the city centre. Noparuru's husband rarely visited her. He was, like Noparuru, a heavy drinker. He was at times seen pushing his supermarket trolley through the streets in the white neighbourhoods, or the city centre, in search of something that he could either eat, sell or barter. Edith helped Noparuru sometimes by giving her food, and also invited her over for the Christmas barbecue because she had nothing to eat. Although the neighbours sometimes felt sorry for Noparuru, she just as often irritated them. She was disrespectful, never helped other people, and showed no sign of appreciation when others helped her. She was one of the poorest, possibly the poorest, person in the vicinity. Noparuru did not belong to any financial mutual.

Whether they liked each other or not, these neighbours had to try and make the most of their neighbourhood. They had to deal with the poor, irritating, and, at times, crazy neighbours. Although the reputations of neighbours were not pri-

---

7 As will become clear in the next chapter, the risk of default in an ASCRA is small compared with a ROSCA.

marily about money, money did play a pivotal role. People's concerns revolved around money, how to take care of themselves, their children, kin, as well as others who were in need. Tensions within relations, as well as feelings of jealousy, were also often about money, and much of the gossip among neighbours concerned money matters. Money was pivotal for the compliance with the values 'helping each other', 'taking care of oneself', and respect. Thus, morals and reputations centred on that which the poor lacked and desired most.

The neighbours who had a bad reputation – due to the fact that they did not adhere to the fundamental social values, because they literally could not afford to – had to be excluded. Disidentification, through joking, behaving rudely, and personalising the structural problems of poverty, led to social exclusion. At the same time, however, one could not neglect someone completely. This would be a disgrace for the neighbourhood because of the 'dependence of individuals on the standing and the image of groups to which they belong' (Elias & Scotson 1965: 103). The physical and social proximity that became apparent in a shared concern for the neighbourhood's affairs and reputations also gave rise to identification. As De Swaan argued: 'Processes of identification ... occur as a restructuring of concerns, of a person's dispositions to be emotionally affected' (De Swaan 1995: 25). The outcome of the processes of identification and disidentification were ambivalent feelings towards marginal neighbours. This led to a half-hearted inclusion or reluctant solidarity.

## Noparuru: A poor reputation

Just like her neighbours, Noparuru had only lived in the newly established township of Indawo Yoxolo for a few months. She came from the town of Fort Beaufort in the former impoverished Xhosa Bantustan Ciskei. However, with the breakdown of the apartheid state, followed by the first democratic elections in 1994, more and more women like Noparuru left the impoverished towns, leaving family, neighbours, and fellow church members behind, in order to find a job in the city as a cleaner, nanny, or domestic worker. However, Noparuru was one of the many who did not find a job and she ended up becoming the poorest person in the street.

The women migrants in particular quickly established neighbourhood organisations that revolved around money. The events relating to death were a major concern as nobody wanted to be buried in a hostile city without family. Therefore, money had to be saved for a descent funeral back home. This made funerals expensive. Even a simple funeral easily cost a cleaner half a year's wage. Neighbours tried to establish burial societies to provide for the mutual assistance, such as collecting money among neighbours, organizing wakes, supporting the bereaved, and ensuring a proper burial back in the Eastern Cape. However, Noparuru did not belong to any organization although she had approached her neighbours and asked them if she could join. The neighbours did not want someone with a poor reputation to join any of their organisations (cf. Elias & Scotson 1965: 103). They complained that when Noparuru had some money, which was not very often, she was frequently drunk. She was often rude, had a speaking disability which everybody made fun of, and she looked terribly unhealthy wearing the same worn-out cloths every day. Neighbours felt that she did not behave respectfully, was irresponsible, never helped her neighbours, and would be a disgrace to the group. One neighbour told me that at one time she had some rotten meat left that she had not managed to sell in time. She wanted to give it to the dogs which, after sniffing the meat, refused to eat it. Because Noparuru had been without food for a long time she eventually gave it to her and she did eat it. She told the neighbours jokingly how disgusting the meat had smelled and how terrible it was that Noparuru actually ate something that even dogs refused. This story was greeted with feelings of embarrassment and revulsion at Noparuru's poverty, as well as aggression since the gift of rotten meat was very humiliating for Noparuru (see also Bataille 1991).

Neighbours expressed processes of disidentification (see De Swaan 1997 on this term). Through jokes, gossip, as well as abuse, people distanced themselves from Noparuru and feelings of hatred and revulsion dominated. At times, however, neighbours also expressed how they identified with Noparuru. She was, after all, a fellow neighbour and fellow migrant from the Eastern Cape. Moreover, the living conditions of most neighbours were very fragile and many were aware that they were themselves only a few steps away from ending up just like Noparuru. This ambiguity – being 'one of us' while simultaneously 'one of them' – was crucial to understanding the attitude towards Noparuru.

Identifications, ambivalence, reluctant solidarity, and the politics of everyday life revealed themselves most clearly around the cruel occurrence of death.[8] After Noparuru died in hospital on 18 May 1998, it became clear how her neighbours tried to deal with ambivalent relations and conflicting concerns, and how this led to reluctant solidarity. Most neighbours had been unaware of Noparuru's hospitalisation until they heard about her death from her brother, Umzwandile. According to Umzwandile, she died of tuberculosis. It was, however, very likely that she died of AIDS, but people often pretended that AIDS did not exist and instead referred to tuberculosis, often an AIDS related disease. After Noparuru's

---

[8] See Verdery (1999) on the significance of reburial across Eastern Europe and the contributions in Ojwang & Mugambi (1989) on the conflicts around the burial of a Kenyan lawyer. These are inspiring studies on the socio-political processes that surface around death and corpses.

death, Umzwandile asked my research assistant Edith to contact his mother in Fort Beaufort in the Eastern Cape. As she had no phone, Edith phoned her own parents-in-law, who coincidently also lived in Fort Beaufort, and asked them to visit Noparuru's mother and inform her about the death of her daughter.[9] Noparuru's mother was also extremely poor, just like her daughter had been, and Edith's in-laws promised to take some food with them so that she would at least have something to eat that day. Because the communication between Umzwandile and his family went largely via Edith, and because of my familiarity with the neighbourhood, I was able to acquire detailed information about the flows of money and the socio-political processes related to the funeral. Quite unexpectedly, people were confronted with a dead neighbour whose corpse was in a Cape Town morgue, who had left no money, and who had never helped others.

*Struggling neighbours*

After the death of Nophuma who had been hit by a train half a year earlier, Noparuru was the second death in the short history of the neighbourhood. When Nophuma died almost all the neighbours had contributed R10, at the time about one dollar, or more to the funeral costs. Noparuru had not contributed. Now a second neighbour had died and it was felt that a more permanent arrangement had to be made through the formation of a burial society for neighbours only (see also Bähre 2002). As is common after a death, wakes were going to be held at Noparuru's shack until the corps had left the morgue for the Eastern Cape and it were particularly the women who attended these wakes who felt responsible.

Before or after the wakes they talked about the formation of a burial society to provide for neighbours after their death, and also in order to discuss what help should be given to Noparuru. The fact that Noparuru had not contributed to the funeral of the other neighbour who had died half a year earlier made most people feel that she did not deserve help. At the first wake one of the neighbours, Voyiswa, confessed that she still remembered that Noparuru wanted to give R10 but that she had created a problem for Noparuru. She had borrowed money from Noparuru and had failed to give it back in time. She explained that Noparuru had even asked her sister to interfere, but even that did not prompt her to return the money. Voyiswa said that she now felt guilty because if she had given the R10 to Noparuru she would probably have used it for the funeral and neighbours would be less reluctant to help her.

One of the women, Makafreeman felt it did not matter: 'She [Noparuru] is not in our book, so there is nothing we can do.'Others, however, felt that they had to

9 There were a number of reasons for contacting Edith. She had a mobile phone, her affines lived in Fort Beaufort, and she was *umakoti* (married), which made her more responsible to assist in funerals.

do something. Noparuru had no relatives in Cape Town, except for her brother Umzwandile. Her husband was nowhere to be found and was probably pushing his supermarket trolley somewhere in Cape Town. Her sixteen year-old son had joined a gang and her other child was not even a teenager. Her relatives in the Eastern Cape would not have the money to pay for the funeral. The discussion hovered around the willingness and possibilities to do something. When the wake came to an end no conclusion had been reached.

The next day my research assistant Edith and myself gave Umzwandile (Noparuru's brother) a ride to an undertaker. He could organise a funeral in Cape town for R1,679 but he insisted on being paid in advance. He had had bad experiences with people who disappeared once the corpse had been buried. Without money there was nothing he could do. Following the meeting we drove to Umzwandile's house in the neighbouring township Guguletu as Umzwandile had said he wanted to make some phone calls. When we arrived at Umzwandile's house he behaved very awkwardly and uncooperatively. He said he had tried to phone his sister in Port Elizabeth, but we saw how he consistently dialed the wrong number. Finally he asked Edith to phone and have the conversation with his sister while Umzwandile went outside of the house to argue with his tenant. During the following weeks, it became clear that Umzwandile was constantly trying to avoid his family as much as possible. Not only did he not want to talk to his sister, he also told the neighbours that it was Noparuru's last wish to be buried in Cape Town and not in Fort Beaufort. The neighbours did regard this a disgraceful wish. Apart from Umzwandile, Noparuru had no kin in Cape Town and one woman remarked: 'You can't be separated from your family. As an ancestor, you want to visit your family sometimes, but Noparuru doesn't have any family here.' Umzwandile frequently complained to us about Noparuru's neighbours: they did not care about Noparuru at all. He insisted on having the burial in Cape Town and on using his house in Guguletu, not Noparuru's house, for the funeral services.

Time and again Umzwandile asked Edith, but also other neighbours, for help. They had to make phone calls, arrange the undertaker, arrange transport, and so on. From Edith's telephone conversations with Umzwandile's family, from Edith's in-laws in Fort Beaufort, from neighbours in Cape Town, and from talks at the wakes and the funeral that I attended, a better view emerged of the complex web of relations and problems around Umzwandile.

Quite some years ago, I was told by different people that Umzwandile had broken his wife's neck. As a consequence he was fired from his job at a shipping company and, after a court case, for which his sister in Port Elizabeth paid all the legal expenses, he was imprisoned for the murder. When Umzwandile got out of prison, he bought a house in Guguletu with the R30,000 that he supposedly received from his pension plan after he was fired. Umzwandile rented out his house for only R500 per month, and this was his main source of income because high unemployment and a criminal record made it impossible for him to get a job. He had had an affair with the tenant but, to his annoyance, the relationship ended sometime later. At that point he decided he wanted the woman out of his house so he could stay there himself or rent it out to others, possibly at a higher rate.

Umzwandile campaigned for a funeral at his house in Guguletu in order to put pressure on the former girlfriend to leave the house. The wakes, the funeral, and visitors would put pressure on the tenant to leave. In retrospect, I could not help feeling that he wanted Edith and me to visit his place for that reason and not to make phone calls. A white visitor was possibly meant to impress the tenant and I would not have been surprised if he had told the tenant that I was his lawyer.

Umzwandile had other reasons to lobby for a funeral in Cape Town. Not only would it be cheaper, it also would enable him to avoid his family. Umzwandile's sister who lived in Port Elizabeth complained a few times about the lack of financial support that Umzwandile gave to his family. She had had to pay all the expenses of her father's funeral a few years ago, despite Umzwandile having R30,000. She remembered very well that Umzwandile had sent just R500 to his needy mother via a postal order. However, the personal details on the postal order were incorrect and it was consequently returned to the sender. Umzwandile's sister was convinced that Umzwandile had done this on purpose. She also felt that Umzwandile wanted Noparuru to be buried in Cape Town so that he could avoid a confrontation with her as well as with his mother. Moreover, if Umzwandile were to go to a funeral in Fort Beaufort he risked meeting the late wife's family who lived in a nearby village. Although Umzwandile had sat out his sentence for the murder, the family possibly still had hostile feelings towards him and might have wanted to kill him. For these reasons, which mainly concerned conflicts relating to money, Umzwandile tried to have a funeral in Cape Town, preferably with a ceremony at his house.

*Two competing neighbours*

The next wake was attended by lots of people. About forty, mainly female, visitors barely fitted into Noparuru's shack. Even old neighbours from the nearby squatter camp Paula Park had come to pay their respect. Knowing that Umzwandile was struggling and because I wanted to contribute something, I had brought sugar and coffee. Having no sugar, tea or coffee was regarded as the nadir of deprivation. One of the worst signs of poverty was not being able to make a cup of tea with sugar for visitors. The absence of sugar, tea, and coffee at the previous wake had been a dreadful moment: it revealed the absence of hospitality and the inability to help one another.

At the wake, which consisted of the usual sequence of hymns and speeches, the speakers said that Noparuru had been rude at times, but that she had never failed to apologise for her rudeness. One woman recalled that Noparuru had always addressed her female neighbours respectfully by using the term 'mama' and said: 'Noparuru never failed to respect her neighbours.' The references to Noparuru's respectful behaviour hardly resembled people's actual experiences, nor the way they gossiped about her. Nevertheless, on this occasion people did their best to say something sympathetic and positive about a person who, during her lifetime, had neither elicited many opportunities to evoke sympathy in others, nor had been able to make a positive contribution to people's lives.

At the end of the wake a little dish was passed around, as is usual at wakes, and people contributed between five and twenty cents 'to keep the light of the house burning', as the expenses of the wake are referred to. Many were only prepared to gave little and gossiped that Umzwandile was going to use it to buy cigarettes anyway. This reluctance was also apparent in the serving of coffee and tea to the guests. Umzwandile had quarrelled with some women because he did not want to serve the neighbours coffee and tea and had commented that it was 'a waste'. However, a few women had successfully protested. In the following days the coffee and tea rapidly disappeared, much faster than could be expected. Eventually neighbours started to search Noparuru's place, where Umzwandile had started to live, and found several plastic sandwich bags filled with coffee and sugar hidden in the cupboards and under the mattress. We were all very upset that Umzwandile was not even willing to use coffee and tea for his sister's wakes.

In the meantime, Noparuru's next door neighbour, Ma Dlamini, had set up a meeting with neighbours and an undertaker Mr Mnyungulo. This undertaker said he could arrange a funeral in Cape Town for R1,200, which was a very low price, and an excellent arrangement because he did not require payment in advance. Ma Dlamini mentioned to him that the neighbours wanted to organise a burial society and were going to meet the following Saturday. She wanted Mr Mnyungulo to be the permanent undertaker for the members of the burial society. The undertaker seemed to consider Noparuru's funeral as an investment for future clientele provided via the burial society. Ma Dlamini was concerned as a neighbour, but also saw a chance to enhance her status within the neighbourhood and take the lead in the formation of a burial society.

A few days later this undertaker called Edith. He told her that Noparuru's family in Fort Beaufort had contacted a local undertaker called Stompie and that he had agreed to work with Stompie and fly Noparuru's body to Fort Beaufort. He did not yet know how much this would cost because, according to Mr Mnyungulo, it depended on the weight of the body. He first wanted the neighbours or Umzwandile to deposit the money into a friend's account, not his own account.

The next Saturday afternoon, Ma Dlamini organised another meeting where the formation of a burial society was further discussed. The meeting lasted an extremely long time as new neighbours kept arriving all the time and had to be updated on the discussion. The central questions were: 'How much should we collect?', 'whose deaths are covered?', and 'how high are the benefits?' Ma Dlamini, who was initially the central figure at the meeting, proposed calling the organisation Masincedane ('let us help each other').

While the meeting had been going on for quite some time, Ma Zantsi arrived, the neighbour who was believed to have ties with the Big Five and who dominated the Victoria Mxenge housing scheme. She had also publicly taken credit for organising the collection after the suicide of Nophuma although she had had little involvement in it. Ma Zantsi was elaborately updated and Ma Dlamini grew increasingly silent. After a few minutes, Ma Dlamini excused herself and said: 'I would like to leave now, my children. I have flu.' The meeting continued and, finally, the women decided on a R30 joining fee and a monthly contribution of R20. They were going to ask neighbours to donate R10 voluntarily towards Noparuru's funeral expenses, but neighbours were also able to join the burial society without making the payment.

In the following days, Ma Dlamini stopped attending wakes, withdrew from the organisation of the funeral, just like the undertaker that she had introduced, Mr Mnyungulo. Stompie, the undertaker in Fort Beaufort, had phoned Edith and told her that he was not reliable and that it was nonsense that the cost of Noparuru's flight depended on the weight of the corpse. Stompie had contacted another undertaker in Cape Town that she wanted to work with. The neighbours gossiped that Ma Dlamini was unhappy that 'her' undertaker had been excluded and, therefore, halted her involvement in Noparuru's funeral. Moreover, Ma Zantsi was now the woman in charge.

*Respect and disgrace*

The final wake was on Monday 25 May as the following day Noparuru's body was going to be flown to Fort Beaufort. Some neighbours were excited about Noparuru's flight: 'Who would think that Noparuru would ever go on an aeroplane', someone had jokingly remarked. Umzwandile complained to some neighbours that he had no money and, therefore, could not afford to go to Fort Beaufort. Before the wake Umzwandile had sent Noparuru's little son to Edith to ask for sugar for the wake. Due to Umzwandile's 'disappearing act', the coffee, tea, and five kg of sugar were gone within a few days.

About thirty to forty people attended the wake. It was one of my most uncomfortable and disturbing research experiences and I find it difficult to convey why this was so. It basically boiled down to the contradictions that were apparent between how things were, and how they ought to have been. One woman gave a speech in which she claimed to have been very good friends with Noparuru: 'Noparuru used to come to my place and wash my clothing for money. But I lost my job and could not afford to pay her anymore.' She broke out in tears and said how much she missed her good friend Noparuru. But she was clearly exaggerating their friendship. Some people, as well as the speaker, could barely disguise their laughter at this theatrical facade. Although the woman lived only about half-a-dozen streets away from Noparuru, she had never been seen in the area prior to Noparuru's death.

Some of the men were drunk and a few women wore trousers instead of the required skirts, which was commonly regarded as very disrespectful. Some of the younger women were giggling and joking and, if this had been the wake of a neighbour of some status, this would not have been tolerated. At the end of the wake there was a little argument among the younger women responsible for making tea and coffee. None of them felt like making it and they jokingly tried to back out of their obligation, using lame excuses. When they finally returned with tea and coffee some of the men barely disguised how they poured brandy into their cups, notwithstanding that it is a great taboo to drink alcohol at wakes and funerals.

After this wake early in the evening I drove to my White upper-class home and realised I had – at least temporarily – lost confidence in humanity. The contrast between the glorifying speeches and disrespectful behaviour was startling. Poverty, violence, and oppression by apartheid have not helped Noparuru's neighbours to feel good about themselves. It also made it difficult to feel compassionate towards neighbours and relatives all the time. The humiliating events of the day contrasted sharply with the speeches that that emphasized 'helping each other'. Friendship and affection were central to those speeches while, at the same time, one could see that the wake was for a poor, marginal woman who had died of a disease which no-one wanted to name. I had hardly ever spoken with Noparuru. It was just too uncomfortable to be confronted with her desperate situation all the time and it was virtually impossible to have a conversation with her. Noparuru's poverty was very unsettling. Maybe some were wondering what would happen to them if they were to die in this hostile city with high murder rates but without friends and family. The identification with Noparuru as a neighbour, and a poor migrant in a violent place, as well as with the nasty way she was treated, often because the neighbours had little more, seemed to be at the core of the ambivalent feelings toward Noparuru and her death. Some neighbours confided that they felt guilty and felt they had failed the deceased (see also Freud 1984: 86-111). The ambivalent relation to Noparuru was apparent in the way in which respect and disgrace were both prominent at the wake. Respect was expressed through language and the people's presence, while disgrace was expressed through dress and non-verbal behaviour.

Ma Zantsi, the neighbour who had ties with the local mafia, had by now taken over the initiative from Ma Dlamini. However, this did not mean that the neighbours stopped interacting altogether. The neighbourhood was too important to break relations completely or to let them become too antagonistic. This became very clear during the birthday of one of Ma Dlamini's grandchildren a few days later. This was the first birthday ever to be celebrated in the young history of this street and the mother had written a card for her little daughter which said that she hoped that she would become a nurse one day. Ma Zantsi was also present and she gave one of the most expensive presents, which were clothes. When the mother had unwrapped the present she started to cry out of joy and the children all started to cheer. The present revealed that the tensions between the two women did not lead to a breakdown in neighbourhood relations.

The next Sunday Ma Zantsi had called another meeting to discuss the establishment of a burial society, which was fairly well attended, among others by Umzwandile, my research assistant Edith, and myself. Everyone was unhappy about the neighbours' hesitation to provide financial support for Noparuru's funeral and that the wakes had come to an end. Umzwandile continued to argue that Noparuru's body was still in Cape Town and he also felt that the money that was going to be collected should be given to him. Ma Zantsi did not agree: together with some other women she was going to attend the funeral in Fort Beaufort herself and deliver the money. Earlier in the meeting, and in the absence of Umzwandile, she had told everyone that she did not trust Umzwandile and that, therefore, she should bring the money herself. Some women did not want to get into a discussion about who should get the money while others felt that Edith should get the money: She was going to attend the funeral with her husband, my girlfriend Esther, and myself.

Edith left the meeting early and a few minutes later her next door neighbour dropped by. She told Edith that as soon as she had left, Ma Zantsi had started accusing her of spreading lies. Ma Zantsi told the women that Edith was the one who had told the neighbours that the body had left Cape Town and she should have kept silent about it so the wakes could have continued. Edith immediately returned to the meeting and confronted the women with what she had heard. Ma Zantis and Umzwandile explained to her that there was a misunderstanding and that her next-door neighbour had not properly conveyed what had been said. Edith left it at that but was getting tired of these fights and was quite happy not to have anything to do with the money: It would only lead to all kinds of accusations towards her.

During the following days it again became clear that Umzwandile needed money desperately. He had put up Noparuru's plot and shack for sale and the neighbours gossiped that Umzwandile was disrespectful. He could not even wait with making money until his sister's corpse had been buried. Umzwandile had also asked Zama, at the time the husband of my research assistant, to organise transport to the funeral. Zama told me that he felt that Umzwandile wanted him to organise transport in order to avoid financial responsibilities. Furthermore, Umzwandile told me that he was cross with Ma Dlamini for telling the neighbours that

Noparuru's body had left Cape Town. This had made it impossible for Umzwandile to continue the wakes and collect the few cents that he seemed to need so desperately. Eventually, the neighbours in Indawo Yoxolo and Paula Park collected R700, at the time about $100. The neighbours in Indawo Yoxolo, and particularly Ma Zantsi, decided that Umzwandile was going to bring the money to the funeral.

*Quarrelling kin*

About a week later, on Saturday 6 June, Edith, Edith's husband Zama, my girlfriend Esther, and I drove the 1,000 km to the funeral in Fort Beaufort. Zama's family kindly provided accommodation for Esther and myself. Thirteen people were sharing a house that consisted of a living room, a kitchen, one bedroom, and two additional bedrooms at the back of the house. We were privileged by being allotted the most private space, which was one of the two little rooms at the back. Three of Zama's siblings were mentally ill. One woman stood all day as motionless as a piece of furniture in the corner of the living room. A man ran around the house all day laughing like only a madman could, while asking for cigarettes. He had stayed with Edith and Zama in Cape Town, but his crazy and, at times, aggressive behaviour had made him an impossible visitor. The third child, also an adult, was quiet most of the time and walked around with a big smile. All three children had been in and out of mental hospitals for most of their lives and were taking medication. About a year or two later Zama joined his brothers and sister as he also started to suffer from severe mental problems that forced him to take medication and live with his parents.

Noparuru's funeral started the next morning at her mother's place. Her mother lived on a small plot with a small house which had just two small rooms, and no kitchen or sanitary facilities. To accommodate the visitors, she had rented a tent that was put in front of the house. Umzwandile and Noparuru's youngest son had also arrived. Noparuru's oldest son, as well as her husband, had not been found and were not informed about the death of Noparuru. Ma Zantsi was not there either, although she had promised to attend the funeral with some of her friends. It seemed that she had made this promise in order to show how important neighbours were. One after another more people arrived until there were about a hundred people, which was not many, especially if one considers the food that was going to be available. It showed that Noparuru's family did not have a high status in the neighbourhood. The fact that the four of us had come all the way from Cape Town was highly appreciated, and was referred to at the beginning of one of the first speeches: 'Noparuru was with people. We can see that people from Cape Town came, which shows that she was a good neighbour. Even if you have fights or other problems, this is the time to put that aside because you are at a funeral.' Another man addressed the visitors and said:

> You guys have a different colour but we are here together. Thanks for coming. I thank Noparuru as white people followed her. It shows we are the same. Now we preach on the bible. Even if a child cries you have to consult the child. The sensitive part of the person is the heart. Thank you for coming all the way from Cape Town so we can see that we are one nation.

Most of the speeches were about the two white visitors and the two neighbours from Cape Town. Our presence provided evidence of Noparuru's good life among respectful and helpful neighbours in Cape Town:

> It [our presence] shows that you were neighbours; you eat together and cry at the same place. Thanks for accompanying the neighbour. You should know everything about your neighbour. If there is no neighbourhood, then there is no burial. You need unity and love between neighbours, and Noparuru had love between neighbours. We are a disgrace between people. Pray and you [will get] answers. The lord calls all of us: prayer makes you strong. People are being killed!

There was extensive talk about the love among neighbours, the importance of caring for each other in a strange environment, and how caring for others enabled one to feel good about oneself. But here and there the speeches also hinted at disidentification among neighbours, about disgrace among people and the religious support one needed to resist disgrace. The mentioning of 'people are being killed' revealed the conflicts that could emerge. When we left for the graveyard, one of the passengers in my car complained about the many deaths that had occurred lately. The old man had noticed that more people were dying than ever before: 'All our children who are away for work come back in a coffin' due to increasing incidences of witchcraft. He felt it had never been this bad in the past.

When we arrived at Noparuru's grave, it contrasted sharply with the adjacent luxurious grave that had a velvet tent placed above it while more velvet cloth was draped around the hole. The coffin was even going to be placed in that grave using an automatic lift! Noparuru's grave was a simple hole in the ground and the coffin had to be lowered with ropes, which meant that a few men had to climb into the hole to place the coffin correctly. While Noparuru was being buried, we saw the large elaborate procession descending the hill to bury the apparently much more important person in the much nicer grave. People talked about respect and 'helping each other', but also indicated the marginality of this poor woman who, like many other migrants who had left Fort Beaufort, returned in a coffin.

After the men had filled Noparuru's grave, we all returned to the home of Noparuru's mother. Upon arrival, we washed our hands to prevent the spread of death. We ate some corn, drank some lemonade, and waited until we received a meal of cooked sheep, rice, beetroot salad, and pasta salad. It was prepared at the neighbour's place and one of the neighbours told me that they had collected the plates and cutlery we ate with from their own homes. The plates were all made of the same red plastic and it seemed awkward to me that the neighbours all had identical plates. The food looked very good, but Edith refused to eat it. She was afraid that someone had put something in the food that could bewitch her. Before we left, we asked if we could return in the evening to talk with Noparuru's mother about the funeral more privately.

*Photo 4.1* Noparuru's grave

Early that evening, we visited Noparuru's mother. The tent had already been taken down, everything had been cleared and cleaned up, and there was little to remind us of the funeral earlier that day. Noparuru's siblings were also there: Umzwandile, Noparuru's sister from Port Elizabeth, and a young man who still lived with his mother. His mother told me that, although her son was an adult, he could not live on his own due to mental problems. Another son in Khayelitsha, Cape Town, and another daughter in Port Elizabeth had not been able to afford to attend their sister's funeral. Noparuru's mother told us that her neighbours had helped a bit with the funeral. She borrowed two large cooking pots from a nearby school and her next-door neighbour allowed her to use her yard to cook the food. Her own yard was too small because of the tent, the visitors, and because the kraal could not be used as a cooking space. Her neighbours did not collect any money and had only come to eat. From Noparuru's husband's family, who lived in a nearby village, and from her sister, she had received R200.

There had been a lot of tensions about money that morning. Noparuru's husband's family had also arrived at the funeral and they knew that the neighbours in

Cape Town had collected money. They had heard this from Edith, who had talked on the phone with Noparuru's husband's brother's wife in Port Elizabeth. Noparuru's husband's brother's wife, in turn, had informed her affines about the money. That morning, Noparuru's husband's relatives demanded the money from Umzwandile. They had taken guns along and put Umzwandile under severe pressure, but he convinced them that the neighbours had not collected any money at all and that they were misinformed.

Noparuru's sister intervened and was angry with Noparuru's husband's family for the way they were treating Umzwandile and demanding money from him. Noparuru's sister knew from Ma Dlamini that Noparuru's neighbours had collected money. However, she did not know that it had been given to Umzwandile. Therefore, she felt that Noparuru's husband's relatives had treated Umzwandile unfairly. When they told us what had happened that morning, Edith was shocked. Umzwandile had tried to keep the money for himself and had told everyone that he did not have it. Edith immediately told Noparuru's mother and sister that the neighbours in Indawo Yoxolo and Paula Park had collected R700. Both the mother and sister were shocked since they had believed Umzwandile. Umzwandile overheard our conversation from the adjacent room and protested loudly, shouting 'Hey, hey, hey!' He did not want the conversation to continue and did not like it at all that his deceitfulness was being discovered. The atmosphere was far from pleasant and the unease between Umzwandile and his mother and sister was tangible.

Noparuru's mother told us that she was suffering from serious financial problems. I asked her about the plates that were used for the meals and asked whose they were. The sister from Port Elizabeth told us that they were hers, but Edith told her that a neighbour had said that they had collected them. 'This is nonsense!', she said in an angry voice. Because Noparuru's mother received such little support she had had to borrow R600 from a cash loan company at 30 percent interest per month. The company took all her personal details and was authorised to withdraw money from her bank account into which her pension was paid. She used R100 to pay off her television that she had bought on a rent-to-own plan.[10] The remaining R500 were spent on phone calls to Cape Town, the funeral, and the wakes. She complained about Noparuru's husband's family, whose members had promised to help her but eventually did nothing. With great disappointment, she said: 'I would give them some money to buy sugar or tea or other things for the funeral, but they would return empty handed. With nothing and they even ask for more money.' The undertaker charged R2,300 for the funeral, which included the coffin, transport from Cape Town to Fort Beaufort, a simple wooden cross, trans-

---

[10] There was no television or any other furniture at her place, but it might have been at a neighbour's place in order to create space for the visitors.

port to the cemetery in the back of a pick-up truck, refrigeration, administrative costs, and legal fees. This was a good price, especially because Stompie organised the funeral without the usual R500 deposit. As soon as Noparuru's mother could, she would pay two instalments of R500 and continue to pay the rest off in smaller amounts every month. Noparuru's mother was very pleased with this arrangement.

Noparuru's mother's financial situation was downright depressing. The R600 debt at the cash loan office alone cost her R180 interest per month. She owed the undertaker another R2,300, luckily based on better terms. Her pension was about R400 per month, but the payment of pensions was often very irregular and sometimes pensioners had to wait for months, or would not receive their pension at all. Her son earned only R200 per month at his temporary full-time job as a construction worker. Some of the misery could have been avoided if Umzwandile had given her the R700 that was collected in Cape Town, but he had very likely needed the money to get to Fort Beaufort with Noparuru's youngest child. Noparuru's mother was going to be in severe debt for the rest of her life. In retrospect, I am quite sure that she expected me to give her the money that was collected in Cape Town, and maybe even more. The praise that the white visitors had received that morning was maybe not only for their attendance, but also for the money that they were expected to give. It must have been a big disappointment for Noparuru's mother that I did not bring any money at all. Instead, Edith and I contributed to a conflict with her son Umzwandile.

The next day, we returned to Cape Town. In Indawo Yoxolo, the neighbours all wanted to know how the funeral had been and what had happened to the money. Had Umzwandile handed it over to his mother? Edith refused to discuss this with her neighbours. It would be her word against Umzwandile's and she did not want to be involved with this funeral any more. She told her neighbours that they had to ask Umzwandile. After all, they were the ones who had decided to leave him in charge of the money. For many neighbours, however, her silence about the issue said enough.

## Conclusion

To define a substratum of people who were categorically excluded from participation in mutuals was a more complex and precarious task than I had expected. The practice of inclusion and exclusion deviated from the rules of organisations because sometimes status carried more weight than the rules of the organisation. Such 'deviations' from rules were closely related to notions of respect and the status of particular people. The way people looked at fellow neighbours depended on their compliance in 'helping each other', 'taking care of oneself', and respect. These values, and the reputation that was built accordingly, distinguished those who one would like to be close to and be eager to help from those who were regarded embarrassing, disgusting, and who were perhaps even feared. One tried to keep them out of the financial mutuals, although this was a difficult task. Their social and geographical proximity, and maybe also their obnoxious behaviour, forced neighbours to deal with them. The realisation that their own situations differed little from the most marginal people might have made it even more difficult to ignore these marginal and irritating people completely. Therefore, instead of a complete social separation, they maintained ambivalent relations with the most marginal among them. Such marginalised neighbours could not be included completely, nor could they be excluded completely, without their fellow neighbours being overcome with guilt and embarrassment.

Processes of identification and disidentification were pivotal for understanding reluctant solidarity. People frequently attested to the importance of morals, but criticised those who wanted only to be associated with successful and respectable people. Although some of the poor were an embarrassment, one could not turn one's face away completely. 'They' – the stinking and mad poor – were also 'we' – a family member, a neighbour, an *umkhaya* – and ignoring them completely would reveal that one could not live up to important values either. Such identifications and disidentifications resulted in a half-hearted inclusion, and reluctant solidarity among those who depended on each other. '[S]ocial identifications, no matter how intensely held, are essentially multiple and unstable' (De Swaan 1995: 34) and, at different moments, different identifications and disidentifications resulted in reluctant solidarity. The poor were assisted out of a mixture of ambivalent feelings, such as guilt for not being able to take care of the marginal, embarrassment if a member of a street was not assisted, the realisation that they could be in a similar position, the decision about how to spend what little money one had and the difficulty one had respecting a disrespectful person.

The neighbours also had to contend with the ambivalent sentiments that were part of many neighbourhood relations. The ambivalence was based on a number of processes. First, there were the conflicts within and between the values of 'helping each other', 'taking care of oneself', and respect. Morals were structured in a way that ambiguity and conflict were inescapable, especially if one did not have the money to afford them. This in turn contributed to an ambivalent attitude towards neighbours who behaved immorally, even after they had died. Second, the destitute and poor were inescapably present. Whether they liked one another or not, they had to make the most of a new neighbourhood and new relationships. Bauman (1998: 93) points out a view often held of the poor: 'Unneeded, unwanted, forsaken – where is their place? The briefest of answers is: out of sight.' For the neighbours in Indawo Yoxolo, however, this was no option. They had to deal with their poor, irritating, at times crazy and obnoxious neighbours.

Third, the dividing line was thin between a good reputation and a bad reputation, between sanity and insanity, between having a job and unemployment, between participation and exclusion from a financial mutual. This meant that the dividing line between 'one of us' and 'one of them' was equally thin. This meant that many neighbours harboured contradictory feelings towards each other. These were solidarity, upholding the reputation of the neighbourhood, realising that one might need the same kind of help at a later point in time, and other identification processes. Simultaneously, neighbours felt disgust, embarrassment about the poor, shame for one's treatment of the stigmatised, the fearful reminder of one's own deprivation that had to be kept at bay, and other disidentification processes. The poor could not be kept out of sight and, let us not forget, the person who was slightly better off might quickly become one of them.

Money played a pivotal role in the processes of identification and reluctant solidarity. Without money, it was impossible to behave appropriately. As studies on poverty and unemployment have shown, it becomes increasingly difficult to maintain a social network without a job (for example, see Howe 1998). Conversely, social relations increase one's ability to manage economic adversities and find sources of income (Granovetter 1973; Moser 1998). Without money, one could not help others, could not take care of oneself, and could not behave respectfully. Money also led to tremendous and horrifying competition in which people tried to gain control over flows of money by identifying with certain others. Some of the neighbouring women wanted to gain power and prestige by organising the financial mutuals, or simply to get their hands on the money. Umzwandile, in particular, used the relationship with his sister to put pressure on the neighbours and to ensure that sugar, teabags, chicory coffee, Noparuru's plot, as well as R700 came under his control.

Conflicts could be caused by only small amounts of money. Ten rand was not a lot of money, even if one only earned R800 a month. Many households, that is a total of seventy, were therefore willing to donate R10 to Noparuru's funeral. However, in total, the R700, which was roughly a monthly salary, was enough to lead to terrible competition, envy, threats, intimidation, and many other strategies to influence people. The fact that some were willing to resort to such severe measures signifies the extent to which people had to deal with the threatening triad of violence, economic insecurity, and volatile relations. No wonder that it was difficult to discuss the consequences of poverty with Xhosa migrants. This was not only because I was wealthy and rich, but also because poverty revealed some of the less valued and embarrassing human characteristics. Xhosa migrants established financial mutuals in an attempt to safeguard their money, manipulate its directional flows, and pulled together in relatively small, private, and dense social configurations. However, the way in which this had to be done was far from harmonious.

# 5

# Maintaining mutuals: Hope for islands of trust

## Introduction

Distrust was an inevitable part of public life in South Africa. Historically, the colonial government and apartheid were characterized by violence, intimidation, corruption, and a fear of spying neighbours. Distrust, however, was also present in post-apartheid South Africa. Moreover, in the Western Cape, 81 murders and 160 rapes per 100,000 people were reported to the police (SAPS 2000) in 1999. Due to a lack of confidence in the judiciary system and a fear of public stigmatisation, the actual occurrence of rape must have been much higher. Of 4,000 women interviewed in Soweto (a township of Johannesburg), one in three said they had been raped the past year (BBC 1999). South Africa has the world's highest murder and homicide rates, the world's highest assault rate, as well as the highest rate of reported rapes.[1] Economic insecurity is, for example, apparent in the fact that the country has the 9$^{th}$ highest Gini Index in the world,[2] while health is under great pressure due to, for example, a prevalence of HIV/AIDS at a rate of about 29.5%.

---

1 See http://www.nationmaster.com. Colombia rates first with 'intentional murders' but South Africa ranks first as regards all the other types of murders and homicides that are listed.

2 According to the World Bank 2005, see data on the Human Development Report website http://hdr.undp.org/statistics/data/indicators.cfm?x=148&y=1&z=1

South Africa is therefore part of the world's region that is currently being hardest hit by this disease.[3]

Racial relations were also governed by distrust. A survey revealed that more than half (56 percent) of black South Africans interviewed felt that Whites were untrustworthy. More than half also found it difficult even to imagine being friends with a white person. For Whites the percentages were lower (a third and 19 percent respectively) (Mail & Guardian 2001).[4] Distrust further intensified in conjunction with the many economic uncertainties. I regularly met African men and women who told me that they had not received their salaries at the end of the month, or that they had received far less than their contract had stated. High unemployment promoted theft and fierce struggles over the allocation of money. As Franz & Keebe Von Benda-Beckmann (1994: 7) argue in their discussion on insecurity: 'Insecurity concerns not only the material aspects of life [but also] people's feelings of trust and existential security.' Why do many women, and quite a few men, put large portions of their meagre incomes into financial mutuals in a society in which there are so many reasons to distrust others?

In an emerging democracy, such as South Africa, it is crucial to have trust in transforming government bureaucracies, newly established local governments, new economic activities, and new citizens that were previously confined to Bantustans. Based on research in varying Eastern European countries, Sztompka (1999) and Völker & Flap (1995) found that, during the communist regimes, people tended to close themselves off in relatively smaller networks in an attempt to stay away from unknown and untrustworthy people and institutions. After the political transition in the DDR, these networks shrunk even further, just like the trust within a person's dense network (Völker & Flap 1995: 105). In Poland, after an initial decrease in trust, the shift from an authoritarian to a democratic state eventually led to an increase in trust as people stopped relying exclusively on close knit relations (Sztomka 1999). Putnam (1993: 2000) strongly argues that trust built in relatively small voluntary organisations can eventually lead to trust in society at large as well as in the government: 'Good government in Italy is a by-product of singing groups and soccer clubs, not prayer' (Putnam 1993: 176).

Financial mutuals in South Africa are such small informal groups. This raises the question of whether financial mutuals should be regarded as enclaves of trust in an otherwise distrustful society (and if so how are these enclaves maintained). Or can, as Putnam argued on civic traditions in modern Italy, trust in financial mutuals help to overcome the dilemmas of collective action and establish trust in the state

---

3 See http://www.avert.org/safricastats.htm. Based on antenatal testing by the end of 2004. See also the website on the reliability of these statistics.

4 This survey was carried out by the Institute for Justice and Reconciliations (IJR) and its results were based on 3,727 interviews.

and society at large? This debate has become increasingly poignant since the United Nations and the World Bank have transformed this debatable argument into poverty alleviation policy. [5]

## Masifunde

The case of Masifunde reveals the inventive ways in which neighbours contained risks and managed relations with their fellow members. Many Masifunde participants were introduced in the previous chapter because Masifunde was organised by the neighbours of Noparuru. A study of Masifunde showed what the suspicions and risks were, how they arose, and what kind of action participants took to deal with them. This case study makes it possible to avoid ideal type relations, or assume rational, altruistic, normative, or other types of behaviour. Instead, it reveals the way in which participants deal with emerging problems, how they call on each other for help, put pressure on fellow members, and what the consequences of the dense social networks were for trust. [6]

Already by the end of 1997, the neighbours started to talk about 'setting up something'. Many women were interested in a financial mutual for their children. The financial mutual could cover the costs of tuition fees, school uniforms, books, and stationary. The women also hoped that it could teach children how to handle money. Instead of the mothers saving money, they wanted their children, at least in

---

5 See Fine (1999), Woolcock (1998), Rothstein (2000), and Putnam (1993) for the analysis of state transformation and development in relation to trust and social capital. See Hechter's (1987: 123) 'two stage theory of institutional development: In the first stage, individuals form groups to attain joint private goods, like credit and insurance, but to do so they must also establish formal controls, which constitute a collective good. Once these are in place, a second stage becomes possible. The group's resources, now protected by the existence of formal controls, can be diverted … to the production of further collective, or even public, goods.' Rothstein (2000) refers to collective memory to bring forward the importance of past experiences and memories in contemporary behaviour. Memories and knowledge of people and state institutions have a perpetuating effect. Once such institutions are not trusted, it becomes very difficult to change such perceptions because, as Rothstein points out, such views can be manipulated politically. See Bebbington *et al.* (2004) on social capital in the World Bank as well as the declaration of the United Nations Year of Microfinance 2005 that strongly relies on social capital. See Fung (2003) and Mouritsen (2003) on social capital, voluntary association, and democracy in which Putnam's work has played a crucial role.

6 See also Webb (1989) and Buijs & Atherfold (1995) on the centrality of personal relationships and trust in South Africa. See, among others, Vélez-Ibanéz (1983) on *confianza* in Mexico and how this is dependent on people's relationships.

name, to save and learn about money. The mutual was aptly called Masifunde: 'Let us learn.'

In the beginning of January 1998, women neighbours and some of their children met at Ma Dlamini's place, the woman who had tried to play a prominent role in the funeral of their poor neighbour Noparuru but who was side tracked by the politically more prominent figure of Ma Zantsi. During the past months the women had had the opportunity to get to know each other and Masifunde would help to strengthen neighbourhood ties. The first meeting was on Saturday 25 January, 1998. A participating mother had to pay R10 per week for each child that she enlisted. Many women had indicated that they wanted to join, but only ten turned up. The women made a list of thirty-five children that were going to save (eventually the number grew to forty). Most of these thirty-five children were not present. Although Masifunde was supposed to help children save, the mothers were the ones who usually saved for their children. Many women had children in the Eastern Cape who were also listed and some women told me confidentially that they 'invented' children that did not exist in order to save more money. Zanele, who did not have children, saved for someone she had made up. The mysterious man was jokingly called Mr Sicu, which did not mean anything and simply sounded funny, but his identity was kept a secret. For some time, the neighbours rumoured that he was Shooter, one of the political figures in the area involved in the struggles around the Big Five. Later it seemed to concern a neighbouring boy. The women often made jokes about the invisible Mr Sicu: 'Where is Mr Sicu today'; 'I hope Mr Sicu has enough money to come to this meeting next time'. For some women, 'saving for children' was a strategy to conceal that they actually saved for themselves. They put forward their most prominent social ties, that between mother and child, to pursue and legitimise their own ambitions and gain control over money.

Family members, other than the women's children, were not allowed to join. Many women did not have stable relationships and instead competed with partners and kin over resources (see also Bähre 2002b). Financial mutuals were established as a protection against financial claims from husbands, boyfriends, and relatives. By allowing them to participate, the women were afraid that they would start to rule the financial mutual and not pay off the loans properly. Trust was also regarded as gender-based. For the women, trust had to do with the responsibility of the home and particularly the responsibility for cooking. Because men could not cook, they were, just like children, considered to be irresponsible and, therefore, less trustworthy. High unemployment among men made it difficult for them to be responsible and take up their roles as fathers and husbands.[7] Other male respon-

[7] See Buijs & Atherfold (1995: 55, 58, 63-64, 77) on the trustworthiness of men, and Bank (1997) on women's position as related to cooking.

sibilities, such as those concerning ritual and kinship, had no place in the urban environment. Male authority seemed to be based on violence and money (wages) instead.

The first formative meeting of this financial mutual led to heated discussions about loans. Edith, who was appointed treasurer of the ASCRA, and Noxolo, who owned the little shop in the street, opposed loans at that time. They wanted the members to contribute four or six times, deposit the money in a bank, and only provide loans once there was sufficient money in the bank to function as collateral. At first, many women agreed with Edith and Noxolo while only two out of the ten women wanted to borrow immediately. They argued that Masifunde was not able to collect enough money in order to open an account anyway. Therefore, they wanted the money to be divided as loans, possibly to make sure that one member, in this case the treasurer, would not steal the fund. Mandy, in particular, insisted on borrowing R50 and seemed to need it really badly. After some time, she said she had visitors at her place and left the meeting, but it appeared that she was in fact angry and wanted to express her dissatisfaction. Noxolo opposed Mandy particularly fiercely and broke off the discussion: 'We are going to open the account and by the first weekend of the month we can discuss how much to borrow, if to borrow, and so on.'[8]

Mandy returned a bit later and continued to complain about the loans saying that 'there is a rule added by new members, like Edith. I don't like it that borrowing is discussed again. The loans were agreed upon before.' Edith, however, persisted, to the amusement of some of the children: it was funny how an older woman was teaching the teenager a lesson. Edith told Mandy: 'You have to get used to this. We discuss things. At meetings we discuss things because we are not afraid of you. We will agree on things and we have to consider the opinions of new members.' Noxolo added in Edith's support: 'Nobody wants to lose money at the end of the year. After we have voted we don't have to argue anymore. If you force things it means that what you have to say does not have any power.' Mandy kept objecting, but it was obvious that she was in a minority and that she would not win her point. It was decided that the rules about borrowing money were going

---

8 As the owner of a shop, she had some ideas about who to trust and who not. After some time, Noxolo had stopped giving meat to some customers on credit, even if the customers were members of Masifunde. To test Noxolo, Edith had once sent her child to Noxolo to ask her for meat. The child returned with Noxolo who was carrying meat. Noxolo told Edith that she was willing to give Edith meat on credit because she trusted her. After all, Edith's husband and Noxolo's husband belonged to the same clan. But Noxolo asked Edith to keep quiet about it. Edith, who was not interested in the meat, told Noxolo that she had changed her mind and did not need the meat after all. Through such 'games' people got to know each other's reputation and test each other's trustworthiness.

to be discussed in more detail at a future meeting. It was also agreed to have penalties, namely R2 for not attending the meeting, 50 cents for being late, and 25 cents for disturbing the meeting. After this discussion, the women collected money which amounted to R193.75. Edith received the money and wanted to sign for it. She did not want to take the risk that members would accuse her of stealing some of it. Edith was also asked to open the account for Masifunde. The start of the financial mutual was a bit chaotic and people were still figuring out who would join, what the rules would be, and if one could borrow or not.

The members of Masifunde met again the following Sunday. Twenty-one women and children attended because word had got around that this was the last meeting at which one could join. Noxolo – the owner of the shop – was absent. Later she told me that she got tired of the hassles at the meeting and could have done without these quarrels. During the previous week, Edith and the two other committee members (Zanele and Ma Dlamini's daughter, Margaret) had not managed to get together in order to open a bank account. Edith had asked me to keep the money because she was afraid that it might be stolen. She wanted to show the money at the meeting to avoid possible rumours that she had spent it. Anxiety concerning such possible allegations was also the reason for carefully examining the financial records of Masifunde. Edith was unsatisfied with the way in which the payments had been recorded because it was easy to write down contributions without having paid for them. She did not like the fact that the records were being kept at Ma Dlamini's place either because her daughter, Margeret, was on the committee. If money went missing, it was likely that Edith was going to be held accountable.

At first, the women collected the contributions which brought the total amount to R1,050. Again, the women discussed whether loans should be provided or whether the money should go into the account. After a long discussion, they decided that each child could borrow a maximum of R50. The remaining money would go to the bank as collateral. The names of the children were called in alphabetical order and the women indicated whether they wanted a loan. Some were not present at the meeting and could, therefore, not borrow money. They did, however, make sure that they paid the contributions by asking fellow members to pay on their behalf.

Breaking up the money into smaller portions through loans reduced the likelihood of default. It was easier for the women to repay a small loan and it was hardly worthwhile absconding with a relatively small amount of money. Moreover, giving loans to everybody strengthened the interdependencies of the participants, which in turn increased social control.

*Opening an account*

That same week, the committee members (Edith, Margaret and Zanele) and I went to the city centre of Cape Town to open a bank account. Usually, the women had to rely on a taxi (a minibus with a fixed route) or train, which was time consuming and unsafe, especially when carrying a lot of money. This time I was able to pick them up and we then went to town together. It was a bit of an outing and the atmosphere was jolly, but not at the bank: it felt uncomfortable for the poor women to enter the impressive banking offices along Adderly Street, where most employees were white.

We had to visit about six banks before Masifunde could open its account. Most banks required a minimum deposit of R1,000 for a savings account or a thirty-two-day notice account. The women preferred a thirty-two-day notice account because the interest was higher and it was easy to give thirty-two days notice before withdrawing money by the end of the year. However, Masifunde had given loans to its members and there was not enough money left for the minimum deposit. Nedbank even required a minimum deposit of R5,000 for a thirty-two-day notice account. The clerk explained that they also had to pay a 'maintenance fee' of R14 per month for a regular savings account with a deposit under R4,000. This was way beyond the reach of the members of Masifunde.

The Allied Bank was an exception. This bank did not require a minimum deposit for a thirty-two-day notice account and the interest was 13 percent per year. Everybody was relieved but, when the paperwork was done, the last bureaucratic hurdle was insurmountable. The lady behind the teller asked if anybody was registered for outstanding debts, for example due to missed instalments at clothing stores, or hire purchase. After Edith had translated this to Margaret and Zanele whose English was insufficient for understanding the conversation, Margaret suddenly remembered that she had forgotten her passport. The account could not be opened and we left the bank. Margaret, however, had not forgotten her passport and quietly admitted that she was registered for debts that she had failed to pay off. She did not want to talk about it and felt very embarrassed. The quest for a bank that was receptive to the needs of the poor had to be continued.

When we arrived at another bank, an embarrassing situation developed again. A White woman approached us and treated the three women as if they were complete idiots. Although Edith was proficient in English, the woman started to talk very loudly and slowly, and exaggerated her articulation: 'CAAAN WEE MAAY-BEE HEE-LUP YOUHOU?', she asked. Even when it was very clear that Edith's English was good, and after the employee failed to explain some of the rules, she added: 'Let me find someone who can explain in your language!' Since the women felt that they were not getting anywhere, they left the bank feeling upset.

Finally, we ended up at the Standard Bank where the women were able to open a group account. The employee promised to send a calculator and an administration book as a present, but it never arrived. The bank also wanted a copy of the organisation's constitution, which could be submitted later. The employee said that, as soon as the balance exceeded R1,000, they could easily change it into a thirty-two-day notice account. In order to make this change possible, the three women had to sign at the bank. It was impossible to sign the papers now and hand them in later when there was sufficient money. It was, however, difficult for the three women to take an afternoon off to change the account, because two women worked irregular hours and one was still attending school and was responsible for some household tasks. Eventually, it took half-a-year before they were able to change the account and receive some more interest on the money.

Many groups faced similar problems, i.e. the amount of money was too small, banking fees were high, transport had to be organised, or a committee member was registered with a debt. But the many hurdles were overcome nevertheless because one did not want to give the money to the treasurer, who might not want to keep it anyway out of fear of spending it or of theft. It was also dangerous to lend out all the money, which would not require a bank account. The members needed some financial collateral to ensure that the loans plus interest were returned. The combination of saving at the bank and providing limited loans to members ensured that the risk of default was minimised, while cheap credit was still available.

*Social control and flexibility*

A few months later, the initial confusions within Masifunde had disappeared. Usually about thirty women and children attended the meetings, which now ran in a smooth and structured manner. On 3 May, Masifunde collected R7,352.20 in 'stage money' (the fixed weekly contributions) and loans, while another R1,300 was in the bank. The members worried about robbery given that such a large sum of money was lying on the table. Many members would have to work a year in order to earn this much. It was for this reason that, when a man asked to enter the place he was refused, which was exceptional under normal circumstances. As an excuse, a woman shouted: 'You can't come in now. We are washing ourselves.' Voyiswa and another woman made a kind of growling noise when the money was on the table. It was the kind of rumbling noise a possessed person would make or if someone sensed the presence of witchcraft. Many women laughed about it and it seemed that the increasing amount of money that was accumulated by the members made everybody nervous.

The large sum of money that circulated among the members did cause some problems as many women borrowed more than they could afford. One woman, for example had to repay her loan plus the accumulated interest of R180, but she only had R160. When she handed over the R160 some women expressed how upset they were since she should have told them immediately about her financial problems and not wait and just give R160 instead of R180. During the quarrel, one woman discretely slipped her a R20 note, which she put on the table, and which ended the discussion. Another woman had previously failed to pay the R100 stage money. This was now regarded as a loan over which she had to pay R20 interest. But the woman only had R60. The women voiced their dissatisfaction clearly: she *had* to pay. The woman proposed borrowing the remaining R60 and paying it back later. Everybody agreed that this was impossible, and that she was only allowed to borrow money when she had no more debts. The discussion faded as other women started to pay their contributions. About half-a-minute later, the woman gave R120. Secretly, in order to avoid further embarrassment, one of the women had slipped R60 to her. Now the debt was an issue between those two women and it was up to them to resolve it.

After a big pile of money had accumulated on the coffee table, the atmosphere became much lighter: 'Yes, I can make it. In December I am going to get fat', one woman joked, while another woman added, 'yes, you are now all making a noise because you can hear the money being counted. Wow, it's a lot of money!' Another woman made a joke about Voyiswa, the woman who had made the rumbling noise earlier. She asked Voyiswa if she felt better now, which Voyiswa could confirm. Some women clapped and cheered when the amount of money was mentioned.

After the money had been collected and counted, it was time to issue the loans. The demand for loans was high. Many also argued that it was good to give loans because interest on the loans would 'make the money grow faster'. Some, however, worried that members were going to borrow more than they could afford. Therefore, they wanted to deposit part of the money, R500 or R1000, into the bank account. Others, again, felt it was not fair that some members were not borrowing much money. They argued that those who did not borrow did not contribute to the fund with interest that made 'the money grow faster'. Nevertheless, while one would share in the interest others had paid, many also realised that it was risky to force members to borrow more than they could afford.

Finally, it was decided to vote on whether R1,000 or R500 should go to the bank. The voting took place in a peculiar way. Someone stated: 'The majority is in favour of R1,000 and only a minority is in favour of R500. Please, let the majority raise their hands.' And, indeed, the majority of women raised their hands and R1,000 was allocated to the bank while the remaining money was distributed as loans. The atmosphere became a little tense when it became clear that the demand for loans exceeded the available money. Some women complained about the R1000 going to the bank. 'At the bank the interest on the money is only two cents', Voyiswa argued. Edith, the treasurer of the organisation, got annoyed and said threateningly: 'I am going to bring R1,000 to the bank and there will be no more borrowing. If you don't stop arguing now, I will go to the bank and make sure that you only get the money in January [instead of December].' The threat worked and the women who wanted to borrow more kept quiet. The uproar indicated that the women were nervous about their money and worried that some might default because they borrowed too much. Some women told me later that they wanted to borrow more money as a precaution against default. If Masifunde was to break down they would then at least not have lost all their money. This strategy, in combination with the desire for inexpensive loans, contained the risk of spiralling the organisation into excessive borrowing. Although the strategy was understandable from an individual point of view, the collectively organised ASCRA could be threatened. The money at the bank could prevent such a self-perpetuating cycle into default.

Edith borrowed R600 for Xoliswa. Xoliswa was also a member of Masifunde but needed a lot of money for construction work on her mother's house in Emaxhoseni. Xoliswa also participated in an *umgalelo* (ROSCA), but had her turn only at the end of the year, which was too late. She had asked Edith to borrow Masifunde money for her, which she would repay, including the interest. Edith felt confident about the arrangement although she remained responsible for returning the money to Masifunde if Xoliswa failed to pay. Edith felt that because Xoliswa was a member of Masifunde as well as of a ROSCA she was certainly going to have the money in the future.

A month and five meetings later, it became clear that some participants had borrowed more than they could afford. It was time to pay back the loans from May, but some did not have the money. Unfortunately, Edith and I were not able to attend the meeting because we were in Fort Beaufort for Noparuru's funeral. But Zanele told us the next day that most members had attended the meeting. Zanele and some other women had visited one of the defaulters at her home. They had found her completely drunk and it was clearly useless trying to talk with her. At the meeting, the members decided that everyone would be given more time to pay back the loans and interest. They were required to pay the interest first and follow that with the capital. However, meanwhile, they did not have to pay interest anymore on the outstanding loan. They collected R8,000 and all the money was lent to the members. This had greatly upset Zanele, as well as Edith. Many members realised that if no measures were taken, the problems of loan repayments would only worsen and Masifunde could collapse. Therefore, the rules had to be discussed again on 21 June.

Unfortunately, I could not attend the meeting on 21 June either because of the violence in Indawo Yoxolo. Edith told me that, although the participants had been given an extra month to pay back the loans and interest, some still had no money. The only thing that could be done was to give time until September to repay the loans and to refuse new loans. Again, no interest was charged on the outstanding debt. The problem the organisation was facing became very clear when all the money was collected, amounting to only R300. It was clear that everybody was holding onto the money, maybe because they were worried about the future of Masifunde. Edith argued that the R1,000 should be put in the bank. In order to convince them, she showed the participants that one automatically took part in a lottery once the balance was over R3,000. This made some women more enthusiastic and it was decided to put R300 into the account. No loans were provided and if people lost confidence in Masifunde, they would stop repaying their loans and the group would spiral down into more problems. The lottery was a pleasant incentive and a good excuse to put more money into the bank, which made the repayment of loans more attractive. The flexibility of the rules ensured that people had the opportunity to repay the loans, and the social control among the participants, who could not avoid each other in the neighbourhood, put enough pressure on them to do so. Adding to the balance in the account ensured that default would result in the exclusion from a substantial amount of money.

*Sharing money*

Unfortunately, my fieldwork stopped because I returned to the Netherlands. Luckily, I was able to return to Cape Town in November 1998, which gave me an opportunity to witness the closing of Masifunde. On the first meeting of November the indebted members received a letter stating how much they owed and asking them to repay before the $16^{th}$. By the end of November, however, some still owed money. There was R16,000 in the bank and R15,785.50 worth of outstanding debts. This worried the members, some had borrowed up to R1,000 and Voyiswa even owed a staggering R1,364! Edith felt that there were too many debts and wanted to make sure she had at least some of Masifunde's money. Therefore, she also borrowed money (R1,000), which she planned to pay off only when the others did the same. Nomfundu, Edith's neighbour, was also at the meeting. Although some had tried to exclude her, she had paid properly and only owed a little bit of money. Nomfundu was clearly not her usual self as she sat quietly, and clearly bruised, in the corner of the room. One of the women said that the day before men had attacked and attempted to rape Nomfundu while she was on her way to the shop just around the corner. They had also stabbed her in the back and stomach. Although I knew that many women felt sorry for Nomfundu, I was quite surprised that the assault was barely mentioned and that nobody expressed any compassion. This again showed how difficult it was to establish trustful relations in Indawo Yoxolo.

The women were wondering how and where they could divide the money safely and asked themselves: 'Should we share at the bank?', 'maybe we should meet at the police station and share the money there'. Many thieves know that ASCRAs divide their money in November or December and might be on the lookout. Some participants privately expressed their fear that one of the members would grab the money from the table and run, or instead pay a thief to steal it for her. Voyiswa bragged: 'I am going to send the police and tell them to get my share from you.' But Nomfundu immediately told her to keep quiet: 'You owe money, you are a liar.'

The meeting of 29 November was poorly attended. Many members wanted to spend Christmas with their family and friends in the Eastern Cape and needed money to pay for the fare and in order to buy gifts. Some were upset that the money was still not divided and that their trip to the Eastern Cape was in jeopardy. Some of the women with large debts had failed to appear at the meeting. An argument developed about the way in which to punish those with outstanding debts. Some felt that they should not share in the accumulated interest. Others, however, disagreed and felt that the money had to be shared equally. The discussion continued for some time and no decision was made, but the threat of a sanction had come across.

Voyiswa's large debt was another problem and the members clearly stated that she would receive nothing if she did not pay. Voyiswa reacted aggressively as usual and told them not to worry about the debt because she would have the money soon. Voyiswa had a valid reason for withholding her payments. A few months previously, Voyiswa had taken Nothemba, a befriended neighbour but not a member of Masifunde, along to the meeting. It was very unusual to take along non-members, particularly when nobody had been informed beforehand. However, Voyiswa was as forceful as ever and nobody dared to complain. There were only a few women present at this meeting and Voyiswa made a strong case for a loan to Nothemba. Some women objected but Voyiswa insisted and promised to be the guarantor for Nothemba. The women did not have the courage to oppose Voyiswa and, against the rules, they lent Nothemba R602.

A few months later, Nothemba had still not returned the loan and the members of Masifunde held Voyiswa responsible. Voyiswa, however, had also taken out a big loan months earlier and had never repaid it. Voyiswa's loan already exceeded her share so there was no money that they could deduct from her share to cover Nothemba's debt. The only way to get the money back was to press Nothemba. Some members had already paid Nothemba a visit and had managed to extract the promise that she would pay soon. She could only give R200 that she got from selling her refrigerator. She explained that she was about to sell her plot and leave Indawo Yoxolo. As soon as she would receive the money she would pay Masifunde. The women were not convinced and actually worried that Nothemba would leave Cape Town. As collateral, they took the small black and white television from her house. Nobody, however, dared to keep the television at their place until Nothemba paid her debt. They decided to let Voyiswa take care of the television. After all, it was her friend. In addition to the television, they wanted to take Nothemba's curtains, but the women agreed that this was too embarrassing.

The last opportunity to collect debts was on 6 December. During the collection of stage money the meeting was structured and business-like as usual. The notes were handled carefully and each type of banknote was put in separate piles. In order to make neat piles, the images on the notes were all faced upwards. Stage money equalling R1,170 was collected and the women really enjoyed seeing and handling the money and started making jokes. It was a recurring reaction once the money was on the table. The women became nervous, laughed, made jokes, and behaved more disorderly. Pumla excitedly said: 'Oh, I don't know if I have the money [that she owed Masifunde]. I will go to the docks to sell my body.' Zanele said this was a good idea, but Pumla told her: 'You don't have much chance. Your thighs look like pieces of Kentucky fried chicken.' Nomfundu, who was quiet most of the time, told Pumla, 'Yes, and then you are going to get AIDS!' Voyiswa who did not get along with Nomfundu, saw her change to say something nasty to her: 'Oh, Nomfundu; you are already infected with HIV. It is just a matter of time until it shows.' Many women giggled and it was a bit embarrassing for Edith to translate this conversation. Nomfundu did not give up that easily and told Voyiswa, 'you know, Voyiswa, your vagina stinks because you have more than a hundred boyfriends. My vagina is clean and tight so watch out or your boyfriends will come to me.' Voyiswa continued to irritate people and it seemed that she was making jokes about me as well. But others teased her more and a few women said: 'Voyiswa doesn't wear any underwear. That's why it smells in here.' The joking and teasing of Voyiswa was most likely inspired by her debts and the problems she got Masifunde into. The vicious remarks revealed that financial mutuals were not always cosy and that some of the women did not trust one another.

R9,633 was collected and the members were very pleased. One of the women felt that Masifunde did so well because of my presence: a white person at the meetings surely must have meant good luck. Others agreed and it seemed that I was a kind of mascot to them. Edith put all the money in an envelope. A few members admitted that they had gone to the Standard Bank a few days ago. They knew that Edith had given notice at the bank in order to withdraw the money. The women admitted that they were worried that Edith might have already withdrawn the money and was going to steal it. They were relieved when the money was still in the account. As a joke about Edith's trustworthiness, Voyiswa added: 'Yes, Edith, I was wondering why you look so pretty today and are wearing such nice clothes. I was wondering what had happened with the money.'

The orderly meeting ended disorderly, as usual. Although the big pile of money took some members' worries away, they were still anxious about dividing the money. The plan was to divide the money equally among the forty children that the women had enlisted, regardless of how much each had borrowed and contributed through interest. The outstanding payments were going to be deducted from the child's share. Some women could not understand the decision and started to scream and shout. Therefore, Edith explained it several times over again and slowly everybody began to understand it and felt it was a fair system. They felt that those with debts should also receive a share of the remaining money and should not be punished twice (first by deducting the debt, second by being excluded from sharing the proceeds of these deductions).

By the end of the meeting, Voyiswa's friend Nothemba had still not arrived. The women felt that it was time to take action and visit her and force her to pay. It took some time before about thirteen women walked to Nothemba's house, only a hundred metres away from the meeting place. Everyone felt very embarrassed about it. Upon arrival Voyiswa started shouting and screaming, which made the neighbours come out of their homes to see what was going on. Nothemba was not there and a neighbour said that she was taking her child by bus to the Eastern Cape and would return later. Voyiswa and some of the younger women set up a search in Indawo Yoxolo in order to force her to go to the meeting. They wanted to find out if Nothemba was hiding at a friend's place somewhere. After a few hours they returned unsuccessfully and it was decided to meet and deal with Nothemba the following Tuesday.

On the subsequent Tuesday, the special Masifunde meeting started at seven o'clock. Several women took the opportunity to pay off their remaining debts and another R1,330 was collected. Before the meeting started, a few women had paid a surprise visit to Nothemba and told her to accompany them to the meeting. Nothemba looked quite terrible and I could not help but feel sorry for her. She had been beaten up and her eyes were swollen. I could not find out who had done this, but the rumour was that it was related to her debts. Everybody felt uncomfortable and nobody dared to mention the loan. Finally someone had the courage to ask: 'Why have you still not paid the R402?' Nothemba explained that she had wanted to pay last Sunday. She was participating in an *umgalelo* and it was her turn, but she did not receive anything because she had failed to contribute to a member's turn. She did not go to the Masifunde meeting because she did not know what to say, except that she had no money. She had heard that they had tried to find her at her place last Sunday. She was not at home because she was on her way to her brother in Langa to ask him for money, but he was not at home. She also went to a friend in Indawo Yoxolo, who was not home either.

Everybody kept quiet for some time and Maggie asked: 'What do you expect us to do?' Nothemba said that she just needed a few more days and would pay on Sunday. The women did not accept this: 'We are waiting for you and your money. That is the only reason why we still have not shared the money', and another woman added, 'you are not a member. If you were a member we would know what to do, but now we do not know what to do and have to fetch you at your place.' Voyiswa was amongst the most critical, saying: 'I signed for you, but not so they could deduct the money from my share.' To the members she said, 'Nothemba has to pay. I refuse to stand for her. She doesn't care about anything. She didn't even come to me to explain what was going on.' Voyiswa started to cry in order to express her disappointment in Nothemba. But it was obvious that she was faking and some women could not help but giggle. Later Voyiswa admitted to me that she was making a show out of it because she wanted to teach Nothemba a lesson.

Everybody was at a loss about what to do next. 'She can't stay here forever. We have to go on with our meeting and she doesn't live here [in this house]', one woman remarked. It was Zanelle, one of the committee members, who made a proposal: 'We have to get something out of your house.' 'But what should I do?', asked Nothemba, who was close to tears. Now the criticism was directed at her. 'You do not respect us. You make it very difficult for us.' 'We should not wait but fetch things immediately.' 'We should get the curtains so we can sell something.' 'You never told us you had financial problems. We cannot trust you and you don't care.' 'Let us take more than only curtains. Let us take something that costs more than R400 to force her.' Voyiswa continued with her theatre, trying to cry although she could not hold her laughter. Voyiswa wailed. 'If I had R400 I would pay for you but I don't have anything. Oh my God! I have learnt my lesson and will never do something like this again.' The vicious remarks were very humiliating for Nothemba.

It was time to go with Nothemba to confiscate her belongings, but nobody seemed to dare and we hesitated before finally walking to her place. When we arrived, we barely fit inside because her shack was so small. Nothemba had very few belongings and the curtains were about the only thing that was worth taking so two women took them off the rails. Nothemba went into the kitchen to take her pots and pans. While she was out of hearing distance Zanele whispered: 'Jihu, this woman is poor. This is a disgrace.' Taking a woman's pots and pans was regarded as the last resort and it was embarrassing that they could not take anything else. There was a little colour television that had not been there before and Nothemba explained that she borrowed it from her boyfriend. Because Nothemba had so little, the women also took the television. This was a bit risky because Nothemba's boyfriend was an ally of the Big Five, although he was a marginal figure. The women told Nothemba that she would get all of it back after she paid off her debt. Otherwise, her belongings were going to be sold among the members. We left quietly and embarrassed and some were giggling about this awkward situation.

The following day, Masifunde met again. The participants were quite nervous, excited, as well as relieved that everything was going well. The women had to wait before the thirty-two days were over and the money could be withdrawn, and some still had to pay some debts. The events of the previous day were discussed and, although the women felt it had been rude, they believed they had had no other option but to confiscate Nothemba's property. Zanele also had problems concerning a debt. She lent R200 of her Masifunde loan to a friend who, including interest, now owed her R400. She and her friend Pumla had visited her a couple of days ago. Because she had no money they took her refrigerator. One of the women reacted by saying: 'You had better watch out Zanele, she might beat you for taking her refrigerator.' But Zanele said she did not care and laughed and said: 'What I liked about it was that Pumla and I could carry the refrigerator by ourselves.' Zanele had sold the refrigerator for R450.

Voyiswa was also present at the meeting and, to my great surprise, she put R1,300 on the table. Her debt was R1,364 so virtually all her debt was paid off. She promised to pay the remaining R64 the following day. Voyiswa's payments were clearly related to Nothemba's debts. Because Nothemba's belongings were confiscated, Voyiswa did not need to worry anymore that they were going to take her money. By staying indebted, Voysiwa had mobilised Masifunde to put Nothemba under pressure. After Nothemba's belongings had been confiscated and were available for sale, Voyiswa's problems were over. Other women also paid their outstanding loans. Their debts were much smaller and could easily be deducted from their shares, but they wanted to pay nevertheless. It seemed that they were worried that they might get less than they were entitled to if they still had debts, and were also concerned about their reputations. The total amount of Masifunde money in the bank and in cash had become R31,025. This was an amazing amount of money. The women were very excited about it, which is easy to understand considering that many Xhosa had to work three years for this without spending any money, if they at least had a job.

Nothemba did not turn up and the confiscated goods were sold. Everybody wanted something because the prices were very low: R130 for the black and white television, R150 for the colour television, R70 for the curtains and R70 for the aluminium pots and pans. Everybody was excited about this and people screamed and argued about prices. Xoliswa joked: 'If we fetch Nothemba's iron we can sell it as well and lower the prices even further.' Voyiswa would have liked to have taken Nothemba's small bookcase that she could have sold to her boss for R150.

Ma Zantsi's daughter wanted the colour television that had belonged to Nothemba's boyfriend, but she was scared because Nothemba's boyfriend had visited her mother the previous night. He had said that he was going to hurt the woman who was going to buy his television. Some considered Ma Zantsi to be a Big Five supporter, just like Nothemba's boyfriend, and wanted to be careful. They did not know if the threat was serious and a wild conversation developed. The women screamed and shouted and argued about what they should do with the television. Many women wanted to buy something and a small fight broke out. The noise level increased so much that I had to leave the overcrowded shack and stand outside for a few minutes to get some air. I just could not bear this screaming anymore as it physically hurt my ears. Some of the women noticed me leaving and used it in the argument. 'Hey you! Shut up and keep quiet. You even made Erik leave with your noise.'

The women agreed to visit Shooter immediately after the meeting to talk with him about the television, just to be on the safe side. He was one of the political figures in the area who at that time was associated with the United Democratic Movement and who had a problematic relation with the Big Five as was described in chapter four. The women asked me to come along but I politely refused. I could not stand the shouting and screaming anymore and I also felt it was too risky. The story had spread already that I had been in the party that had confiscated Nothemba's belongings. The women walked away but returned after going ten metres to ask me again if I could join them. When I insisted on staying behind, they told me that my presence would give them more courage and confidence. They said it had also made them feel more powerful and courageous when I joined them to confiscate Nothemba's belongings. It became clear that I was not the passive bystander that I tried and preferred to be. Instead, my presence, even without saying anything, influenced the members of Masifunde. They probably would have visited Nothemba anyway, even without me, but it seemed that my presence had made it a bit easier for them. They decided to visit Shooter anyway, although I did not accompany them. He told them that he would not interfere when they would sell the colour television.

Finally, they decided to divide the money on Friday 11 December. I offered to pick up the three committee members and take them to the Standard Bank in Adderly Street. The fee for withdrawing the money and closing the account was more than R500 and significantly cut down the interest earned which had been R277 over the last month based on an amount of R17,174. For safety reasons, the women divided the money at my home in the Observatory suburb. The total amount was R34,717.38, while another R1,506 was still owed. Edith kept separate books because she was worried about members altering the book at Ma Dlamini's. Each of the forty children received R905.58. Because the largest debt was only R300, it could easily be deducted, which meant that the collateral at the bank had been sufficient.

The money was put into envelopes with the names of the children and we left for Indawo Yoxolo. In the car, Zanele told me that it was very attractive to borrow money from Masifunde 'but it is not a blessing'. It was attractive to borrow money and lend it to others and let them pay for the interest but the risks were not a blessing. Zanele gave the example of a weekly R50 ROSCA that she, Dolly, Margaret, and Xoliswa (all members of Masifunde) had started with a few other neighbouring women. Dolly had borrowed money from four Masifunde members but she refused to pay it back. Zanele said:

> Dolly is rude and she screams. One of our women is soft and quiet and does not have anyone to help her put pressure on Dolly. She is not going to get her money back. Dolly had also caused problems in our R50 *umgalelo*. She refused to pay when it was Xoliswa's turn because she knows that Xoliswa is also soft and will not put pressure on her.

I had heard before that some suspected that Xoliswa and Dolly had tampered with the Masifunde books which, if it was true, might make it even more difficult for Xoliswa to coerce Dolly. Because of Zanele's story, Edith was suddenly reminded of a R180 loan to a member of Masifunde. Edith had issued the loan some months ago but the woman had still not paid it back. She had also failed to say anything about it to Edith. Edith took R180 out of the woman's envelope and wrote a note that reminded her of her debt. While other women had similar problems with fellow members, they had to sort it out themselves, Edith could use her position as a committee member to get her money back.

We met the Masifunde members at a secret place in Indawo Yoxolo. I dropped them off and left again immediately. If I had stayed my blue Mazda would have attracted criminals and increased the risk of robbery and, just in case of an attempted robbery, I preferred to be elsewhere. Later I heard that the sharing went very well and that the meeting took only a few minutes. Many women were pleased with the organisation and started it again in January 1999.

## Containing risk

The case of Masifunde reveals a number of measures taken to contain the risk associated with the financial mutual. First, it was important that there was money in the bank which was not accessible to the members. The only risk then would be that the three committee members would steal the money together. The money at the bank also functioned as collateral against loans. Whenever the loans increased, it also became important to increase the amount deposited at the bank to ensure that the loans would not exceed the savings. The members were willing to overcome many hurdles in order to open an account, such as travelling time, travelling expenses, legal limitations of opening an account, banking fees, as well as embarrassing treatment by bank employees.

Second, the relative rigidity and flexibility of the rules were inherently faulty. The rigidity meant that the stage money – as the minimum contribution was called – was fixed and not open for negotiation, and that loans had to be paid back. The flexibility concerned the amount of loans, the exact time of repayment, the amount of interest on extended loans, and the amount of money in the bank. Flexible rules prevented default but, when changed, they could never be enforced individually or applied only to individuals. Decisions were made democratically and everyone had to obey the new rule. This combination of flexibility and rigidity allowed members to avoid default or non-contribution and thus prevented excessive risk.

Third, and contrary to my expectations, lending money to fellow members was not excessively risky. I expected loans to increase risks because more people could default. However, the loans prevented a situation in which only a few women were in charge of a large sum of money. Distributing part of the fund made it less advantageous to abscond. It also avoided pronounced inequality, which could attract witchcraft.

Fourth, the members of Masifunde tried to keep political figures out and, in their dealings with outsiders, they trivialised the significance of the financial mutual. The political groups, particularly the dangerous Big Five, only once played a role after the colour television of the boyfriend of a non-member had been confiscated, just before the money was divided. By staying away from politics in Indawo Yoxolo, the risk that political divisions would dominate the relations within Masifunde decreased. It also made it less likely that political groups would use the financial mutual for political purposes.

Fifth, certain categories of people were excluded because they could challenge the obligations inherent in financial mutuals. Just like many other financial mutuals, men were not allowed to participate in Masifunde, despite the fact that some men would have liked to have joined. Male authority, just like kinship hierarchies, could easily overrule the obligations that members had towards each other. They might simply refuse to pay and there would be little that the women could do to force them to. Kin, except for a few adult daughters who lived with their mothers, were excluded for the same reason. If kin, and especially affines, a boyfriend or husband were to join, this would seriously undermine trust. It would be nearly impossible to overcome the obligations and loyalties of such relations.

Sixth, different forms and degrees of aggression and violence, varying from rumour and social control, to coercion, physical violence, and confiscation of property, were vital in order to contain risks (cf. Smets & Bähre 2004). The case of the confiscation of Nothemba's property revealed what the members were capable of, even if it was uncomfortable and embarrassing for them. Women who failed to pay were put under pressure at meetings, were visited at their homes, and risked the confiscation of their humble belongings. In one case, the mutual jointly confiscated the humble possessions of a woman who was not even a member, and it is possible that they also beat her up.[9] In other cases it was left to the individual member to get the money back because it was not regarded as the mutual's responsibility. For example, it was up to Zanele to sort out her problems and she and a friend confiscated the refrigerator. In many cases, the threat of sanctions was

9 Lukhele (1990: 36) describes how a man was robbed of the money of a burial society and was found hanging from the rafters of a railway station three days later.

enough because people were aware that members who had lent money were willing to use pressure which they would not dare to use in other circumstances. The threat of the mutual and one's fellow members forced the individual member to get her money back from neighbours or friends. One wonders if Zanele would have dared to confiscate the refrigerator if she did not need the money to pay off her debt with Masifunde. Therefore, the social constraints within the group could also influence the social constraints outside of the group.

## Co-operation without trust

If people co-operate, they can take measures to contain risks, but risks can never be ruled out completely (cf. Coleman 1990: 91; Misztal 1996: 18). Crozier and Friedberg (1977: 6) express strong views on the dilemmas of establishing organisations: 'Considering the context of not only bounded rationality, but also of bounded legitimacy ... and of bounded interdependence... it is a miracle that organizations exist at all.' Sztompka (1999: 13) expresses an equally gloomy picture. He states that 'without trust we would be paralysed and unable to act' and cites Hardin (1993: 519 in Sztompka 1999: 25): 'With a complete absence of trust, one must be catatonic, one could not even get up in the morning.' The fact is that Xhosa migrants *do* get up in the morning, often very early, and deal with distrust and the problems that occur in financial mutuals. Although many neighbours did not trust each other, at least not all the time, they established financial mutuals that mostly functioned very well. This raises the same question, which Gambetta (1988: 217n6) so clearly posed: 'We should ask why uncooperative behaviour does not emerge as often as game theory predicts' (cited in Putnam 1993: 160).[10] However, should the dilemma of collective action indeed be sought in the dynamics of trust and social capital? A closer examination of cooperation in small social networks reveals that such a theory is in danger of romanticising co-operation. To overcome an overly pessimistic view of organisations as put forward by rational choice theorists, as well as an overly romantic view as advocated by the social capital debate, it is necessary to acknowledge the ambivalence of social relations. By taking account of ambivalence (strong and contradictory feelings) in

---

[10] Smelser (1998: 3) noted five 'ingredients of rational choice': '1) unconstrained actors try to maximize; 2) actors possess complete information about their tastes, their resources, and the availability, quality, and prices of products, as well as about job opportunities and other market conditions; 3) actors calculate and behave rationally … 4) tastes are "given" – that is, they are stable and not to be explained – … 5) the interaction between two actors, the buyer and the seller, produces an equilibrium point at which exchange occurs, and at this point supply and demand and utility and cost converge.'

human relations and towards institutions one gets a better insight into people's actions (see Smelser 1998).

A closer look at the way in which Xhosa migrants value relations provides some answers to their willingness to co-operate in a society where distrust is the rule rather than the exception. The interdependencies between neighbours and fellow members of financial mutuals, in particular, meant that many had mixed feelings towards one another. These ambivalent relations made it difficult to predict someone's behaviour completely, especially if one had a close relationship with him or her. On a few occasions, some men and women shared their reflections about the way they understood social relations. Such occasions were not common and therefore the material presented here might come across as slightly haphazard snapshots. I prefer, however, to present it in this loose fashion than to pretend to give a clear, unambiguous and possibly idealistic image of Xhosa's understanding of trust and social relations. Nevertheless, it is important to reveal such reflections on trust and social relations because they enable one to grasp why the men and women risked such substantial amounts of their meagre incomes.

Nofurniture, for example belonged to a financial mutual and told me that she suspected that the organising committee had stolen money. She was angry and tried to do something about it, but she failed. Nevertheless, she joined again the following year with some of the same committee members. When I expressed my amazement at her decision to take the risk again she said: 'What else can one do?' Another woman told me that she had lent money to a neighbour although she did not trust her. The neighbour kept asking her for money and she finally gave in and lent her R150. As she expected, the neighbour never repaid the loan. When I asked her why she lent money to someone she did not trust, she replied: 'To trust someone you sometimes have to take a risk. What else is there to do?'

Sometimes men and women conveyed that people, including themselves, encompassed good and evil characteristics. This seemed to be a fundamental and fairly unchallenged understanding of all humans. In the course of the research, I sometimes felt naive and alien when I expressed the view that people were basically good until proven otherwise. On such occasions people looked at me in amazement and I slowly started to adjust my thoughts.

For example, in October 1997, Edith and I visited Ma Ntshona. She was known to be a Big Five supporter and was involved in a scandal for having stolen R3,600. The money belonged to members of Victoria Mxenge, a group of mainly women who saved money together to build houses. We had tried to meet Ma Ntshona before, but she was never there, even though we had made an appointment. It seemed that she was trying to avoid either Edith or me. We tried again and found Ma Ntshona accompanied by three women in front of her shack. They were waiting to be picked up and brought to a Victoria Mxenge meeting. The atomsphere was uncomfortable and Ma Ntshona was visibly nervous. After we exchanged polite greetings, one of the women who had accompanied Ma Ntshona asked Edith: 'Doesn't it worry you that people now see you standing here with Ma Ntshona?' Edith, who knew that Ma Ntshona was accused of stealing money, replied that this was not our business: 'Every person has good and bad.' The women agreed and one of them replied, '*Injalo*', that's how it is.

A similar remark was made when we visited Ma Zibiya, a neighbour in Indawo Yoxolo who worked as a live-in domestic worker in the affluent, and therefore White, suburb of Tokai. During the week, Ma Zibya's neighbour, Nobuntu, took care of the children because Ma Zibiya was only allowed to go home for the weekends. When we arrived at Ma Zibiya's place, she was having tea with some friends. She laughed and enjoyed seeing us and said: 'Ah, there we have the Paparazzi! Where is your camera?' Obviously this was a playful reference to my paparazzi-like behaviour. Clearly I was probing into other people's lives. The remark was also inspired by the death of Princess Diana. On the radio they had heard about her death in a car crash, which was possibly due to the paparazzi who were pursuing her. Listeners had phoned to the radio station and said: 'It was all due to the pepperonis that Lady Di is dead.' And another man had said: 'You know, it are the Pavarottis that killed her.' These remarks made Zibiya and her friends laugh. After Zibiya shared the joke with us, she told us that she had heard that Lady Diana was not only good. Before the radio programme she thought that Lady Diana was only good because she cared for children and tried to help people in need. But now she had heard on the radio and read in the newspapers that she also had bad sides which, according to Zibyia, only came out after her death. She was relieved to find out that Lady Diana was also a regular person, 'Like every person: the bold *and* the beautiful'. Through reference to this popular soap series about rich people who are constantly fighting and deceiving one another, Zibiya emphasised that every person has good sides and bad sides, even Princess Diana.

If people consist of good and evil, you should know that you cannot always trust them. It even implies that you cannot completely trust yourself either, because you might also harm others. The conflicts about the flows of money and competition over money revealed that people were sometimes ruthless, and sometimes could not prevent harming people by not helping them. The ideology of *ubuntu* as well as the dynamics of witchcraft both revealed how good and evil were interpreted as a part of people and their interactions.

*Ubuntu* can mean a lot of different things to different people. It is a useful but also a very politically charged concept. Therefore, it is important to explore this concept a bit further and be slightly cautious when using the term in a social science context. *Ubuntu* means humanity and is an ideology that emphasises respect for fellow human beings while stressing the inclusiveness of African communities. Sometimes people also refer to this ideology in order to explain altruistic or respectful behaviour. One has to be cautious when using the term *ubuntu* to understand social relations. In post-apartheid South Africa it has become a synonym for development and encompasses a romanticised vision of the rediscovery of African values (cf. Van Kessel 2001). *Ubuntu* has come to stand for anything positively African. Archbishop Tutu played a pivotal role in putting *ubuntu* on the map. As the chairman of the Truth and Reconciliation Commission, he emphasized African morality and self-worth and highlighted *ubuntu* as a way to deal with pains of the past, work towards forgiveness, and envision a common future of interdependent people (see Battle 1997). *Ubuntu* has to be approached carefully because of its romanticised, one-dimensional notion that is now fashionable in politics and business.[11]

In the course of my research, the African migrants never referred to *ubuntu* to explain their behaviour and instead emphasised *ukunceda*, or 'helping each other'. But when I asked whether this could also be understood as *ubuntu*, they agreed and were surprised that I knew about this term. *Ubuntu*, although it was not often used in daily conversations, embraced the ideology of respect, helping each other, and solidarity. As Buijs & Atherfold (1995: 75) found among members of financial mutuals in the townships of Grahamstown, South Africa:

> [R]eputation is especially important in the context of ubuntu or the ideal of humanity … [which] recognises that human relations and human survival are paramount values and that material possessions are seen as the means whereby these values can be achieved.

The proper names of financial mutuals, such as Masizakhe ('let us build each other'), Mascedane ('let us help each other'), Masonwabe ('let us be happy') also indicated the importance of this ideology.

---

[11] For example Mbigi (1997) applies ubuntu to 'Africanise' the work force. Sindane & Liebenberg (2000), and Tusenius (1998) provide some examples of the glorification of ubuntu in the wake of the African renaissance. Van der Merwe (1996: 15-16) gives a very broad, unempirical, and idealistic vision of the role of ubuntu for financial mutuals in South Africa: 'Die idee van "ubuntu" is 'n gemeenskaplike ideaal wat aan alle Swartmense suid van die Sahara betekenis aan lewe en realiteit gee. Hierdie konsep word dikwels as die geestelike grondslag van alle Afrika-gemeenskappe besckou. … Stokvels is een van die wyses waarop die beginsel van "ubuntu" uitgeleef word en mense mekaar ondersteun en help om te oorleef in omstandighede van nood.' Another example can be found in Kimmerle's (2000) review of Ramose's (1999) 'African philosophy through ubuntu': '"be-ing" in African philosophy is based on a "conception of the universe as a musical harmony" and that the "dance of be-ing" is an invitation to participate actively in and through the music of "be-ing"' (Kimmerle 2000: 192). For a critical examination of the African renaissance see Hammond-Tooke (1998). Since Tempel's Bantoe-filosofie (1946), which tried to comprehend the notion of ntu in Congo, such notions have been heavily debated and criticised. See Okafor (1982) for a discussion of Tempel's work.

The expression *umntu ngumntu ngabanye abantu*, means 'a person is a person by means of other people' is central to the ideology of *ubuntu*. *Ubuntu* highlights the interdependencies of people and how social configurations determine, or at least influence, one's future. When I asked people about their motivation for particular forms of action, it was common to reason from a relational point of view. The expectations of others, especially kin that lived over a thousand kilometres away, were an important reason for establishing financial mutuals and, through new social relations, direct flows of money.

The ideology of *ubuntu* reminds one of Fortes' (1983 [1959]) understandings of fate and destiny among the Thallensi. For the Thallensi, fate and destiny were very much a result of people's interdependencies and particularly relations with ancestors: 'A man's Destiny, then, consists of a unique configuration of ancestors who have, of their own accord, elected to exercise specific surveillance over his life-cycle, and to whom he is personally accountable' (Fortes 1983: 21). Moreover, Fortes (1983: 23) writes that: 'Destiny ancestors are benevolent not out of affection for their descendants but out of self-interest and because they have the power. Their solicitude is gained not by demonstrations of love but by proofs of loyalty.'

For the Xhosa, relations with ancestors encompassed good and evil. Personal well-being depended on the ambivalent relations with ancestors. Ancestors could give protection but could also withhold protection when they were not respected and recognised through ritual. The migrants in Indawo Yoxolo were new. Hardly anybody had performed the ritual beer drinking that could ensure ancestral protection. This increased their vulnerability. Neglecting ancestors could have serious repercussions, as Hirst (1997: 220-221) noted:

> When the ancestors are neglected, they withdraw their protection (*ukukhusela*) from their descendants, making them open to witchcraft/sorcery (*ukuthakhatha*) and thus subject to illness … According to experienced diviners, the various symptoms suffered are directly related to difficulties in relationships with significant others.

While the ideology of *ubuntu* emphasises the positive way in which people can help, forgive, and support one another, the experience of Xhosa migrants was much more ambiguous as, for example, shown by the reluctant solidarity described in the previous chapter. According to the notions of 'helping each other' and *ubuntu*, people can 'construct' each other and support each other and establish a positive sense of well-being and humanity. However, witchcraft shows that it is definitely possible to do the opposite. As the threatening triad reveals, people can also influence each other in destructive and dehumanising ways.

In her study on the spread of AIDS among Zulu youth, Leclerc-Madlala (1997: 377) refers to the '"flip side" of the Afrocentric ethos of *ubuntu*' that promotes common misery. She describes how those who were infected with HIV, or believed to be infected, wished to infect others as well. A nineteen-year-old student explained: 'By giving it [HIV] to others, I won't be going down alone. That's my only hope', while another nineteen-year-old male also had the desire to infect others with HIV, 'This disease is horrible. The only good thing would be if we're all together. *Ubuntu*, we share … if we are people we must share' (Leclerc-Madlala 1997: 371). The conversations with youth about AIDS and *ubuntu* led Leclerc-Madlala (1997: 372) to pose the question: 'Could there be a "dark underside" to the process of *ubuntu*?'

The danger of *ubuntu* also emerged in relation to marriage. In the course of the research I had attended only one wedding because people rarely got married, and if they did it was a jural marriage. During a conversation with a few men and women I discovered the reason for this was related to gifts:

> If a man has a girlfriend, she will be jealous of the bride. The jealous girlfriend might give a present, such as clothing or money that is treated with herbs (*amayeza*). This gift causes the newlyweds to spend money like crazy and they will end up in misery. *Ubuntu* can be dangerous sometimes.

On another occasion, a woman told me that her sister once received R30 from someone out of the blue. She was surprised because she had not indicated to that person that she needed money. She visited a diviner (*igqirha*) who explained to her that the woman gave her the money in order to harm her. When she told me the story she added: 'So you see: *Ubuntu* can be dangerous sometimes.' Money was particularly vulnerable for use in witchcraft and people were thought to put witchcraft medicine on the money to harm others. Thus, circulating money in a financial mutual definitely had its dangers.[12] For this reason, people would sometimes keep money from a suspicious source separate in order to prevent it from contaminating other notes and coins. By spending it as quickly as possible one diminished the risk of being bewitched by it. In other words, wealth needs to be avoided because it can lead to jealousy. Jealousy is a problem because it can lead to witchcraft and therefore undermines trust. The paradox here is that trust is needed in order to 'create' wealth through co-operation in financial mutuals while that same creation of wealth undermines trust.

*Ubuntu* and witchcraft were related because both indicated how people were influenced through relationships and, just like people hardly spoke about *ubuntu* and preferred 'helping each other', they hardly ever discussed witchcraft openly but instead spoke of the dangers of jealousy. People seemed to be aware that one could not be in complete control of oneself, and they realised their own kind-heartedness *and* malignancy. Jealousy was the emotional component of witchcraft, and it is an emotion that was difficult to control, even if one tried very hard. Jealousy, followed by guilt when one feels responsible for the misfortune of others appears to underlie self-accusations. Grandma Doris told me how she witnessed a

---

[12] See Taussig (1980) on such dangers in South America.

case of a self-confessed witch. Grandma Doris' twelve-year-old daughter had tragically suffocated from the smoke caused by a fire that had burned her shack to the ground. Soon after the child's death, her neighbour ran out onto the street and screamed and shouted and moved wildly. She publicly blamed herself for the death of Grandma Doris' daughter. The woman had opened the bible and the power of the bible had caused her to reveal herself as a witch.

Self-accusations were rare but did occur (see also Niehaus 2001).[13] People saw humans, including themselves, as consisting of good and evil. They were good natured as well as malicious, could contribute to other people's lives in a positive way, but were also capable of destroying others by, for example, uncontrolled jealousy. This had significant consequences for people's understanding of trust. It was inherent in people's understanding of their entrenchment in social configurations that relations were ambivalent. Therefore, one could not always trust one another, and one could not even entirely trust oneself. This was a basic fact of life and any form of interaction and co-operation. Sometimes things go wrong: *Injalo*, that's life, *c'est la vie*, *zo gaat het nu eenmaal*. Because people were aware of these risks in life, it was enough to maintain them, and they did not expect them to be eliminated. People can have multiple, conflicting feelings about one another and nevertheless co-operate. The participants entrusted large parts of their income to others without trusting them all the time, and without entirely trusting themselves.

## Conclusion

Financial mutuals can be regarded as 'islands of trust' but only to a certain degree. The threatening triad of violence, economic insecurity, and volatile relations urged people to organise into confined, dense, social networks that did not extend beyond a radius of a couple of dozen metres. They at least could be controlled to some extent through gossip and rumour and physical proximity.

The contradiction between a distrustful society in which trustful financial mutuals flourished is, to some extent, false. The threat of violence and confiscation

---

13 Geschiere (1997: 12) rightly argues: 'Most anthropologists still tend to reduce discourses on witchcraft to an unequivocal opposition between good and evil, even when the local terminology hardly lends itself to this.' Among the Xhosa, *ubuthakati* (i.e. witchcraft) has a negative connotation but is also a discourse that highlights the desire for wealth. A diviner (*igqirha*) might also be a witch (*igqwirha*) and the herbs (*amayeza* or *umti*) that are used can be both dirty and clean, depending on their use. Therefore, I wish not to reinforce simplistic oppositions of good and evil but show how good and evil work can be done through similar techniques and social processes.

show this more than anything else. The same violence that undermined trust in South African society could, under certain conditions, contain risks in financial mutuals. Although financial mutuals certainly built up social capital, it was also the threat of violence that offered the control that was needed. Acts of violence, intimidation and confiscation were legitimate yet problematic within the context of financial mutuals, but are difficult to reconcile with the maintenance of good governance and legitimate bureaucracies. Therefore, the political transformative capacities of financial mutuals in South Africa are small. It did not seem very likely that trust in financial mutuals could lead to trust in society at large or in political institutions.

The organisers of financial mutuals established strategies that contained risks by managing social relations. The case of Masifunde revealed the strategies that people used to manage relations with fellow members: the money at the bank was used as collateral against default, the combination of flexibility in rules and rigidity in its application also implied risk. By dividing the fund into many small parts and lending it to many members, mutual dependencies were emphasised while absconding with the money became less advantageous. The mutuals steered clear of political division in the township. No kin – except for a few daughters – or boyfriends and husbands were allowed because the hierarchies in these relationships were threatening to the members' mutual obligations; the threats of violence and confiscation were severe repercussions in case of default.

These measures, however, could not eliminate risks. Financial mutuals were part of a violent, threatening, and distrustful society, although the members made attempts to separate themselves and their money by creating 'islands of trust'. The threat of violence was even necessary to deal with default. Distrust and threats were endemic to society and an inevitable part of social relations, also among the members of financial mutuals. The dense social networks among the participants were subject to risks but also gave rise to complex interdependencies that in turn created an ambivalence within these relations, similar to other social configurations, such as kinship.

Because ambivalence is central to the social configurations revealed, one could co-operate without trusting others completely. It makes it possible to grasp why one was willing to risk being harmed by others. People understood themselves and their interdependencies with others as a mixture of good *and* evil forces that were not always under control. Distrust was, therefore, an inevitable part of life. Sometimes you cheat and sometimes someone cheats on you and then you pick up the pieces, get back on your feet, and continue living. *Injalo*; that's the way it is.

# 6

# Spending money: Consumption, friendship and friction

## Introduction

Throughout the year, many African women, but also men, contributed substantial amounts of their sparse income to financial mutuals. It was not uncommon for them to reserve a quarter of their monthly salary for the mutual. Contrary to the ambitions of many development agencies, hardly anyone used the money for business purposes. The reluctance to use money for business purposes should, however, not come as a surprise. Setting up a business in the informal economy is difficult and risky and the income is unlikely to be comparable with the wages of an unskilled or semi-skilled worker.[1] Moreover, violence in places like Indawo Yoxolo makes it difficult for businesses to succeed, especially if one does not have the protection of local Mafia-style leaders. It actually puzzles me that, while many foreign investors are reluctant to invest in South Africa's economy, uneducated and inexperienced migrants are expected to invest their money in businesses in an unprotected informal economy.

Virtually all the money was spent on consumables and one can roughly distinguish three categories, namely clothing, rituals, and food. Clothing should be understood as a very broad category. It includes dresses, school uniforms, and so on, but also items considered to be 'clothing for the house', such as refrigerators,

---

[1] See, for example, Rahman (1997) and Reinke (1999).

stoves, cooking utensils, crockery, and duvet covers. Often, money was used to contribute to the costs of rituals, such as funerals, initiation of sons, or rituals that were held in order to evoke respect towards the ancestors. Finally, money was used to buy food. Ma Zibiya, for example, belonged to several *imigalelo*, of which one was a monthly grocery ASCRA. In December, the members collectively bought a massive amount of groceries at the nearby MAKRO store, including sugar, rice, flower, washing powder, cooking oil, milk powder, and dried beans. She also received R527 in cash. After she had received the goods and money she took most of the food to her mother's place in the former Transkei. The cash was used in order to buy a bull that was slaughtered to honour her deceased father.

## Status and conflict

Why is consumption so important for Xhosa migrants? Spending money on consumables certainly generates economic advantages. It protects you against adversities and food can be bought more cheaply from wholesalers, without having to take a loan (see Heidheus 1994; Lont 2000b; 2002; Miracle *et al.* 1980; Scofield 1997).

At least as significant as the economic aspect of consumption is its social significance to Xhosa migrants. An important function of consumption is being and feeling less poor and being able to hope for a better future. Consumption enables people to feel better about themselves, distinguish themselves from others, and show a lifestyle that evokes respect and status (Bourdieu 1984: 1992; Lamont 1992: 68-70; Veblen 1899). The Xhosa migrants were pre-occupied with consumption and, particularly under the conditions of poverty and despair, it was important to distinguish oneself from others through one's consumer habits. For example, when I visited a second-hand store in the township Philippi, one of the clients wanted to buy the largest radio. I asked the client why she preferred that particular radio, to which she responded: 'It is the largest radio. I know it is only competition, nothing more, to see who has the biggest radio.'

Food was also important for respectable behaviour as the provision of food to visitors showed hospitality. Moreover, food led to fatness.[2] Men readily explained that gaining weight meant gaining the good of the public opinion. During a conversation, a man once jokingly referred to his belly, as well as mine, as 'a lot of public opinion'. Status and respect were closely intertwined with food and other forms of consumption, which could only be afforded by participating in financial mutuals.

---

2 See, among others, Masquelier (1995) on consumption, particularly sweetness and its pivotal role for the Mawri in Niger to grasp changes in society.

Distinction, status, and respect through consumption did not go unchallenged by those who did not share in them. For example, while having tea at the home of one of the residents in Indawo Yoxolo a man walked in with a mobile phone clipped visibly onto his belt. The phone attracted everybody's attention. People wanted to see and hold it and find out how it worked. Soon it became clear that the man did not know how his phone functioned and that it was not even connected to a network. Everybody laughed, and with a look of dismay, the owner of the phone had to listen to humiliating jokes about the way he had been bragging.

Status, consumption, and lifestyle were also at the core of critical remarks made against another resident in Indawo Yoxolo. One of Edith's neighbours was the only one in the street with a brick house. It had four rooms and stood out beautifully against the surrounding shacks and ten square meter RDP 'matchbox' houses. During a casual conversation on the street, the neighbours started to gossip about their neighbour with her large house. They complained that she did not greet them anymore and would only reciprocate a greeting, never start one. Another woman said that she had noticed that, since the neighbour had lived in this big house, she had changed the way in which she walked. To clarify her argument she mimicked her neighbour by parading slowly in front of us, head up, while wiggling her behind. Everyone laughed at this little show. Another woman complained that she had failed to recognise her neighbour the other day because of her different walk, 'She now thinks she belongs to a higher class', 'she thinks she is better than us'.

Consumption, as a status indicator, was accompanied by envy, jealousy, and dismay. Consumption worked well as a means of distinction, but this distinction was felt to be problematic, especially among people who were fairly close to one another. To have a lot of possessions and to show off without shame was regarded as bragging (*ukubreka* or *ukuqhayisa*). The person who brags, the *brekgat*, i.e the 'bragging ass', was the one who bought the biggest and most desirable products in order to compete.

The literature on the colonial encounter and modernity has given ample attention to the dynamics of consumption, social relations, and socio-political conflict (see among others Appadurai 1986; 1997; Burke 1995; contributions in Comaroff & Comaroff 1993; 1999; Fisiy & Geschiere 1996; Masquelier 1995; Meyer 1995, 1998, 1999; Taussig 1995; Thoden van Velzen & Van Wetering 1991). Although only in passing, financial mutuals in South Africa have also been compared with the potlatch (Buijs & Atherfold 1995: 42; Kuper & Kaplan 1944: 84). Bataille (1991) and Wolf (1999) convincingly argued that this $19^{th}$ century gift giving institution among the Kwakuitl contains an element of warfare and rivalry.[3] A gift

---

[3] See also Mauss' (1954: 35) reference to gift giving as the 'war of property' and 'the war of wealth'. See also Thoden van Velzen & Van Wetering, especially on the secret dumping place of possessions of convicted witches in the forest of Suriname,

forces the recipient to make a more valuable counter gift. In the potlatch, there was rivalry and competition over who could give the most and thus had the most prestige and rank. Due to new sources of wealth and insecurity, the potlatch increasingly became a space to compete and fight with goods (Wolf 1999).

This perspective on consumption (status and conflict) provides an interesting approach to financial mutuals. Financial mutuals are too easily portrayed as 'solidarity groups'. At first glance, consumer practices that are part of financial mutuals can be understood as expressions of belonging and mutual help which, as will become clear in this chapter, does not do justice to the complex social dynamics of consumption in financial mutuals.

## Zolani Club: The price of a bed

Comaroff & Comaroff (1999: 293-294) state that 'there is this perplexity ... about the very nature of human subjects, about their covert appetites, about dark practices of the heart that show themselves in spectacular new fortunes and orgies of consumption'. Indeed, there is much uncertainty about the powers that bring about wealth and enable consumption. The case of the financial mutual Zolani Club revealed much more clearly than a fragmented account how consumption was regarded as pivotal to social tensions. However, in order to understand this perplexity – and here I share Moore's (1999) methodological caution on the imaginative interpretation made by Comaroff & Comaroff (1999) – I submit that the inquiry must be rooted in ethnography.

Zolani Club was part of one of the largest and most sophisticated financial mutuals that I encountered during my fieldwork. The name of the club was derived from the word *ukuzola*, 'to stay cool, to relax'. Zolani Club meant something like 'the ones who stay cool', which they did by giving money to one another. It was a ROSCA and the members met three Sundays per month in a classroom at Chumise High School, Khayelitsha, Site B (*ukuchumise* means 'to produce a lot of fruit'). One of the members of Zolani Club introduced me to the organisation, and I had ample opportunities to go to their meetings, have conversations with members, visit them at their homes, which were mostly in Khayelitsha, and pick up some of the rumours and gossip. It was only an intimate knowledge of the relationships between the members that enabled me to see the other side of Zolani Club, and to see that the club was not only about happy people supporting each other with gifts, respecting each other and distinguishing themselves from others through con-

---

on the embeddedness of consumer products in conflict (Thoden van Velzen & Van Wetering 1991: 154-156).

sumption in a carefree fashion. It revealed that the support that members gave each other was neither unconditional nor unproblematic.

*Photo 6.1* Some of the members of Zolani Club

*Financial arrangements*

The 31 participants of Zolani Club made financial contributions to each other in a number of ways. Each meeting was oriented around a 'birthday'. The 'birthday' was fictitious and had nothing to do with the member's actual date of birth. The contribution to a birthday depended on a variety of factors. In 1998, Zolani Club was divided into three subgroups of about ten members each. On the occasion of a birthday of someone within the same subgroup, one was obliged to contribute at least R100. If the member belonged to one of the other two subgroups, a minimum gift of R10 was sufficient. This gift money had a special name – 'stage money' – because it was needed before one was to be allowed 'on stage', that is, allowed to come forward and start giving. Two secretaries recorded all the contributions in two books. One book was kept for the individual member, the other for the organisation.

In addition to stage money, participants were encouraged to give additional money or goods, such as cooking utensils and soap or even larger presents such as refrigerators or stoves. The prices of any items given were also recorded. The extra amount of money and goods given beyond 'stage money' was called *ukuskora*, derived from 'to score'. This extra amount offered depended on the individual participant and her relationship with the recipient. Nevertheless, recipients were expected to reciprocate all contributions with a gift worth at least the same amount.

Besides 'stage money' and 'scoring', there were other ways of receiving on a 'birthday'. Zolani Club was part of a network of ROSCAs called Noluthando (meaning approximately 'the group/person is based on love') initiated in 1984. At least six other ROSCAs were part of Noluthando, each with its separate board, uniform, meetings, and organisers. Within this network of groups, it was possible for one group to visit a birthday celebration hosted by another group. To attend these celebrations, a R2 admission fee had to be paid which covered some of the expenses for food and drinks. On top of the R2, visitors were encouraged to give whatever amount they preferred. Like the gifts coming from within the immediate group itself, gifts from members of other groups within the Noluthando network were also written down by the secretaries, and were expected to be reciprocated at the appropriate time. Thus, by contributing to the birthday of another group's member, one created the obligation for another to attend one's own birthday with a contribution of at least the same amount.

To create even more opportunities for giving and receiving, participants created a fictitious or 'quasi'-kinship system. Each member had a 'mother', a 'grandmother', 'sisters', and often also 'daughters'. Although participants did not use different terms for kinship within the organisation – the situation made it clear who was who – I will distinguish these 'organisational kin' from biological family with the use of quotation marks; 'mother', 'grandmother', and so on. In order to join Zolani Club, the aspirant was required to declare an intention to join and choose a 'mother'. Every woman in the organisation wanted to have as many 'children' as possible and often asked, before the meeting took place, if anyone would like to become their 'daughter'. Still, it was up to the 'daughter' herself to decide on who her 'mother' would be. By choosing a 'mother', the member automatically placed herself in a social web that included 'sisters', a 'grandmother', and possibly even a 'great grandmother'. Furthermore, 'aunts' (the 'mother's sisters') and 'nieces' (the 'mother's sister's daughters') were also part of the picture. Nevertheless, because the quasi-marriage of quasi-kin was non-existent, there were no quasi in-laws. For many, this last aspect was important.

At a member's birthday, it was quasi kin in particular who provided plenty of money and presents. The 'mother', 'grandmother', 'sisters', and 'children' asked what the member would like to have for her birthday. The minimum amount given in addition to the stage money depended on the amount that had to be reciprocated from previous exchanges. Again, if you owed someone because of what you had received on your last birthday, it was obligatory to reciprocate with at least the same amount. In many cases, though, much *more* than the original amount was given, thus creating a new and larger debt.

Quasi-kin could be of the same subgroup, the same club, or could be members of other clubs within Noluthando. This flexibility made it possible for a 'daughter' to take part in a different ROSCA than that to which her 'mother' belonged. This system of groups within groups (clubs within Noluthando, for example, and subgroups within clubs) gave the organisation room to grow. If too many members joined a single club, the cycle of the ROSCA became longer – and a lengthening of the cycle has been shown to be erosive to the mechanisms of trust and social control within the group (see also Bähre & Smets 1999: 2004). But a subgroup could leave the ROSCA and establish a new ROSCA within Noluthando. The new ROSCA maintained its reciprocal relations with quasi-kin and other clubs and subgroups by attending and giving presents at the appropriate birthday celebrations. Though it was not possible to have more than one 'mother', it was possible for a member to leave her 'mother' in order to become the 'daughter' of another member. Though rare, this did happen, and it caused considerable difficulties.

Another way to contribute to a participant's birthday celebration was by 'playing' money. This could be done by anyone, and most of the time the amounts of money in question were relatively small (such as R2, although amounts up to R40 were also played). When the money was given, an announcement was made, such as, 'With this money, I want to say happy birthday', or 'With this money, I want the guests to start a song'. This played money was also registered by the secretaries and entered the ledger of social obligation and reciprocity.

Although the ability to accumulate large amounts of money and goods within a short time was a major attraction of the organisation, there were still risks attached to this fortune. One member confessed having sleepless nights because she had received money and presents worth far more than what she could afford to reciprocate within a year. She had expressly asked for small presents, but her 'mother' in particular gave much more than she could have imagined. Members tried a couple of different strategies to prevent such sleepless nights and to manage their obligations within Zolani Club, but these strategies were not always successful. For example, it was possible to limit the number and costs of group relationships by not taking any 'daughters' or by giving small presents or no presents at all. Indeed, some members only contributed the minimum 'stage money' necessary and, most of the time, abstained from 'scoring' and visiting other clubs. The consequence of this cautious engagement with group exchange was that one had fewer and less intensive reciprocal obligations – and, therefore, a minor status within the group. Another strategy to limit one's obligations was to save the money that had been given on a birthday. Instead of spending the money, some immediately put it aside, to be used for another member's birthday. To keep the money until later, though, required not only a safe place to keep the money, but also a substantial level of restraint on the part of the individual. For those on formal incomes it was also possible to purchase a gift on credit. However, the high interest rates in South Africa (which, at the time of the research, were approaching an annual rate of 24 percent) meant that such a gift would be far more expensive than its immediate price tag. Buying gifts on credit was a high risk strategy, for if a loan was not paid off regularly, the ever-accruing interest on the borrowed amount could easily become unmanageable.

Another strategy to prevent the increase of one's money circulating in the organisation was to talk with the 'birthday girl' before the celebration. The concerned member could explain her financial problem and try to make a deal – perhaps to pay later, or to pay back the debt over two birthdays without receiving a birthday present in the interim. If an agreement was reached, the debtor had to explain at the birthday meeting why she had no money, apologise for the situation, and promise that the present would come later. At one meeting of Zolani Club that I observed, a woman could not afford to pay the R600 she owed her 'mother'. She told the members and her 'mother' in particular: 'I am sorry, sorry. She/you[4] [her 'mother'] made it possible for me to have some education and for me to say "good morning *umlungu*". [Umlungu means 'white person'. By saying this, she was explaining that she now knew some English ('good morning') and could therefore interact with white people.] I can only give R30 and will give the rest of the money at her next birthday.' This situation was an embarrassing one that elicited sympathy from others in the group. Because of the shame involved in not being able to pay, participants often went to great lengths (and great costs) to avoid such a situation.

Yet another strategy for managing one's finances within the organisation – and even to benefit from it – was used by Nokwanda. She had been a member since the beginning of the group in 1984 and, with her twenty-two 'children', she was a well-known and respectable woman whose presence in the group was always felt. Together with her husband, she lived in an eight square metre room in her employer's premises. She used her ROSCA money to lend to her neighbours, who were also from Qumbu in the former Transkei. During an interview, someone interrupted to repay her R1,300 she had previously borrowed. This repayment included the 30 percent monthly interest (generally regarded as a fair rate). Nokwanda told me: 'This is how I keep my money.'

In addition to the measures that individual members took in order to manage financially, the organisation deducted R500 from the money that was collected at the birthday celebration. The R500 was collateral and could be used to settle outstanding debts. In general, these measures worked well. Default was rare, debts were mostly settled and, if problems occurred, they involved individual members and did not damage the future of the organisation as a whole. The dense web of

---

[4] In Xhosa the noun *u* signifies both she/he and you singular.

financial obligations strengthened the organisation's survival and it was actually difficult to stop giving and receiving and leave the organisation.

Some financial strategies were clearly unattractive and expensive. The fact that people nevertheless resorted to such strategies reveals how important the social relationships established through the ROSCA were and how powerful the bonds were between members. From its financial role alone, one could see that the organisation gave mutual support and cemented social relations via money and presents. But these ties could gag as well as they could bind. The organisation and its criss-crossing obligations came to be, for some members, a source of stress, sleepless nights, and indebtedness.

*History*

In order to acquire a better understanding of Zolani Club and its network of people and organisations, I spoke with Nokwanda. The way in which she conveyed the history of this financial mutual revealed how important the gift of money and consumption was for the establishment of close relations. Nokwanda told me the following story:

'The *umgalelo* was established in 1984. We started in a small group and attended meetings at the member's room. Some members were sleep-in domestic workers, so there could be no singing because of the noise. The *umgalelo* was very popular and we started growing, so we called a meeting. This was in 1986. They gave permission to meet at a hostel in Langa,[5] the oldest township in Cape Town. We started with R12 stage money per month. A year later, in 1987, we called the organization *Nompulelelo*, meaning something like 'the improvers'. We could really see the improvement. If you had R500 that was a lot of money in those days. Things went up, including the stage money, which was set at R22. Prices also went up. In those days the maximum amount payable on someone's turn was R1,000.

In 1988, the connection to Bhayi (Port Elizabeth) developed. It went via Radio Bantu, now called Radio Umhlobowene. You give regards or dedications to friends in other parts of the country via the radio. You can send a postcard or letter to the radio, which they read during broadcasting. After regards and dedications had been sent between Cape Town and Port Elizabeth, we asked the radio station for telephone numbers from the people in Port Elizabeth. We didn't know each other at all. We had the phone numbers and we started to send each other dedications by phone and started talking to each other. We started talking about *imigalelo* and we gave each other advice. We still haven't met.

Mother Nomfuneko Godana, who lives in Port Elizabeth, was fifty-two years old at the time. She proposed having 'children'. She phoned the radio and said that

---

[5] In 1986, a state of emergency was declared. This severely restricted meetings and one needed permission from the authorities to get together.

she was looking for 'children'. We were a bit confused. When one is at school one would play at having schoolmates who are your mothers and children, so we knew about it. But still it was confusing to us what it had to do with *imigalelo*. At a meeting with members of her organisation in Port Elizabeth, she explained how it works. You give your 'children' a lot of money and the money comes back. It lets the family grow. We thought, if it works in Port Elizabeth, we also have to try it here in Cape Town. Via Radio Bantu the people in Port Elizabeth started to announce the birthday of their members. We were surprised and Nomvumekaya, one of the members of the organisation in Port Elizabeth, said on the radio: 'I would like you, Nokwanda, to be my child.' She had left her telephone number at the radio station. After I phoned the radio to ask for Nomvumekaya's number I phoned her in Port Elizabeth. Nomvumekaya explained to me about the ideas Nomfuneko Godana had and what she said about quasi-children and mothers. I liked it and I called a meeting in Langa to inform the members of our organisation. They had also heard about it on the radio and they were curious and very interested.

It was going to be member Sowati's turn on the second of March 1989. Everybody was looking forward to see what would happen and if she really would send presents and visit her from Port Elizabeth. Nomvumekaya was her 'mother' and she phoned us to let us know that she would go to Cape Town for Sowati's birthday. Unfortunately, she couldn't come as one of her children was ill, but she had sent a present by mail. At Sowati's birthday, the chairlady opened the present: everybody was curious as it came from far. It was a dress and R50. Now everybody wanted a 'mother'! Mother Sowati phoned to Port Elizabeth to thank Nomvumekaya and she told her that the other members in Cape Town also wanted a 'mother'. At that time, people from Port Elizabeth were proposing and welcoming 'children' from Cape Town. But still we had not met each other.

After three years, everyone had 'mothers' and 'children' and 'grandchildren' and people from Port Elizabeth would contribute. That's how we got to know each other and bring money. We gave birth to many 'children'. Our organisation, Nompumelelo, grew much bigger. I decided to take some people to start my own group called Nanoxolo, meaning 'bright place'. This was on 17 February 1990. I also had grandchildren and my grandchildren started Zolani Club. There are now many different clubs such as Mazizake Club, meaning 'Let's build ourselves', Sinethemba, meaning 'Let's have hope', Siyathemba I and II, meaning 'We have hope', each with different uniforms.

Every member has a mother, but even if you are not a member, you can have a mother. On your birthday, your real one, they will come to your place and give money and presents until you become interested in the organisation and will join.

Before I joined this organisation, I had two rondawels [huts] at home in the Eastern Cape. Now I have a nice place with furniture. Before I have my birthday, my twenty-two 'children' get together and contribute and buy something I want. They pay cash at the store and if they don't have enough money they have to buy on credit. If the amount the children collect is not enough, one 'child' opens an account for hire purchasing with, let's say R400. The 'child' pays the instalments. Then, if it is the mother's turn to give her daughter she will give R400. The extra expense the child had, because she bought on credit and had to pay interest, is the child's responsibility. This helps a child to buy a nice present, but the danger is that you make too many debts and get yourself into financial problems.'

Nokwanda was very pleased with the intimate relations that she had with her twenty-two 'children' and many other members. Her status in the financial mutual contrasted sharply with her status as a semi-skilled worker sharing a room with her husband that barely fitted anything more than a bed, a wardrobe, and a colour television. The presents of the members were so important that, in one instance, the gift *was* the relation. The members of the financial mutual did not even know the quasi-kin in the Eastern Cape and they already started to exchange presents. Nokwanda's account of the history of this financial mutual shows how important these relations were and the trouble people went through to get in touch with each other, against the grain of apartheid policy, in order to create affective bonds that were modelled after kinship ties.

*Friendship and support*

Thandi lived with her three children in Khayelitsha, site B, in a three-room shack made of wood and corrugated iron. She had applied for a government housing subsidy and received a 'site and service plot' – with a toilet, a running-water tap, and a pre-paid electricity connection – on which she could build her shack. The plots were quite small, and between the plots were dirt roads that filled with muddy pools in the rainy season. We first met Thandi in December, when it was dry and hot. Thandi worked part-time as the housekeeper for a doctor. She had a problem with her leg (caused by several car accidents) so she received a disability grant. She was married, but had left her husband because she felt that men in general, especially husbands, were troublemakers. He was violent, and he had held her at gunpoint several times. This was a bit too much for her and she eventually left him: 'That's why most women only want a boyfriend. It is easier to leave them than to leave a husband. That's why you become a member of a club like Zolani. Men only cause problems.'

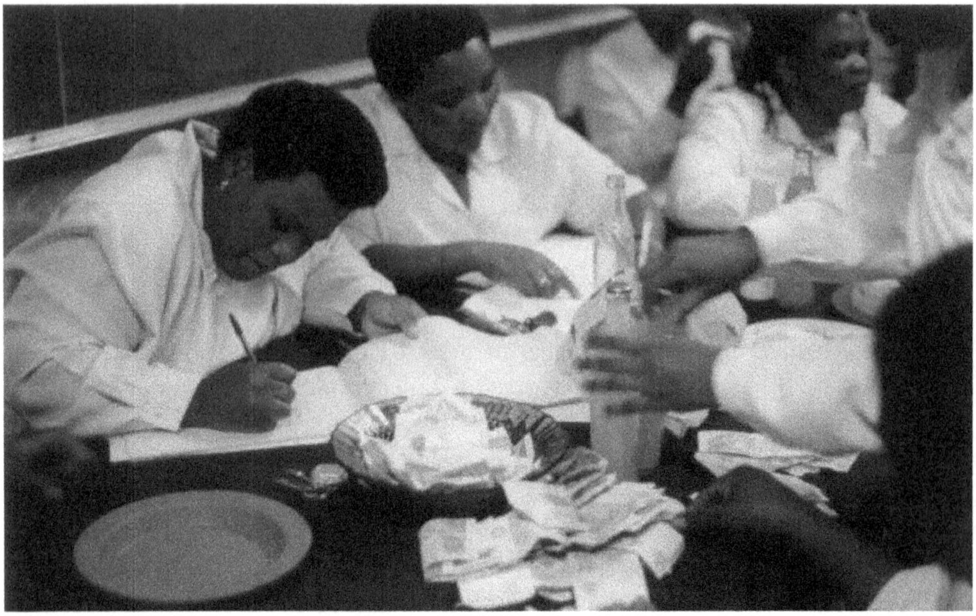

*Photo 6.2* Bookkeeping at Zolani

Thandi was the 'daughter' of Nokwanda and had 'daughters' herself – Linda, Nobuntu, and Bukelwa.[6] Thandi and I met for the first time on her birthday in early December 1997, at which she was given a total of R7,931. She also received presents such as a two-door refrigerator, a room divider, a stove with cooking plates, cupboards, cutlery, soap, a salad bowl, a duvet cover, and many smaller items. She was proud of her possessions, and saw them as proof of the supportive and respectful relations between the participants. All in all, she received about R20,000 worth of goods and money at the celebration. Considering her meagre income, this amount was incredible. Her job as a cleaner and her disability grant could have been no more than R1,000 per month. She admitted that she had not expected *this many* presents – especially not from her 'mother', Nokwanda. Because of the quantity of gifts, she had many a sleepless night after her birthday.

---

6 It was difficult to gain insight into these relationships. They were, of course, personal relations and loyalty between quasi-kin made research difficult. The advantage of my situation was that Thandi and Edith Nokwanele Moyikwa used to be neighbours in the past. Moreover, they belonged to the same clan, which made it easier to get to know and trust each other. However, that also meant that Thandi's 'children' associated us primarily with her, a view that Thandi actively supported by trying to attend all the interviews we had with her 'children'. Certain information was therefore difficult to collect and this specific social constellation influenced the things that people did, gossiped, or kept quiet about.

On many of the occasions that we went to visit Thandi, she was not at home because she was working or visiting her 'daughters', who lived in the neighbourhood. If she was home, friends from the Zolani Club were often visiting her. It was obvious that the financial mutual and her 'children' within it were very important to her. She had only been a member for one year, but already most of her spare time was taken up by visiting 'daughters' and other group members, attending the meetings of ROSCAs, buying presents, and engaging in other similar activities that were part of her overall participation.

One day, en route to a meeting, we began to compare Thandi's quasi-family to her real family. To her, an advantage of the quasi-kinship was the absence of affines in the ROSCA. She explained that the most important difference between quasi-family and real family was that, in the quasi-family situation, jealousy was absent and individuals could trust one another. She was often aware of distrust within her real family and saw that people could, and often did, treat each other badly. This was not the case in Zolani Club. In contrast to the situation with real family, one could leave Zolani. Thandi explained that the members realised that a member could leave and therefore had good reasons to treat members nicely. In Zolani Club, everyone cared for each other and helped each other out. All of this enthusiasm, she insisted, was not only rhetoric since it could be readily witnessed in practice. When one of the members of Zolani Club lost all her belongings because her shack had burned to the ground, for example, sympathetic members offered household items and helped her re-establish her household.

Linda (Thandi's 'daughter' and Nokwanda's 'granddaughter') had three 'children'. Like Thandi, Linda had moved to Khayelitsha, site B, about two years earlier, and Thandi and Linda often visited each other. However, unlike Thandi, Linda lived in an area in which there was no subsidised RDP housing – which meant that there were no individual plots with private toilets, water, and electricity. She lived with her two children and her sick husband, Benjamin, who worked as a security guard when his swollen legs permitted him to work at all. In early 1998, Linda began working as a cleaner in a hospital in Cape Town. It was a part-time, temporary position, but Linda hoped that she would be appointed on a permanent basis once her initial probation period was over.

Although one was not really supposed to switch 'mothers', Thandi was not Linda's first 'mother'. Linda had had a previous 'mother' in Noxolo Club – who had also been Bukelwa's 'mother' – but neither 'daughter' was happy with her for long. They felt that she favoured some of her other 'children' more than them. With regard to birthdays, for example, this 'mother' would ask some of her 'children' exactly what they wanted, while Linda and Bukelwa would receive anything their 'mother' felt like giving, without the luxury of being asked. After a little more than a year, both women confronted and then abandoned their 'mother'. In July 1997, both women became Thandi's 'daughters' and joined Zolani Club.

Because they became Thandi's 'daughters' on the same day, they considered themselves 'twins'. Thandi, in contrast to their previous 'mother', was good, kind, and worthy of respect.

## Linda's birthday

On Sunday 8 March, Linda's birthday celebration took place in Zolani Club. As always, the meeting was held in a classroom at a high school in the township Kayelitsha. The celebration was to last all afternoon. There were about forty to fifty people in attendance at the beginning of the celebration (almost exclusively women), and more arrived during the course of the meeting. Manxoto chaired the meeting. The first meeting that I attended, I was dazzled by all the action. People were constantly arriving, speeches were held, songs were sung, and people danced in circles, as is sometimes done at the independent churches. Often, attendees lined up to give presents to, and speeches about, Linda. Though the scene appeared chaotic at first, after some time the authority of the chairperson became apparent through the din.

The basic structure of the ceremony was provided by a succession of speeches by individual members, combined with songs – mostly church songs – accompanied by lively clapping and dancing. There was a clear order governing the groups and people who could, in turn, come forward to offer money and presents to Linda. Even in the midst of all the rumours and excitement, the chairperson was well able to provide everyone their turn while at the same time she supervised the secretaries, and made sure the correct amounts were recorded in the notebooks. When, at one point, the atmosphere of the birthday celebration became too hectic, the chairperson adopted the manner of a judge, forcefully slamming an empty Coke bottle on the table before her while shouting 'Silence in the court!'

When a number of women had arrived, one of Linda's 'daughters' started a song about God's protection. Everyone joined enthusiastically in the singing, while dancing and clapping their hands. In the middle of this performance, another group, visitors from Hout Baai who had also come to celebrate Linda's birthday, entered the classroom. They joined in the singing and later started their own song, clapping and dancing as well in accompaniment of the expanded group of participants. There was constant emphasis on the fact that the meeting was for Linda. The chairperson addressed the group from Hout Baai who, of course, already knew it was Linda's birthday:

> I greet the organisation that just came in. I just saw an organisation coming in and I was surprised. We welcome you. Stay and enjoy with us. We are playing here, we are playing for Linda Masekwana, Thandi Sodinga's daughter under the word of God that is written in the book of Psalms Chapter 31, Verse I, 'In thee, O Lord, do I seek refuge;

let me never be put to shame'. I ask you to share with us what you have been eating on your way here.

The group members introduced themselves and then another song began. After some time, Manxotho again hit the table with her Coke bottle to silence the group: 'I stop you for the people's reports. Anyone who has a report from someone else should say it now. We've just started, there were no announcements yet.' Various women stepped up and apologised on behalf of those who were not present, 'Mandisa will be late, but she is coming'; 'Nomava is not feeling well'; 'Nobanzi too'; 'Peter is also coming but you all know he has a problem [often, having a problem means a death in the family]'; 'Nosandise said she will be late or maybe won't make it. She has a problem'. Manxotho then said, 'I mean, I'm doing this to keep the people calm in spirit. Now let us sing.' Pinky began clapping and singing a song that, like the previous one, emphasised protection:

So I wish I could walk
with you, king who has sympathy
to go up the hills
and the deepest darkness
Ma ma ma ma, etc.

When the song had finished, Linda kissed some of the participants (I was surprised by this display of affection because one never sees individuals kissing one another in public). The whole meeting very obviously revolved around Linda. Most of the time, she stood near the window and watched what was going on. just like most of the other women on their birthdays, she did not directly participate in the singing and talking, nor did she receive the money and gifts directly. The participants in the celebration expressed warmth, comfort, and protection by comparing Linda with a baby. One member provided this image: 'I greet the woman who is bathing [Linda]. I also saw her. Do not worry. I picked this money up, but the Lord loves me.' After saying this, she kissed Linda as another song started, 'Mercy came from Golgotha'.

The chairperson's language also cast Linda in the role of baby: 'Now, I am asking [sub] group A to come and wish the baby a happy birthday. I repeat, group A must come forward. Time goes quickly and we started late today.' After a song, the chairperson continued, 'Is this everyone from group A? Here is a paper with names of the people who owe. Come, group A. I do not even have money to prepare a place (*ukundlala*) for you guys.' To 'prepare a place' meant that one gives a small amount of money, mostly a few rand, before the bigger present was given. One by one, the members of group A came forward to prepare a place and to praise one another. For example, Pinky approached and offered R2 while reflecting on the importance of the group: 'With R2 I am asking everyone here to look at group A and their relationship with me. They are everything.' Having said this, Pinky then kissed all the members of group A. In addition, Nombuyiselo gave

R2 to prepare a place and she also kissed the members of group A. The mini-ceremony of 'preparing a place' was considered a game and a form of competition, with people trying to outdo one another in their contributions or the level of silliness of what they had to say. One member of group A, for example, approached and said: 'With R20, I will shake your hand.'

At last, all of the members of group A had made their contributions. Manxotho said: 'A is finished. Let us clap hands.' Hands were clapped in a pattern: two sets of three claps followed by a single clap. After group A had receded, the members of group B came forward. One of the members said she would not bathe Linda. Instead, she would pamper her and also take care of her like a baby. Nomyameko, also a member of group B, came forward with R40 and said: 'With R20 I shake a hand and with R20 I pay back. You [Linda] helped me so much.'

After group B had finished their offerings, the other groups contributed in the same way, so that all of the groups had their turns to offer praise and money to Linda. For example, a member of group D came forward to prepare a place and said:

> The people are surprised to see someone who is loved by many people. My name is Pamela Cwabe. Now I can feel that, oh God. My 'mother' is not here but my 'grandmother' is here. I am a 'granddaughter' of Nokoyo Nowethu. Oh! How beautiful my 'mother' is. Oh no, I don't want to mention my beloved 'grandmother'. When they said 'Happy' [the speaker's nickname], I thought they were going to read from the bible. I turned around to look and I felt I was myself. Noonde Dubisiko, Nokwanda, Sowati, and Mildred Mbhalo. I am Happy to my 'grandmother' Linda Notwala. Oh, oh, I hear your words. I wanted to preach but my 'mother' is gone with my spirit. I love my 'mother'. I cannot control myself. She is quiet, like me, and well structured, like me. I'll pay back an amount of R16 and enter with R5. You have helped me.

The whole meeting took more than four hours and constituted a stream of mutual compliments and a showy collection of money and presents for Linda. In this way, money was used to create and to demonstrate intimate relations of friendship between members, as well as to support the impression (or the 'illusion', it might be ventured) that all is safe for members of the Zolani Club.

However, the finale was still to come. While a 'child' was welcomed by her new 'mother', Thandi and a few other women entered the classroom and began to sing about the power of the blood of the lamb. During the song, some women drew up sheets and moved school desks in order to uncover Thandi's 'birthday present' in the corner of the classroom. It was a suite of furniture that included a double bed with a headboard, a bedside table, a dressing table, a mirror, and a duvet cover. Participants were astonished by this great present. Some of the women went to sit and recline on the bed while Thandi accompanied Linda to the bed and urged her to sit on it as well. Linda's 'sister' gave her a hug while Linda's husband, Benjamin, approached and sat next to Linda. Many cheered, screamed, and some even climbed on the school tables to make sure that their admiring view of the new bed was not obscured in any way. After some time, the chairperson provided the necessary closure: 'With one rand I want to say something. My stomach is sore. Let me say it again. My stomach is sore. Please, sit – like that. My stomach aches; these are my 'children'. This is my 'son' [referring to Linda's husband].' Thandi added: 'All organisations in the house and all our visitors, I thank you.'

More people arrived, though, and joined in the excitement. Another song began, 'Jesus cried tears'. The chairperson shouted to the newcomers:

> People and the organisation that come in now, we are playing here. We are playing for Linda Masekwana. Linda, come to your place [in front of the room] now so that the people can see you. Come, let us build the wall of Jerusalem'. The chairperson held up a birthday card that had been written for Linda and read it aloud, 'Again, a word from her daughter. Isaiah, Chapter 41, Verse 10: "Happy birthday, mum. Do not be afraid, for I am with you. From your child Mayoli".

'Now, let us ask what you have been eating on the road', she asked the newly arrived people. The crowd started singing again, but after some time the chairperson stopped them – again, by hitting the table loudly with her bottle. Many wished to say something, but now it was Thandi's turn. Before she could say anything, however, a 'child' prepared a place for Thandi to speak with an offering of R10: 'I want to prepare a place with R10 for the mother who is going to talk here.' It was very noisy, so the chairperson again had to urge people to be quiet: 'I am asking the dishes [in the back people were preparing a meal] not to make a noise when the 'mother' of the 'child' is going to speak. She is going to speak until blood comes out. I ask you and the chairs to be quiet!'

Thandi was at last allowed to speak:

> People, I greet the visitors. I greet Erik, my best friend. I greet Nokwanele, my child. Visitors, I have already greeted you and the club. At this moment my child [Linda] is standing in front of you. I am your mother. There is nothing I brought you except love. I only brought you love. You know that I love you. Listen to the words written in the book of Neimiah 2: 17. Those words, my child, are asking for help from you my children: "Come let us build the walls of Jerusalem". My mother [Nokwanda] is not here. With R100 I prepare for that thing I saw you were in need of.

After some interruptions – including that by the chairperson herself, who said 'you should know that person [Thandi] loves you' – Thandi continued: 'This present is from Nokwanda. Do not open it. You will open it at home.' While Thandi kissed and hugged Linda, the chairperson added, 'This is a present from your 'mother'. She wrote: "Happy birthday, my child". She really loves you.'

The celebration was almost finished. Participants admired the bed as they stood in line for the food and drinks that were offered (paid for by Linda and prepared by the group members). The secretaries were counting the money collected that day, and the chairperson announced the total amount:

> We are finished now! Listen now, do not make a noise! Sit down, I am going to talk to you inside the house and those who are outside. I will not speak loudly. I will use my normal voice, so *please*, do not make a noise, *please*, be quiet because I will not scream for those who are outside! It is R4,123. Okay, in the meantime we are finished, aren't we? Linda Masekwana's 'sister', stand up and come near me please. Please, give this money to Linda and tell her the members of Zolani Club have lent it to her.

Linda's 'sister' carried the money bowl to Linda while saying: 'I greet the organisation. I was sent by the organisation to give you this money. They said they lend you the money so please use it carefully.' The chairperson then took the money bowl from her and spoke again: 'To everyone including the visitors: Here is your money. I will not talk too much because I know you know you have to pay the people's money back. Linda, you are a housewife and do not let us hear that you are fighting with my son[7] because of this money. This is my son, do not play with him, do not fight over this money. This is other people's money. Do important things with this money.' She handed over the dish with the money to Linda who began singing of compassion and the end of sin.

For the first time that day, Linda had an opportunity to say something:

> I greet the club of Zolani and all my visitors inside and everyone in the house. I thank you. I won't cry today as I used to do. I thank you and next week I will do the same for someone else. Thank you, I will not cry. What you are doing is very nice and you must never change because when I joined this organisation I liked you. When I visited this organisation I saw this is an organisation that does not choose people but sings for everyone. I joined this organisation because I liked it and I will not leave it. Thank you.

Now, everyone was permitted to begin eating, drinking, and chatting and over the next few hours people began slowly to leave for their homes. Some, though, had to hurry home, because transport was difficult and dangerous, especially after seven o'clock in the evening.

In the ROSCA, money was constantly being changed into smaller coins and this allowed frequent, and relatively small, donations to be made regularly. This permitted maximum performance and attention within the ceremony with a relatively small amount of money (cf. Kiernan 1988: 460). The above account of this meeting shows that money in Zolani was used for mutual support. The quasi-kinship ties, the celebration of Linda's birthday, the constant gifts of money and presents, the metaphor of Linda as a baby surrounded by caring 'mothers' – it all demonstrated the mutual importance people felt for one another. If one limits the analysis to the activities at the meeting and what people would explicitly give as their reasons for participation in the activities, one does get the impression that the ROSCA is a socially constructive force. From this account, then, it is clear that poor African migrant women establish a home, a substantial sense of security, and

---

[7] Linda's husband was the chairperson's 'child'.

perhaps even a touch of euphoria, even as they reside in a new and dangerous city. Consumer products and money were pivotal to the creation of such an environment.

*After Linda's birthday*

A few days after Linda's birthday celebration, we heard from a member of Zolani Club that Linda was ill. She was hesitant to talk about the issue, but she suspected that Linda had been bewitched. The first question that came up was, of course, 'By whom?' She thought it might have been someone from within Zolani Club itself.

We visited Linda the very same day at her home. The place was very crowded with people – her husband, Benjamin, and her children, two of Linda's brothers, Benjamin's sister, and Thandi were all there. Linda was very confused. Her eyes blinked nervously, and – something highly unusual for her – she was moody and argued constantly with her husband. She told us that, at times, she was so happy and full of love, while, at other times, she was angry and used abusive language. Crowds especially made her cry and she had lost the desire to eat. She wanted to listen to gospel radio all the time and insisted on praying for people. She told us that she could see who needed help. At work, she would place her hands on colleagues and patients in order to pray for them. She almost lost her job because she had suddenly covered her supervisor's eyes with her hands while her supervisor was driving the company car.

After Linda had received the money from Zolani at her birthday celebration, she had lent money to anyone and everyone who asked for it. The amounts lent were as high as R500, and she hardly knew some of the borrowers. Because of her illness, she had even forgotten, in some cases, to whom she had lent the money, and it appeared that a lot of it would probably never be given back. Linda went to a doctor for medication.[8] He wrote a note, for the purposes of her employer, that Linda was suffering from anxiety and depression. Linda also consulted a diviner (*igqirha*), who indicated that there might be two causes for her illness. It might have been jealousy that made her ill (possibly the jealousy of a neighbour), or the illness/crisis could be a sign from the ancestors who wanted to urge Linda to become a diviner.

In the course of the next few weeks it became clear that there were a number of versions of what might be the problem with Linda and who might be responsible. In the rumours and gossip that circulated, notions of witchcraft were prominent. People started to wonder about who could be jealous of Linda and who might have harmed her. It became apparent that various individuals had different versions of

---

8 He prescribed her Betapan for sleeping, Ethipromine, and multivitamin pills. To me, the symptoms suggest that Linda was suffering from bipolar mania, also known as manic depression.

the truth according to their relationship with Linda. In many versions, the bed played a central role in explaining Linda's misfortune.

*The neighbour?*

In the past, Benjamin had had affairs with Linda's neighbour. It was not exactly clear, though, if the affair overlapped with, or was exclusive of, Benjamin's relationship with Linda. In any case, the tensions that this affair had caused between Linda and her husband had been expressed mostly indirectly. Now that Linda was ill, she insisted on medical attention, but her husband felt that this idea was nonsense. Instead, Benjamin proposed moving to another place (probably to avoid a sticky confrontation with the neighbour). However, Linda wanted to stay and, in my presence, told her husband the following:

> No. You are diabetic, you are sick. I am not going to Valkenburg Hospital [a mental hospital]. I will only go to the clinic, Lentegeur Hospital. I am not mad. I don't want to leave this place. I don't want to talk about it. I love my husband. The girls at work hate me because I tell them about Jesus.

Later she argued with her husband and told him, 'You shut up. Just go to your girlfriend', to which he replied: 'Stop it, else I might even go to her.'

That same day, Linda's brother shared an experience he had had. Linda had left the room when Linda's brother explained why he was temporarily staying at Linda's place. He had a fight with his wife, as well as with his girlfriend:

> I had a fight with my girlfriend who pressed charges against me. But when the police came to see me I was not at home. I was not hiding and I did try to find the inspector that handled the case but the case number was lost. They think I am running away, but I am not. I also had a fight with my wife. I took R15 from a vase, but my girlfriend said that I took R65. I did not, but when I took the R15 a R50 note fell out of the vase on the floor. I found it later and put it back in the vase, but my wife refuses to believe me: She insists on saying that I took R65 and returned the R50 later.

After having listened to the story, Thandi said that it was very bad to be married and also have a girlfriend and Linda's husband added: 'Your girlfriend is trying to end your marriage', which Linda's brother agreed with. Linda's brother tried to convey diplomatically to Linda's husband that he was also destroying his marriage because of his affair with the neighbour.

The suspicions of the affair were confirmed by an incident involving a radio. In December the previous year, Benjamin had sold the couple's radio to their neighbour without the consent or knowledge of his wife. I was told that this kind of transaction was unheard of because if a woman wanted to have something, she was supposed to ask another woman. Asking Benjamin for the radio – and especially keeping quiet about the transaction to Linda – was regarded as positive proof of a sexual relationship between them. The neighbour not only had the motive for bewitching Linda, but also had the opportunity to make Linda ill. She came to admire Linda's new bed, and she told Linda that she would have liked to buy it. But Linda and her husband refused to sell it because they wanted the bed for their place in Emaxhoseni. Some of Linda's friends pointed out that it was exactly at this point that Linda became ill.

Tension with the neighbours also became clear when Edith and I left after one of our visits. A group of young men were standing in front of the suspected neighbour's shack and one of them shouted: 'This white man should not come here anymore. Next time we will put a tyre around his neck and burn him.' Edith jokingly replied that they should not think this bothered us.

It was unclear what Linda thought about the allegations towards her neighbour, and her illness certainly did not make it any easier to get information from her. She did say that she used to be good friends with her neighbour, but now wanted to avoid her; she also added that she was angry about the affair. For a few days she stayed with Bukelwa, her 'twin sister' who lived a few blocks away, while at other times she insisted on staying at her own place. After a few weeks, Linda and her neighbour visited each other again and Linda told us she never suspected her neighbour of using witchcraft.

*Colleagues at work?*

Linda was very happy to start her temporary cleaning assignment at the hospital, especially in the light of the fact that local competition for jobs was so fierce. She got the job through a fellow member of the Independent Church who was a supervisor at the hospital. Linda was acting awkwardly, and bothering colleagues and patients alike with her praying, kissing, and talk of witchcraft. The white manager of the hospital had to take action so that she did lose her contract, 'I am a Christian myself', she explained to me when I phoned her, 'but this really scared me'. The manager first dismissed Linda, but was later willing to give her another chance to keep her job.

In the first two weeks of her illness, Linda accused some colleagues at work of employing witchcraft in order to take her job away. Linda's supervisor agreed with Linda on this and felt that Linda had a special gift:

> She can predict and see things. Linda told me that she was sure the bus would be on time that particular day. This is rare, because most of the time the bus is too late. She said she was going to pray for it. And the bus came on time! Also our colleagues at work use dirty medicine.

Linda could apparently see who took along 'dirty medicine' to practise their witchcraft, but the supervisor told Linda that the accusations she had made caused problems. Linda was also accused of using witchcraft, and people suspected that she rubbed her own 'dirty medicine' on people as she placed her hands upon them in prayer.

After a few weeks, when Linda had improved and had obtained a permanent position, she told us that the problems with her colleagues were now over. She had lied to her white manager that the laying on of hands was an old habit from church that she had stopped. The problem, Linda explained, was that one of her colleagues had a friend who was unemployed. This colleague was envious of Linda because of her job, and wanted Linda to vacate her job so that a space would open up for her friend. Linda was convinced that this colleague was a witch.

*Thandi?*

Implying that a person may be involved in witchcraft is a serious business. Being called a witch carries with it a tremendous stigma and the potential for ostracism. It can even lead, in some cases, to the accused being killed. Although I use a pseudonym in my writings, I still find it difficult to write down the suspicions regarding witchcraft that I heard and sensed about someone I know personally, like Thandi. The discourse on witchcraft is very powerful and potentially destructive.

The main current beneath the flow of rumour was this: who might want to harm Linda? Thandi told us that she did not believe in witchcraft. Instead, she explained, Linda had had a problem with her nerves – not only because of her husband's illness, but also because her sister had died a few weeks before. Thandi told us: 'I have more than Linda, but people are not jealous of me. There are demons of witchcraft. If you believe in it, it has power; but if you don't believe in it, like me, it doesn't have any effect on you.' Thandi's denial of witchcraft might be because the bed, after all, had been a gift from her. She did not want a diviner to investigate Linda's problems because she did not think witchcraft was the cause. Thandi's evasion of the witchcraft issue might, however, also be interpreted as an attempt to conceal her own role. As someone quizzically asked me: 'Why would Thandi say she doesn't believe in witchcraft?' My only response to this could be: 'Maybe because she is a witch?'

Some people expressed the view that it was someone within Zolani who harmed Linda. Such accusations were made very carefully, and no names were mentioned because many nearby were friends and quasi-kin. Talking too overtly about this would immediately implicate Thandi because she, after all, had given Linda the bed. Linda's sister-in-law thought that my videotaping of her birthday celebration had made some people envious and when Linda received the bed, many members within the group became emotional, excited, and perhaps even envious, as well. Many stood on the desks in the classroom and shouted, sang, and clapped.

A few weeks later, when Linda was feeling better, another link to Thandi became apparent. Linda showed us a tea set she had bought for the birthday of the Zolani Club's chairperson, who was also Benjamin's 'mother'. 'Last week', Linda confided to us,

> It was her birthday, but we couldn't attend the meeting. We will give her the present tomorrow and she will be very happy. People talk a lot and there must be a lot of rumours that we have not yet given her a present. People like to gossip, which is very irritating. There is also a lot of jealousy because some children are better treated than others. Especially 'mothers' – they can cause a lot of problems.

Edith and I both thought she was referring to her own 'mother', Thandi, but we did not dare ask for verification of our suspicions. The dependencies within Zolani Club and the complex quasi-kinship ties made it very difficult to discuss existing tensions and possible problems. Linda did say, though, that someone, or maybe even more than one person, within the Zolani Club was jealous of her new bed. She remembered how everyone had climbed upon the school desks, clapping and cheering. 'I did not feel good when this happened. I know they were jealous', she said. And on the videotape of the event, one could see the rapid flickering of her eyes.

*Linda's husband's family?*

In November 1998, about eight months after Linda's illness (and after I had returned to the Netherlands for four months), I again set out to meet members of Zolani. Although Linda's situation had improved, she was still not well and she still had the same symptoms from which she had suffered in March, although they had subsided somewhat. She was very quiet and introverted at times, but also talked a lot of nonsensical speech, repeating questions and at times rapidly flickering her eyes. We heard from one of her neighbours – Linda was not supposed to inform us of this herself – that her husband, Benjamin, had died the previous October due to the complications of his diabetes. We offered our condolences, and Linda started to cry (her tears were highly frowned upon by her friends).

The death of Linda's husband had led to a renewed round of witchcraft-related rumours. Later, at a barbecue attended by members of all of the organisations of Noluthando, Thandi assured us that there had been a lot of problems surrounding Benjamin's death. Linda and Benjamin had never been legally married, nor were they married according to Xhosa custom. There had never been any *lobola* payments made. However, according to Thandi, Benjamin's family recognised their relationship.[9] In any case, Linda was still legally married to the father of her two children. Although they had separated many years ago, they never legally divorced, and this had been what prevented Linda and Benjamin from marrying.

After Benjamin's death, Linda went to Emaxhoseni to attend the funeral among members of his family. This was a horrible experience for her, as they treated her badly (even trying to strangle her at one point). They accused her of killing

---

9 From an economic point of view, this makes sense, because the husband's family is burdened with paying *lobola*.

Benjamin for the money. Benjamin's employer had organised life insurance, which was due for payment to Linda upon his death. Linda's affines accused Linda of killing Benjamin for the insurance money, and claimed that the money was rightfully theirs. They forced her to go to the bank and withdraw money. They got hold of a total of R10,000, after which Linda managed to get word to the employer to stop depositing money in her account until she was back in Cape Town.[10] Linda's affines also wanted the celebrated bed that Linda had received from Thandi during her birthday celebration at Zolani. Benjamin's father's younger brother (*utata uncinci*, meaning 'little father') was especially aggressive towards Linda. Although previously Thandi had strongly denied any role possibly played by witchcraft, she was now convinced that Benjamin's family, fatally jealous of Linda and her new bed, had bewitched her.

## Conclusion

Together, participants in Zolani Club attempted to realise their desires, namely to have wealth and luxury, to be a baby, a caring mother, to have society without affines, to live in the solidarity and protection offered by 'the walls of Jerusalem', even in the midst of a dangerous and unstable society. The Zolani Club used money and consumption to create a social space where, even if only temporarily, women could forget the pains of their sometimes violent lives on the socio-economic margins. As the name suggests, the financial mutual was a place for *ukuzola* – 'to stay cool, to stay relaxed'. In the state of crisis experienced by many South Africans, an oasis of relaxation is a necessity rather than a luxury – a much-needed refuge that helped participants to manage their lives financially and socially.

In a situation of poverty, violence, and hardship, hope for a better future seemed to be important. The purchasing of consumer products that represented an affluent lifestyle, such as refrigerators, status furniture, cutlery, duvet covers, or body lotions revealed the ambition for a better future. The consumer products provided social and economic upward mobility and everybody who was in a position to buy these products would do so. Through consumption, the destitute and uprooted Xhosa migrants could distinguish themselves from the more desperate migrants around them. Consumption provided respect, prestige, and self-confidence to people who had to do without this most of the day. In line with

[10] I have heard more often about struggles over money after a death and the money always seemed to disappear or was appropriated by other kin. It was impossible for me to check this story and find out to what extent it was truth or more of a fantasy (about kin hiding money and wealth).

Bourdieu's argument, participants in financial mutuals forced each other into a consumption pattern associated with a higher class and comfortable life.

One needs, however, to sensitise a theory of consumption as well as financial mutuals to possible conflicts between people and the micro-political problems of distinction. While there is ample attention for conflict concerning the distribution of resources or productive forces of the economy, no theory on conflict and consumption has been properly developed. For example, Bourdieu's (1984) seminal work on consumption and distinction does not devote much space to an understanding of conflicts relating to consumption, reputation, and status.[11] Among the members of the financial mutuals, consumption was part of social conflict and competition between neighbours, kin, colleagues at work and fellow members of the organisation. Status and prestige were forms of inequality and could therefore cause social tensions. Furthermore, sharing and giving away consumer items could turn out to be a form of rivalry and competition. These two functions of consumer products – possessing and giving – were closely intertwined with financial mutuals. Possessing consumer products meant they could not be given away or shared, which could be regarded as selfish, unhelpful, and a form of distinction that was not appreciated. Giving away could also increase status and respect, but the objects of desire were lost, possessed by someone else, and giving was a way to gain power over others. The rumours surrounding Linda's illness revealed that power over others could be destructive and not necessarily constructive.

Linda's bed was the central focus of the accusations circulating about witchcraft. The bed was the most expensive present offered and it summarily became Linda's most valuable possession. The bed can be interpreted here as a symbol of intimacy – the intimacy between husband and wife, between Benjamin and his neighbour, between Linda and her neighbour, and between Linda and her quasi-kin, particularly her 'mother', Thandi. The intimacy of the object coincided with the intimacy at the core of both the positive *and* the negative in social relationships – in other words, mutual support and understanding *as well as* jealousy, envy, and rivalry.[12]

---

[11] An important exception is the rather philosophically oriented work on consumption by Bataille (1991).

[12] Comaroff & Comaroff (1999: 288) highlight the fierce generational opposition where the young are anxious about the wealth of the older generation and accuse them of witchcraft. Generational opposition, rivalry, and anxiety also exist among quasi-kin. 'Mothers' have to be careful to treat their 'daughters' in the right way and 'daughters' keep an eye on their 'mother' to make sure no 'daughter' is favoured above the others. However, among Xhosa migrants in Cape Town, generational opposition among quasi-kin is only one dimension of the witchcraft rumours. Witchcraft rumours also examine other dependencies, such as those between neighbours, 'siblings', in-laws, and colleagues at work.

However comforting it may be at times, the sense of protection and solidarity provided by these groups is far from all embracing. On the contrary, even these groups could only temporarily keep the dangerous outside world at bay. For some, the financial obligations stemming from membership of Zolani Club caused indebtedness and sleepless nights. This led, for example, to Linda's illness. Money and consumption were desirable, but also dangerous because they emphasise the inequalities between people who nonetheless depended on each other and invested in intimate mutual relationships. Rivalry among quasi-kin was a constant possibility, and 'mothers' had to be extremely careful not to evoke envy among their 'children'. The ambivalence of the quasi-kinship relations meant that within the organisation gossip and envy were just as likely as mutual support and understanding. Although consumption made it possible to create bonds of friendship and feelings of self-worth, it simultaneously led to envy, jealousy, and tensions among interdependent people. Consumption, therefore, could only partly fulfil people's hopes and dreams, only temporarily allowed for a boundary with the violence of the outside world, and meant that conflict was part of the acquisition of status and respect.

# 7

# Conclusion

## Transformations

A study of financial mutuals among Xhosa migrants captures pivotal changes in post-apartheid South Africa. It reveals the consequences of liberation from apartheid, such as massive migration, the state in its guise of development, and the formation of a neighbourhood by people who, during apartheid, were forced to live outside of the state in Bantustans. I examined the way in which destitute and uprooted people dealt with what which they lacked most, and which compelled them to go to South Africa's urban and industrial centres, namely money. They organised financial mutuals in order to manage money vis-à-vis kin, neighbours, and home-people. To women migrants it was essential – and more so than for the men – to influence the flows of money because these had such severe consequences for their relationships.

Flows of money had become part of interdependencies even during the colonial conquest. The introduction of the capitalist economy, along with diseases and natural disasters, virtually destroyed the Xhosa subsistence economy. Apartheid led to a further incorporation of Africans into a society in which they were forced to be marginal and were denied socio-economic and political freedoms. Money was introduced through wage labour, labour migration, taxation, and new forms of consumption, which subsequently altered kin relations.

From the 1980s onwards, popular protest, ongoing migration, and the limitations of state control made it possible for more Africans to live in industrial areas and cities such as Cape Town. In-between jobs and during vacations, migrants returned home with money and beautiful stories of Cape Town's wealth and riches. Even if people knew better than to believe such stories, poverty caused ever more people – women in particular – to earn some money in Cape Town to survive and to support kin. The change from a subsistence economy to an economy in which the capitalist mode of production was pivotal had drastic effects on people's relationships. Kinship dependencies changed because new sources of wealth challenged existing hierarchies. Conjugal, affinal, as well as consanguineal relations were full of tensions that frequently focused on the allocation of money. Flows of money played a pivotal role in the maintenance of sound relations. The lack of money therefore made it impossible to fulfil obligations and establish enduring satisfactory relations. Fatherhood was heavily contested, women's relations with affines were full of tensions concerning money, and intimate relations between men and women were mostly short-lived, unstable, and violent.

Labour migration led to a new type of identification centred on migrants from one area (*abakhaya*) who used to establish financial mutuals together. Unlike many other contemporary African societies (see for example Kane 2001b), the establishment of financial mutuals among fellow migrants became less important. The reason for Xhosa migrants to stop creating new financial mutuals among *abakhaya* was that *abakhaya* were not neighbours anymore. Apartheid legislation forced *abakhaya* to be neighbours. This, in turn, meant that there was sufficient social constraint among them to establish financial mutuals together. With the breakdown of apartheid legislation, *abakhaya* were no longer necessarily neighbours, which made it difficult for them to establish financial mutuals.

In the townships of post-apartheid South Africa, such as Indawo Yoxolo, neighbours – although they were new and unknown – could establish financial mutuals because of the physical proximity that was needed for social constraint. 'Neighbourhood' had become a social configuration that was distinct from kin and *abakhaya* relations. These three relationships (kin, *abakhaya* and neighbour) were precisely the relationships that people attempted to maintain, negotiate, or discard through participation in a financial mutual. By saving, accumulating, and sharing money in financial mutuals, the participants could negotiate flows of scarce amounts of money within and among their personal relationships. In other words, the neighbours established relations in financial mutuals that offered social constraint. This configuration ensured that a large sum of money was available at a specific time, which the participant could use for his or her own purposes and share with people she or he felt were important.

The circumstances in which neighbours established financial mutuals were far from favourable. One key problem was violence. A major cause of violence, although it was not the only one, was the presence of the post-apartheid state in its guise of development. The ideology of development differed vastly from its practices. The ANC wanted to overcome some inequalities of apartheid by developing housing, education, health, and so on. Development was an attempt to include into society those who had been excluded and marginalised in the past and to let them share in the joys of liberation. Instead of to liberation, the development processes, at least in Indawo Yoxolo, led to a system of control of 'communities', which policymakers falsely envisioned as homogenous and harmonious. A few 'community representatives' locally known as 'the Big Five' were in charge of the development projects and resorted to intimidation, corruption, and violence to get their work done and remain in power. Unsatisfied residents organised – fairly limited – opposition but, due to the continuous support the 'big men' received from the development institutions and political factions, this opposition was largely unsuccessful. It might be the case that the incorporation of some of the Big Five into local government, as has already taken place, eventually will cause a shift towards patronage in the future. Local political leaders may then attempt to bind clients by distributing resources in exchange for political support and not rely anymore on Mafia-style rule. However, it does not appear that the incorporation of 'big men' in local government will cause the violence to decrease.

What do these changes have to do with financial mutuals? The incorporation of colonial conquest, apartheid, violence and local politics into the analysis revealed a central reason for people to establish financial mutuals. Xhosa migrants made efforts to create an 'island' where one could feel secure, be appreciated as a fellow human being, and where it was possible to behave respectfully towards each other. The confinements of the relatively small, close-knit groups could function, at least to some extent, as a shield against the outside world and as a way to establish some kind of freedom through the management of scarce money.

It helps to compare relations with rubber bands tied in knots (see Goudsblom 1974 who uses the image of the air cushion). By establishing a new knot of rubber bands (a financial mutual) these rubber bands pull, as it were, on the members and force them to put the money in the group and put stress on other rubber bands (certain kin or neighbours). This, in turn, urges other people to do likewise. A person thus influences the strength of, and stress on, her or his 'rubber bands'. By allocating money (received from the financial mutual) to specific people, for specific purposes, and at specific times, 'rubber bands' are used to strengthen or stretch other 'rubber bands', and some might even snap altogether. This limited 'pulling', 'stretching', and 'snapping' of relations is the limited freedom that the management of money in mutuals provides for.

Unlike the Tswana independent church that Comaroff (1985) studied during the apartheid days, financial mutuals should not be regarded as a form of political resistance. Financial mutuals were migrants' attempts to withdraw from political life and to escape from the hostile environment, even if only temporarily, and deal with immediate concerns. The group had to provide protection against the hostile outside world, and to some extent it managed to do so. The close-knit web of relations in financial mutuals made it possible to separate oneself from the hostile world of political conflict, assault, unsatisfactory relations, and poverty. The density of the network also provided social constraint to self-constraint in that the participants 'forced' each other to hand over a contribution to the financial mutual. This made it possible to influence flows of money and relationships, and thus separate oneself from certain people.

Withdrawing into close-knit networks that deal with immediate concerns is not unique to the Xhosa migrants in Cape Town. Kiernan (1974: 82) found among Zulu Zionist churches that 'one of the foremost concerns … is to protect … against the township as an African community by drawing and maintaining boundaries setting off its membership from the rest of the population'. Similar contractions of relations around immediate concerns have been found in Brazil (Reis 1998), communist Poland (Sztomka 1999), and the DDR, as well as post-communist eastern Germany (Völker & Flap 1995).

What is typical for the Xhosa migrants in Cape Town was the particular concern around which these social configurations could emerge. In places such as Indawo Yoxolo there were virtually no churches and no sense of belonging. Rituals all took place in Emaxhoseni and male migrants, in particular, had to miss out on the status and sense of belonging that rituals provided. In Cape Town, people's kin were absent and kin were not a social configuration that was part of day-to-day life. Fatherhood was heavily contested and mothers often had to send their children to kin in Emaxhoseni. Local politics were characterised by violence and did not provide prestige or a dense social network in which daily concerns could be managed, at least for most migrants. The migrants organised themselves around money because it was so important to their lives and because nothing else was available. There were no unions or other workers' organisations, no age-based groups or ethnically based societies, and no soccer clubs. The migrants worried about money and money was the main resource around which they organised their lives.

The lack of alternatives was also evident in the migrants' morals. Money was so pivotal to the lives of Xhosa migrants that values, morals, social boundaries and interdependencies could only crystallise around money. It was for money that the migrants had come to Cape Town, it was money which they lacked most, and it was money that was at the core of their relations.

## Ambivalence

There was an innate downside to the way in which the Xhosa migrants managed money and social relations. They tried to close themselves off from the threats and dangers surrounding them by establishing close-knit networks in financial mutuals.

The close-knit networks increased the interdependencies of the members, which made these relations prone to ambivalent feelings. Such strong and contradictory feelings – friendship, support, warmth, but also rivalry, jealousy, and distrust – meant that there were also conflicts between members. Many of people's problems that participation in a financial mutual was supposed to solve – such as poverty, insecurity, uprootedness, violence, and people's claims on money – were thus reproduced within the group and around the group's participants. If one looks beyond the ideology of financial mutuals, and instead examines specific cases, it becomes apparent that tensions, rivalry, competition, and jealousy were inherent in this social configuration. Participants who, in many respects, care for one another and like one another had simultaneously harboured hostile feelings towards one another. In her study of ROSCAs among Surinamese Creole women in Amsterdam, Van Wetering (1999: 73) rightly poses critical questions on the interpretations of cultural practices as 'resistance' and instead reveals the ambivalences embedded in these relations.

That contradictory feelings were part of financial mutuals comes to the fore in a wide array of relations and social situations. These are the dynamics of gender, women's participation and kin, the establishment of social boundaries in relation to three core values (helping each other, taking care of oneself, respect), the inability to trust others – and oneself – completely, and the mixed feelings that accompanied consumption. If one closely examines these dimensions of financial mutuals, it becomes clear that all these dimensions of financial mutuals were fraught with ambivalence.

Financial mutuals allowed women in particular to control their money and thus have power over relations. They had to deal with the demands of boyfriends or husbands, with needs of, and claims by, the extended family, with the responsibility over children and with requests for money from neighbours. These claims were mostly legitimate, but they just did not have enough money. Because money had an impact on the kind of relationships migrants had, redirecting flows of money created tensions. The social constraint to self-constraint vis-à-vis the other financial mutual members made it possible to ignore certain claims. One could not share because the money was 'locked up' in the financial mutual. At a certain time, money became available and one could have some say as to what, with whom, and when to share. The money could be spent with people with whom one wanted to associate and invest in particular relationships. Women spent money on their own children and first-degree female relatives, while they tried to avoid claims from within their own extended kinship network, claims by boyfriends/husbands, and by in-laws. The women's attempts at managing flows of money were not unchallenged and contributed to ambivalent, and sometimes outright hostile, feelings vis-à-vis kin and neighbours.

The three key values (helping each other, taking care of oneself, and respect) that were central to the creation of social boundaries, were just as ambivalent. In order to establish and maintain proper relationships, it was of the utmost importance to show respect. For some people, however, it was very difficult to reciprocate respect. The very poor and marginal had to live off begging and cheating, deal with violence and alcoholism, and frequently suffered from mental problems. In such circumstances, it was impossible to show respect. The poorest did not form a separate class, and were not even very different from other neighbours. Maybe some slightly better off neighbours had once been exactly like these bothersome and destitute neighbours, or realised that they might well become like them should misfortune cross their paths. This identification process meant that the 'irritating poor' were not completely neglected, but somewhat included and taken care of. But this solidarity had its limitations.

In addition to disidentification – a contempt towards the poorest neighbours – (de Swaan 1997) people had only few financial means for solidarity. They were unable to treat everybody respectfully or help them all the time. There were too many people with severe problems and too little money to help them, while people also needed to take care of themselves. The choices were difficult, stressful, and contestable. The identification and disidentification processes with the neighbouring poor led to ambivalent social configurations and reluctant solidarity.

Ambivalence was also important in order to understand trust. Participants entrusted their money to fellow members and knew that they risked not receiving it back. The threatening triad of violence, economic insecurity, and volatile relations meant that there was a great deal of distrust in society. Members tried to contain risks in financial mutuals and tried to establish trust within the financial mutuals. Nevertheless the risks for default, or theft, could never be avoided completely. Members did not co-operate because they entirely trusted each other and it was often violence, rumour, confiscation of property, and social constraint that limited the risks. Financial mutuals did not have the capacity to create trust beyond the vicinity of the neighbours whose door one could see. Even those living only a few dozen metres away, at most, were not trusted completely.

The participants co-operated without much trust in each other because they realised that it was their only option. They were aware of their own capability to support as well as harm others. They knew that there was always the risk of witchcraft, jealousy, and envy within interdependencies. The few, yet significant, cases of self-confessed witchcraft revealed that people knew that they themselves, maybe without wanting to do so, could be evil and harm others. Distrust was inevitably part of life because people were aware that relations encompassed good *and* evil. The ambivalent relations meant that trust could never be established completely and participants co-operated in financial mutuals without completely trusting others, and even themselves.

The phenomenon of consumption was also vulnerable to social conflict, jealousy and rivalry. Through consumption, made possible by financial mutuals, people could strive for a better lifestyle, self-worth and respect. A bigger house, a cellular phone, or furniture showed that one belonged to 'a higher class', as neighbours told me. Consumption at funerals and initiations, just like the many goods that migrants took along on their visits home, were part of a person's status in society, and evoked respect. For that reason – i.e. using consumption to increase one's status – it led to social tensions. Accumulation was at odds with sharing, which evoked friction among interdependent people. Moreover, the act of giving consumer products and money could be an aggressive one. It forced the fellow member to reciprocate with a counter gift of at least the same value, even if that person could not afford it. The interdependencies that were established by giving and receiving created not only friendship, solidarity and self-esteem, but also jealousy, rivalry and rumours about witchcraft.

To sum up, financial mutuals were an attempt by Xhosa migrants to close themselves off from the violence, economic insecurity, and anxiety that surrounded them. By withdrawing into a close-knit web of relations, they hoped to keep the outside world at bay and create positive relations. They used money, being the reason why they had come to Cape Town, to increase their control over their lives, to create social boundaries, intimacy, solidarity, self-worth and friendship. However, the interdependencies that were part of financial mutuals, and actually needed for social constraint, meant that aspects of the ugly outside world were incorporated into the financial mutual. The interdependencies within the financial mutuals, as well as the influence of financial mutuals on the migrants' interdependencies with kin and people living in proximity, gave rise to ambivalent relations. It was not possible to completely control money, or have complete power over relations with others, or over oneself. Financial mutuals were, therefore, the backdrops to rivalry, distrust, jealousy and frictions as well as islands of solidarity, trust, and friendship. Thus, poverty did not result in extensive unifying bonds of solidarity, but in small bonds of ambivalence.

## Experience as methodology

Research among uprooted African migrants who lived in violent and insecure circumstances had its obvious methodological constraints. It is important to reflect on these methodological constraints because they are so much part of the insights that emerged during the course of the research. Methodology is not simply a 'tool' that can be separated from the insights that it generates. The reason for focusing on methodology in the conclusion is that it is intrinsically linked to the insights that I was able to gain during the research.

Instead of ignoring such constraints, or even worse, ignoring the many Africans that try to make a life in South Africa's urban and industrial centres, these methodological issues have to be made explicit. Quantitative ways of gathering information, such as surveys, were impossible because of the level of distrust and my inability to move about freely. Qualitative research methods were also limited. The extent to which I could participate in the lives of Xhosa migrants was severely restricted. I was often dependent on a few people, particularly on my research assistant, and although I could not do the research without them, these dependencies also had their drawbacks. Due to violence and my dependency on people, I had to adjust the course of the research, not always advantageously.

In a world where violence and conflict are part of the lives of many, the methodology issues of research in dangerous situations have to be addressed more thoroughly than is currently the case. If social sciences fail to address these issues, they will leave substantial parts of the world population aside and neglect a broad array of social phenomena. Research institutes have to pay more attention to the repercussions of neglecting violence, or of restricting one's academic interest to studying only a limited number of places and phenomena in the world. My experience was that the budgetary constraints of researchers and research institutions make it difficult to uphold necessary standards of safety. For example, it was difficult for me to negotiate funds to ensure that I had a car and did not need to do research on the scooter that I was initially offered. In research institutes, it should be common practice to concentrate on safety and security in a structured way and learn from the experiences of fellow researchers. Consultation or 'debriefing' of those returning from the field is a service which is not provided at universities and research institutes, unlike other professional organisations that have people working in (potentially) violent circumstances. Moreover, I was initially inclined to downplay the risks of the research myself, so that it would not be branded unfeasible. Instead of avoiding these issues and restricting the scope of social sciences, a lively debate on methodological issues and responsibilities is needed.

Notwithstanding the constraints that violence imposed, the qualitative research that I did, particularly case studies and limited participant observation, was well suited to bringing the dynamics of financial mutuals to the fore. Especially my own experiences as a researcher, which I have tried to make explicit, provided central insights. Let me clarify how experiences drew my attention to the migrants' attempts to close themselves off from society, as well as the ambivalence within interdependent relations.

During the research I started to perceive my environment differently. As Green (1995: 108) aptly put it:

> Gradually I became to realize that terror's power, its matter-of-factness, is exactly about doubting one's own perceptions of reality. The routinization of terror is what fuels its

> power. Routinization allows people to live in a chronic state of fear with a facade of normalcy at the same time that terror permeates and shreds the social fabric.

I realised that I tried to distinguished between 'real risks' and 'acceptable risks', and tried to identify unjustified paranoia. Although some places and situations surely were more dangerous than others, I started to realise that 'real risks', 'acceptable risk', and 'safety' were socially constructed categories. Conversations about risks, dangers, and safety were actually an attempt to control the dangers and imagine that there were spaces that were not violent. As became apparent during my work on this thesis, these spaces did not exist, at least not for Xhosa migrants, but the distinctions were nevertheless important. For me, as a fairly well protected researcher, it was also a relief to be able to envision spaces and situations that were safe. It helped me to legitimise the research to others and provided a sense of security, which to some extent was false.

This experience allowed me to appreciate the fact that migrants used financial mutuals in a similar fashion. They were a way to construct a safe and secure environment, even if that was to a large extent imagined. It was part of the management of normality (see De Swaan 1990 on the concept in a different context). Through my definitions of 'safety', 'real risks', and 'acceptable risks', I was doing the same as Xhosa migrants. The realisation that feelings of safety were largely a social construction, albeit a vital one, allowed me to enquire further along these lines and appreciate what the consequences of violence were for the migrants' life.

Furthermore, I initially found that the politics and violence in Indawo Yoxolo, as described in chapter three, put severe constraints on the research. It was an obstacle that prevented me from studying financial mutuals. In retrospect, however, I wonder how I could even have attempted to neglect the importance of violence for the organisation of financial mutuals. It was actually a defensive strategy against anxiety-inducing experiences (see Devereux 1967: 83). I tried to ignore violence because it was unsettling and disturbing. Just like the Xhosa migrants, I attempted to shut out violence and politics. The residents of Indawo Yoxolo did the same and had even more reasons to try and shield themselves against the horrific living conditions and the fears and anxieties that these brought about. They also tried to use financial mutuals for that purpose. Conceptually, I could turn the obstacles of violence and political manoeuvring – that were preventing me from studying financial mutuals – around and regard them as key sources of information about these mutuals. The importance of violence in the analysis of financial mutuals initially revealed itself through experience. My experience – of my own attempts to isolate from violence and unsettling events – made me sensitive to a major function of financial mutuals for Xhosa migrants and enabled me to pursue this theme in conversations and case studies.

The pivotal place of ambivalence for the analysis of financial mutuals was also apparent from my own experiences. The constraints that violence put on my research consequently meant that I was very dependent on others. I could not decide for myself where to walk, nor whom to talk with and at the time of day that was convenient to me. The violence made me more dependent on others than fieldwork under safe and relaxed circumstances would have done. Some also depended on me, and through this I experienced the ambivalent feelings that were part of such interdependencies. I was sometimes irritated by the way Africans perceived me, or tired of trying to challenge racial boundaries, just like the migrants in Cape Town sometimes expressed their feelings of resentfulness to me, a White, rich, and nosy man with a car. At the same time, my dependency on the people among whom I did the research meant that I really appreciated their willingness to help me with the research and cherished their friendship and support. This was particularly so vis-à-vis my research assistant Edith. This inspired me to wonder whether participants of financial mutuals had to deal with feelings of ambivalence towards each other. The interdependencies meant that sometimes I would irritate them, and they would irritate me. After all, that was what co-operation, even for this thesis, was all about. Even if I liked certain people very much and valued the relationship, I could still have mixed feelings towards them. Conversations and case studies revealed that this was central to their organisations and understanding of social relations in a hostile environment.

These experiences were a useful start, but not enough in themselves. They allowed me to explore avenues that, had I not undertaken fieldwork or ignored uncomfortable experiences, would have remained indiscernible. Experiences, therefore, have to be made explicit – and all too often they are not – and the researcher should reveal how they provided insight into people's actions, and their motives (cf. Devereux 1967; Hastrup 1993, 1995; Jenkins 1994; Van de Port 1998; 1999; Thoden van Velzen & Van Wetering 1991; Thoden van Velzen 1995). The scope of social science is limited if experiences are disregarded, neglected, or concealed. Experience is a precious methodology that needs to be developed further because, if one fails to do so, particular dimensions of social phenomena will be left unexamined.

# References


ADAMS, D.W. & D.A. FITCHHETT, eds. (1992), *Informal finance in low-income countries*. Boulder: Westview Press.

ANC (1994), *The reconstruction and development programme: A policy framework*. Johannesburg: Umanyano.

APPADURAI, ARJUN (1986), Introduction: commodities and the politics of value. In: A. Appadurai, ed., *The social life of things: Commodities in cultural perspective*, pp. 3-63. Cambridge: Cambridge University Press.

APPADURAI, ARJUN (1997), *Modernity at large: Cultural dimensions of globalization*. Minnesota and London: University of Minnesota Press.

ARDENER, SHIRLEY (1995), Women making money go round: ROSCAs revisited. In: S. Ardener & S. Burman, eds., *Money-Go-Rounds; The importance of rotating savings and credit associations for women*, pp. 1-19. Oxford and Washington D.C.: Berg.

ARDENER, SHIRLEY & SANDRA BURMAN, eds. (1995), *Money-Go-Rounds; The importance of rotating savings and credit associations for women*. Oxford and Washington D.C.: Berg.

BÄHRE, ERIK (1996), *"We organise each other": Financial self-help groups and civics in the Townships of Cape Town, South Africa*. Masters thesis, Utrecht University.

BÄHRE, ERIK (2000), The price of a bed: Migrants and money in Cape Town. *Etnofoor* XII(2): 55-77.

BÄHRE, ERIK (2001), Housing for the urban poor in Cape Town: A post-apartheid dream or nightmare? *Global Built Environment Review* 1(1): 33-44.

BÄHRE, ERIK (2002a), *Money and violence: Financial mutuals among the Xhosa in Cape Town, South Africa*. PhD thesis, University of Amsterdam.

BÄHRE, ERIK (2002b), Witchcraft and the exchange of sex, blood, and money among Africans in Cape Town, South Africa. *Journal of Religion in Africa* 32: 300-334.

BÄHRE, ERIK (2005). How to ignore corruption: Presenting the shortcomings of development in South Africa. *Current Anthropology* 46(1): 107-113 & 117-120.

BÄHRE, ERIK & PEER SMETS (1999), Counting on people: Trust and control in ROSCAs. In: P. Smets, H. Wels & J.van Loon, eds., *Trust and Co-operation; symbolic exchanges and moral economies in an age of cultural differentiation*, pp. 51-66. Amsterdam: Spinhuis.

BAILEY, FREDERICK GEORGE (1971), *Gift and poison: The politics of reputation*. Oxford: Blackwell.

BAYART, J.-F. (1993), *The state in Africa: The politics of the belly*. London/New York: Longman.

BANFIELD, EDWARD (1958), *The moral basis of a backward society*. New York: Free Press.

BANK, LESLIE (1997), The social life of paraffin: Gender, domesticity and the politics of value in a South African Township. *African Studies* 56(2): 157-179.

BANK, LESLIE (1999), Men with cookers: Transformations in migrant culture, domesticity and identity in Duncan Village, East London. *Journal of Southern African Studies* 25(3): 393-416.

BARTH, FREDRIK (1959), Segmentary opposition and the theory of games: A study of Pathan Organization. *Journal of the Royal Anthropological Institute* 89: 5-21.

BATAILLE, GEORGES (1991), *The accursed share: An essay on general economy*, volume 1: Consumption. New York: Zone Books.

BATTLE, MICHAEL (1997), *Reconciliation: The ubuntu theology of Desmond Tutu*. Cleveland, Ohio: The Pilgrim Press.

BAUMAN, ZYGMUNT (2001), *Community: Seeking safety in an insecure world.* Cambridge: Polity Press.

BBC World: Africa (1999), *Sexual violence on the rise in South Africa*, Vol. 1999: BBC News.

BEBBINGTON, A. (1999), Capitals and capabilities: A framework for analyzing peasant viability, rural livelihoods and poverty. *World Development* 27(12): 2021-2044.

BEINART, WILLIAM (1982), *The political economy of Pondoland 1860-1930*. Cambridge: Cambridge University Press.

BENDA-BECKMANN, FRANZ & KEEBE BENDA-BECKMANN (1994), Coping with insecurity. *Focaal* 22/23: 7-31.

BIJNAAR, ASPHA (1998), Wat je zaait, zal je oogsten! Dwang en zelfdwang in Creools-Surinaamse onderlinges. *Amsterdams Sociologisch Tijdschrift* 25(3): 329-370.

BIJNAAR, ASPHA (2002), *Kasmoni: Spaarzame levensgenieters in Suriname en Nederland.* PhD thesis, University of Amsterdam.

BLOCH, MAURICE & JONATHAN PARRY (1989), Introduction: Money and the morality of exchange. In: M. Bloch & J. Parry eds., *Money and the morality of exchange*, pp. 1-32. Cambridge: Cambridge University Press.

BONNER, PHILIP (1990), The politics of black squatter movements on the rand, 1944-1952. *Radical History Review* 46(7): 92-94.

BONNER, PHILIP (1995), African urbanisation on the Rand between the 1930s and 1960s: Its social character and political consequences. *Journal of Southern African Studies* 21(1): 115-129.

BOUMAN, F.J.A. (1978), The ROSCA: Financial technology of an informal savings and credit institution in developing economies. *Savings and Development* 4(3): 253-276.

BOUMAN, F.J.A. (1994b), ROSCA & ASCRA: Beyond the financial landscape. In: F.J.A. Bouman & O. Hospes, eds., *Financial landscapes reconstructed: The fine art of mapping development*, pp. 375-394. Boulder: Westview Press.

BOUMAN, F.J.A. (1994a), Informal rural finance: An Aladdin's lamp of information. In: F.J.A. Bouman & O. Hospes, eds., *Financial landscapes reconstructed: The fine art of mapping development*, pp. 105-122. Boulder: Westview Press.

BOUMAN, F.J.A. & OTTO HOSPES, eds. (1994), *Financial landscapes reconstructed: The fine art of mapping development*. Boulder: Westview Press.

BOURDIEU, PIERRE (1984), *Distinction: A social critique on the judgement of taste.* London: Routledge.

BOURDIEU, PIERRE (1992), *Opstellen over smaak, habitus en het veldbegrip*, gekozen door Dick Pels. Amsterdam: Van Gennep.

BUIJS, GINA & GLEN ATHERFOLD (1995), *Savings and money-lending schemes: How rotating credit associations help poor families*. Pretoria: Human Science Research Council.

BUNDY, COLIN (1979), *The rise and fall of the South African peasantry*. London: Heinemann.

BURGWAL, GERRIT (1995), *Struggle of the poor; Neighborhood organization and clientelist practice in a Quita squatter settlement*. PhD thesis, University of Amsterdam.

BURKE, THIMOTHY (1996), *Lifeboy men, lux women: Commodification, consumption, and cleanliness in modern Zimbabwe*. London: Leicester University Press.

BURMAN, SANDRA & NOZIPHO LEMBETE (1995), Building new realities: African women and ROSCAs in Urban South Africa. In: S. Ardener & S. Burman, eds., *Money-Go-Rounds: The importance of rotating savings and credit associations for Women*, pp. 23-47. Oxford: Berg.

BURMAN, SANDRA & PAMELA REYNOLDS, eds. (1986), *Growing up in a divided society: The contexts of childhood in South Africa*. Johannesburg: Ravan Press.

CARTER, G.M. (1986), The republic of South Africa: White political control within the African Continent. In: P.M. Martin & P.O. O'Meara, eds., *Africa*, pp. 343-359. Bloomington: Indiana University Press.

CLARK, L & J NGOVESE (1975), *Women without men*. Durban: Institute for Black Research.

CMC (CAPE METROPOLITAN COUNCIL) (2001), *A socio-economic profile of the Cape Metropolitan Area*: Cape Metropolitan Council.

COCK, JACKLYN (1980), *Maids and madams: A study in the politics of exploitation*. Johannesburg: Ravan Press.

COLE, JOSETTE (1987), *Crossroads: The politics of reform and repression 1976/1986*. Johannesburg: Ravan Press.

COLEMAN, J.C. (1990), *Foundations of social theory*. Cambridge, Mass.: Harvard University Press.

COMAROFF, JEAN (1985), *Body of power, spirit of resistance. The culture and history of a South African people*. Chicago and London: University of Chicago Press.

COMAROFF, JEAN & JOHN L. COMAROFF (1990), Goodly beasts, beastly goods: Cattle and commodities in a South African context. *American Ethnologist* 17(2): 195-216.

COMAROFF, JEAN & JOHN L. COMAROFF, eds. (1993), *Modernity and its malcontents: Ritual and power in postcolonial Africa*. Chicago and London: University of Chicago Press.

COMAROFF, JEAN & JOHN L. COMAROFF, (1999), Occult economies and the violence of abstraction: Notes from the South African postcolony. *American Ethnologist* 26(2): 279-303.

COMAROFF, JEAN & JOHN L. COMAROFF, eds. (2000), *Millennial capitalism and the culture of Neoliberalism* (Special issue of Public Culture). Duke University Press.

COMAROFF, JOHN L. & JEAN COMAROFF (1987), The madman and the migrant: Work and labor in the historical consciousness of a South African people. *American Ethnologist* 14: 191-209.

CROZIER, MICHEL & ERHARD FRIEDBERG (1977), *Actors and systems: The politics of collective action*. Chicago and London: University of Chicago Press.

CRUSH, JONATHAN (1995), *Power of development*. London: Routledge.

DAVENPORT, T.R.H. (1969), African townsmen? South African urban areas legislation. *African Affairs* 68(271): 95-109.

DELIUS, PETER (1993), Migrant organisation, the Communist Party, the ANC and the Sekhukhuneland revolt, 1940-1958. In: P.D.P. Bonner & D. Posel, eds., *Apartheid's Genesis: 1935-1962*, pp. 126-159. Braamfontein, Johannesburg: Ravan Press, Witwatersrand University Press.

DE SWAAN, ABRAHAM (1990), *Management of normality: Critical essays in health and welfare*. London and New York: Routledge.

DE SWAAN, ABRAHAM (1995), Widening circles of identification: Emotional concerns in sociogenetic perspective. *Theory, Culture and Society* 12: 25-39.

DE SWAAN, ABRAHAM (1996a), *Zorg en de staat: Welzijn, onderwijs en gezondheidszorg in Europa en de Verenigde Staten in de nieuwe tijd*. Amsterdam: Bert Bakker.

DE SWAAN, ABRAHAM (1996), Onderlinges toen en nu, hier en daar. Informele spaar- en verzekeringskassen in het negentiende-eeuwse Westen en in de tegenwoordige buiten-westerse wereld. In: M.v.d. Linden & J. Sluijs, eds., *Onderlinge hulpfondsen: Historische en etnografische essays*, pp. 9-22. Amsterdam: Stichting Beheer IISG.

DE SWAAN, ABRAHAM (1997), Widening circles of disidentification: On the psycho- and sociogenesis of the hatred of distant strangers – Reflections on Rwanda. *Theory, Culture and Society* 14(2): 105-122.

DE SWAAN, ABRAHAM (2000), *De mensenmaatschappij: Een inleiding*. Amsterdam: Bert Bakker.

DEVEREUX, GEORGE (1967), *From anxiety to method in the behavioral sciences*. The Hague and Paris: Mouton & Co.

ELIAS, NORBERT & JOHN L. SCOTSON (1965), *The established and the outsiders*. London: Frank Cass.

ESCOBAR, ARTURO (1991), Anthropology and the development encounter: The making and marketing of development anthropology. *American Ethnologist* 18: 658-682.

FAKIR, SALIEM (1999), Community projects drown in ideology. In: *Mail and guardian*.

FERGUSON, JAMES (1990), *The anti-politics machine: 'Development', depolitication and bureaucratic state power in Lesotho*. Cambridge: Cambridge University Press.

FINE, BEN (1999), The development state is dead – long live social capital. *Development and Change* 30: 1-19.

FISIY, CYPRIAN & PETER GESCHIERE (1996), Witchcraft, violence and identity: Different trajectories in postcolonial Cameroon. In: R. Werbner and T. Ranger, eds., *Post-colonial identities in Africa,* pp. 193-221. London and New Yersey: Zed Books.

FORTES, MEYER (1983) [1959], *Oedipus and job in West African religion*. Cambridge: Cambridge University Press.

FREUD, SIGMUND (1984), *Totem en taboe*. W. Oranje & R. Starke, transl. Amsterdam: Boom Meppel.

FUNG, A. (2003). Associations and democracy: Between theories, hopes, and realities. *Annual Review of Sociology* 29 (1): 515-539.

GAMBETTA, DIEGO (1988), Can we trust trust? In: D. Gambetta, ed., *Trust: Making and breaking cooperative relations*. Oxford: Blackwell.

GARDNER, JANE (1835) Statement of 13.1.1825: *Parliamentary Papers,* xxxix(50).

GEERTZ, CLIFFORD (1962), The rotating credit association: A "Middle Rung" in development. *Economic Development and Cultural Change* 10: 241-263.

GESCHIERE, PETER (1983), Bruidsprijzen bij de Maka in Kameroen: Marxistiese theorieën en de praktijk van antropologies veldwerk. *Ter Elfder Ure* 26(3): 604-638.

GESCHIERE, PETER (1997), *The modernity of witchcraft: Politics and the occult in postcolonial Africa*. Charlottesville and London: University Press of Virginia.

GLUCKMAN, MAX (1971), *Analysis of a social situation in modern Zululand*, Volume 28. Manchester: Manchester University Press.

GOLDIN, IAN (1987), *Making race: The politics and economics of coloured identity in South Africa*. Maskew Miller Longman.

GORDON, R.J. & A.D. SPIEGEL (1993), Southern Africa revisited. *Annual Review of Anthropology* 22: 83-105.

GOUDSBLOM, JOHAN (1974), *Balans van de sociologie*. Utrecht, Antwerpen: Het Spectrum.

GOULDNER, ALVIN W. (1973), *For sociology: Renewal and critique in sociology today*. London: Allen Lane.

GRANOVETTER, MARK S. (1973), The strength of weak ties. *American Journal of Sociology* 78(6): 1360-1380.

GREEN, LINDA (1995), Living in a state of fear. In: C. Nordstrom & A.C.G.M. Robben, eds., *Fieldwork under fire: Contemporary studies of violence and survival*, pp. 105-127. Berkeley, Los Angeles, London: University of California Press.

GUYER, JANE I., ed. (1995), *Money matters: Instability, values and social payments in the modern history of West African communities*. Portsmouth and London: Heinemann & James Currey.

GUYER, JANE I., ed. (1999), *Marginal gains: Monetary transactions in Atlantic Africa*. Chicago and London, University of Chicago Press.

HAMMOND-TOOKE, W.D. (1962), *Bhaca society: A people of the Transkeian Uplands, South Africa*. Cape Town, London, New York: Oxford University Press.

HAMMOND-TOOKE, W.D. (1970), Urbanization and the interpretation of misfortune: A quantitative analysis. *Africa* XL(1): 25-39.

HAMMOND-TOOKE, W.D. (1997), *Imperfect interpreters: South Africa's anthropologists, 1920-1990*. Johannesburg: Witwatersrand University Press.

HAMMOND-TOOKE, W.D. (1998), African renaissance and African religion: The South African case. *Aambeeld* 26(2): 17-20.

HARDIN, R. (1993), The street-level epistemology of trust. *Politics and Society* 21(4): 505-529.

HASHATSE, LEBOGANG (1992), Andrew Lukhele: The New Empowerment. *Tribute September* 36-40.

HASTRUP, KIRSTEN (1993), Hunger and the hardness of facts. *Man* 28(4): 727-739.

HASTRUP, KIRSTEN (1995), *A Passage to anthropology: Between experience and theory*. London and New York: Routledge.

HECHTER, MICHAEL (1987), *Principles of group solidarity*. Berkeley, Los Angeles, London: University of California Press.

HEIDHEUS, FRANZ (1994), Consumption credit in rural financial market development. In: F.J.A. Bouman & O. Hospes, eds., *Financial landscapes reconstructed: The fine art of mapping development*, pp. 33-48. Boulder: Westview Press.

HELLMAN, ELLEN (1934), The importance of beer-brewing in an urban native yard. *Bantu Studies* 8: 38-60.

HOSPES, OTTO (1997), New studies on informal finance: Exploring the-state-of-the-art and the art of the state. *Savings and Development* XXI(1): 5-18.

HOWE, LEO (1998), Scrounger, worker, beggarman, cheat: The dynamics of unemployement and the politics of resistance in Belfast. *Journal of the Royal Anthropological Institute* 4(3): 531-550.

HUNTER, MONICA (1933), The effects of contact with Europeans on the status of Pondo women. *Africa* VI: 259-276.

HUNTER, MONICA (1979), *Reaction to conquest: Effects of contact with Europeans on the pondo of South Africa*. Cape Town: David Philip.

HUTCHINSON, SHARON E. (1996), *Nuer dilemmas: Coping with money, war and the state.* Berkeley and Los Angeles: Universityof California Press.

JAMES, DEBORAH (1997), Anthropology, history and the making of past and place. *African Studies* 56(2): 115-136.

JAMES, DEBORAH (1999a), *Bagagsu* (those of my home): Women migrants, ethnicity, and performance in South Africa. *American Ethnologist* 26(1): 69-89.

JAMES, DEBORAH (1999b), *Songs of the women migrants: Performance and identity in South Africa*. London: Edinburgh University Press.

JENKINS, TIMOTHY (1994), Fieldwork and the perception of everyday life. *Man* 29(2): 433-455.

JONES, SEAN (1993), *Assaulting childhood: Children's experiences of migrancy and hostel life in South Africa*. Johannesburg: Witwatersrand University Press.

KANE, ABDOULAYE (2001a), *Les cameleons de la finance populaire au Senegal et dans la diaspora: Dynamique des tontines et des caisses villageoises entre Thilogne, Dakar et La France*. PhD thesis, University of Amsterdam.

KANE, ABDOULAYE (2001b), Diaspora, villageoise et développement local en Afrique: Le cas de Thilonge association développement. *Hommes et Immigrations* 1229: 96107.

KERRI, JAMES NWANNUKWU (1976), Studying voluntary associations as adaptive machanisms: A review of anthropological perspectives. *Current Anthropology* 171: 23-47.

KIERNAN, J.P. (1974), Where Zionists draw the line: A study of religious exclusiveness in an African Township. *African Studies* 33(2): 79-90.

KIERNAN, J.P. (1988), The other side of the coin: The conversion of money to religious purposes in zulu zionist churches. *Man* 23(3): 453-468.

KIMMERLE, HEINZ (2000), Book review of African philosophy through ubuntu by Magoke B. Ramoe, Harare, Mond Books, 1999. *African Philosophy* 13(2): 189-197.

KOKOALI, G.M. (1986), *Umgalelo and the failure of the church? A study in voluntary associations in Mbekweni, Paarl*. M.A. thesis, University of Cape Town.

KUCKERTZ, HEINZ (1997), *Ukuhlonipa* as idiom of moral reasoning in Mpondo. *African Studies* (Special Issue: Culture and the common place; Antropological essays in honour of David Hammond-Tooke, edited by P. McAllister): 311-348.

KUPER, ADAM (1982), *Wives for cattle: Bridewealth and marriage in Southern Africa*. London, Boston, Melbourne and Henley: Routledge and Kegan Paul.

KUPER, ADAM (1995), Comments. *Current Anthropology* 36(3): 424-426.

KUPER, ADAM(1997), The academic frontier: History and social anthropology in South Africa. *African Studies* (Special Issue: Culture and the common place: Antropological essays in donour of David Hammond-Tooke, edited by P. McAllister): 69-84.

KUPER, HILDA & SELMA KAPLAN (1944), Voluntary associations in an urban township. *African Studies* 3: 178-186.

LAMONT, MICHELE (1992), *Money, morals, and manners: The culture of the French and American upper-middle class.* Chicago and London: University of Chicago Press.

LAUBSCHER, B.J.F. (1959), *Sex, custom and psychopathology: A study of South African pagan natives*. London: Routledge.

LAUGHLIN, CHARLES D. (1974), Deprivation and reciprocity. *Man* 9(3): 380-396.

LECLERC-MADLALA, SUZANNE (1997), Infect one, infect all: Zulu youth response to the AIDS epidemic in South Africa. *Medical Anthropology* 17: 363-380.

LEE, REBEKAH (1999), *African women, urban areas and the development of the apartheid state: The case of Cape Town, 1945-1970.* M.Phil thesis, University of Oxford.

LEEUWENBERG, J. (1977), *Transkei: A study in economic regression.* London: The Africa Bureau.

LEFTWITCH, ADRIAN (1994), Governance, the state and the politics of development. *Development and Change* 25: 363-386.

LI, TANIA MURRAY (1999), Compromising power: Development, culture, and rule in Indonesia. *Cultural Anthropology* 14(3): 295-322.

LONGMORE, LAURA (1959), *The dispossesed: A study of the sex-life of Bantu women in urban areas in and around Johannesburg*. London: Jonathan Cape.

LONT, HOTZE (2000a), More money, more autonomy? Women and credit in a Javanese urban community. *Indonesia* 70: 83-100.

LONT, HOTZE (2000b), Finding the right balance: Financial self-help organizations as sources of security and insecurity in urban Indonesia. *International Review of Social History* 45: 159-177.

LONT, HOTZE (2002), *Juggling money in Yogyakarta: Financial self-help organisations and the quest for security.* PhD thesis, University of Amsterdam.

LONT, HOTZE & OTTO HOSPES, eds. (2004), *Livelihood & microfinance: Anthropological and sociological perspectives on savings and debt.* Delft: Eburon.

LUKHELE, ANDREW KEHLA (1990), *Stokvels in South Africa: Informal savings schemes by Blacks for the Black Community.* Johannesburg: Amagi Books.

MAGER, ANNE KELK (1999), *Gender and the making of a South African Bantustan: A social history of the Ciskei, 1945-1959.* Oxford and Cape Town: James Currey and David Philip.

MAGLIOLO, JACQUES (1998), Changes for funeral schemes. In: *Mail and Guardian.*

MAGUBANE, B. (1973), The "Xhosa" in town, revisited urban social anthropology; A failure of method and theory. *American Anthropologist* 75(5): 1701-1715.

MASAKHANE (1995), *Home truths*. Brochure.

MASEKO, B. (1991), *Mamlambo and other stories*. Johannesburg: COSAW.

MASQUELIER, ADELINE (1995), Consumption, prostitution, and reproduction: The poetics of sweetness in *bori*. *American Ethnologist* 22(4): 883-906.

MASUKU, LOUIS (1995), The Zimbabwean burial societies. In: M. Mandani & E. Wamba-dia-Wamba, eds., *African studies in social movements and democracy*, pp. 279-308. Oxford: CODESRIA.

MAUSS, MARCEL (1954), *The gift: Forms and functions of exchange in archaic societies*. London: Cohen and West.

MAYER, PHILIP & IONA MAYER (1974), *Townsmen or tribesmen: Conservatism and the process of urbanization in a South African city.* Cape Town, London, New York, Toronto: Oxford University Press.

MBIGI, LOVEMORE (1997), *Ubuntu: The African dream in management.* Randburg: Knowledge Resources.

MCALLISTER, PATRICK (1980), Work, homestead and the shades: The ritual interpretation of labour migration among the Gcaleka. In: P. Mayer, ed., *Black villagers in an industrial society: Anthropological perspectives on labour migration in South Africa*, pp. 205-253. Cape Town: Oxford University Press.

MCALLISTER, PATRICK (1985), Beasts to beer pots-migrant labour and ritual change in Willowvale District, Transkei. *African Studies* 44(2): 122-135.

MCALLISTER, PATRICK (1996), Traditional settlement, cultural identity and rural development in the Transkei. In: P. Blunt & D.M. Warren, eds., *Indigenous organizations and development*, pp. 7-20. London: Intermediate Technology Publications.

MCALLISTER, PATRICK (1997), *Ritual and social practice in the Transkei.* (Special Issue: Culture and the common place: Antropological essays in honour of David Hammond-Tooke, edited by P. McAllister): 279-309.

MCALLISTER, PATRICK (2000), *Maize yields in the Transkei: How productive is subsistence cultivation*? Cape Town: University of the Western Cape, School of Government, Programme for Land and Agrarian Studies, Occasional Paper Series: Land Reform and Agrarian Change in Southern Africa.

MCALLISTER, PATRICK & D. DELIWE (1994), *Youth in the Transkei: The demise of traditional youth associations and the development of new forms of association and activity, 1975-1993*: Grahamstown: Rhodes University, Institute for Social Economic Research (ISER).

MCGREGOR, ROBIN (1989), Cash in hand. *Leadership* 8(8): 121-126.

MCNAMARA, J. K. (1980), Brothers and work mates: Home friends networks in the social life of black migrant workers in a gold mine hostel. In: P. Mayer, ed., *Black villagers in an industrial society: Anthropological perspectives on labour migration in South Africa*, pp. 305-340. Cape Town: Oxford University Press.

MEILLASSOUX, CLAUDE (1968), *Urbanization of an African community: Voluntary associations in Bamako*. Seattle and London: University of Washington Press.

VAN DER MERWE, P.H.C. (1996), *Die Stokvel: 'n ondernemingsregtelijke studie.* Volume 26. Bloemfontein: Universiteit van die Oranje-Vrystaat.

MEYER, BIRGIT (1995), 'Delivered from the powers of darkness': Confessions of satanic riches in christian Ghana. *Africa* 65(2): 236-255.

MEYER, BIRGIT (1998), *Visions of blood, sex and money: Fantasy spaces in popular Ghanaian cinema.* Paper Presented to the Workshop 'An anthropology of the imagination or an imaginative anthropology?' at the EASA-conference, Frankfurt, 1998.

MEYER, BIRGIT (1999), *Translating the devil: Religion and modernity among the Ewe in Ghana*. London: Edinburgh University Press.

MIRACLE, MARVIN P., DIANE S. MIRACLE & LAURIE COHEN (1980), Informal savings mobilization in Africa. *Economic development and cultural change* 28(4): 701-724.

MISZTAL, BARBARA (1996), *Trust in modern society: The search for the bases of social order*. Cambridge: Polity Press.

MOLEFE, S.F. (1996), An overview of the characteristics of self-help organisations amongst blacks in South Africa – A historical perspective. *Social Work/Maatskaplike Werk* 32(2): 173-178.

MOODIE, T. DUNBAR (WITH VIVIENNE NDATSHE & BRITISH SIBUYI) (1988), Migrancy and male sexuality on the South African gold mines. *Journal of Southern African Studies* 14(2): 228-256.

MOODIE, T. DUNBAR (WITH VIVIENNE NDATSHE) (1994), *Going for gold: Men, mines, and migration*. Volume 51. Berkeley and Los Angeles: University of California Press.

MOODLEY, LOSHINI (1995), Three stokvel clubs in the urban black township of KwaNdangezi, Natal. *Development Southern Africa* 12(3): 361-366.

MOORE, SALLY FALK (1999), Reflections on the Comaroff lecture. *American Ethnology* 26(2): 304-306.

MOSER, CAROLINE O. N. (1998), The asset vulnerability framework: Reassessing urban poverty reduction strategies. *World Development* 26(1): 1-19.

MOURITSEN, P. (2003), What's the civil in civil society? Robert Putnam, Italy and the republican tradition. *Political Studies* 51(4): 650-668.

NAUTA, WIEBE (2001), *The implications of freedom: The changing role of land sector NGOs in a transforming South Africa*. PhD thesis, Free University, Amsterdam.

NIEHAUS, ISAK (1994), Disharmonious spouses and harmonious siblings; conceptualising household formation among urban residents in Qwaqwa. *African Studies* 53(1): 115-135.

NIEHAUS, ISAK (2000), Coins for blood and blood for coins: From sacrifice to ritual murder in the South African lowveld, 1930-2000. *Etnofoor* 13(2): 31-54.

NIEHAUS, ISAK (2001), *Witchcraft, power and politics: Exploring the occult in the South African lowveld*. London and Cape Town: Pluto Press and David Philip.

OJWANG, J.B. & J.N.K. MUGAMBI, ed., (1989), *The S.M. Otieno case: Death and burial in modern Kenia*. Nairobi: Nairobi University Press.

OKAFOR, STEPHEN O. (1982), Bantu Philosophy: Placide tempels revisited. *Journal of Religion in Africa* 13(2): 83-100.

OLIVER-EVANS, CERIDWEN (1993), *Employment and urbanisation: The impact of the abolition of influx control in the Western Cape*. Cape Town: Southern Africa Labour and Development Research Unit.

OMER-COOPER, J.D. (1994), *History of Southern Africa*. London: David Phillip, James Curry.

PEIRES, J.B. (1989), *The dead will arise: Mangqawuse and the great Xhosa cattle-killing movement 1856-7*. Johannesburg: Ravan Press.

PHILLIPS, RAY E. (1977) [1937], *The Bantu in the City: A study of cultural adjustment on the Witwatersrand*. Lovedale: Lovedale Press.

PUTNAM, ROBERT D. (1993), *Making democracy work: Civic traditions in modern Italy*. Princeton: Princeton University Press.

PUTNAM, ROBERT D. (2000), *Bowling alone: The collapse and revival of an american community*. New York, London: Simon and Shuster.

RAHMAN, SAYEEDA (1997), Reaching the unreached. *The Unesco Courier* (January): 10-11.

RAHMAN, SAYEEDA (1999), Micro-credit initiatives for equitable and sustainable development: Who pays? *World Development* 27(1): 67-82.

RAMPHELE, MAMPHELA (1989), The dynamics of gender politics in the hostels of Cape Town: Another legacy of the South African migrant labour system. *Journal of Southern African Studies* 15(3): 393-414.

REINKE, JENS (1999), Does solidarity pay? The case of the small enterprise foundation, South Africa. *Development and Change* 29(3): 553-576.

REIS, ELISA P. (1998), Banfield's amoral familism revisited: Implications of high inequality structures for civil society. In: J.C. Alexander, ed., *Real civil societies: Dilemmas of institutionalization*, pp. 21-39. London: Sage.

REYNOLDS, PAMELA (1989), *Childhood in crossroads: Cognition and society in South Africa*. Cape Town and Johannesburg: David Philip.

RICHARDS, AUDREY (1951), *Land, labour and diet in Northern Rhodesia: An economic study of the Bemba tribe*. London, New York, Toronto: Oxford University Press.

ROBERTSON, M.K. (1990), Black land tenure: Disabilities and some rights. In: A.J. Rycroft, A.J. Boulle, M.K. Robertson & P.R. Spiller, eds., *Race and the law in South Africa*, pp. 119-135. Cape Town: Juta and Co.

ROSS, FIONA (1990), *Strategies against patriarchy: Women and rotating credit associations*. B.Sc.Hons., University of Cape Town.

ROSS, ROBERT (1999), *A concise history of South Africa*. Cambridge: Cambridge University Press.

ROTHSTEIN, BO (2000), Trust, social dilemmas and collective memories. *Journal of Theoretical Politics* 12(4): 477-501.

ROWLANDS, MICHAEL (1995), Looking at financial landscapes: A contextual analysis. In: S. Ardener & S. Burman, eds., *Money-go-rounds: The importance of rotating savings and credit associations for women*, pp. 111-124. Oxford/Washington D.C.: Berg.

SAIRR (1998), *1997/1998 Survey*. Johannesburg: South African Institute of Race Relations.

SAPS (1998), *Quarterly crime report* 3/98 South African Police Service.

SAPS (2000), Specific crimes per 100,000 of the population for the provinces during the period January to December 1999: SAPS.

SAS (1997), *South African statistics 1995*. Pretoria: Central Statistical Service.

SCHEPER-HUGHES, NANCY (1995), The primacy of the ethical; propositions for a militant anthropology. *Current Anthropology* 36(3): 409-440.

SCHOFFELEERS, MATTHEW (1988), Black and African theology in Southern Africa: A controversy re-examined. *Journal of Religion in Africa* xviii(2): 99-124.

SCHROEDER, RICHARD A. (1999), Community, forestry and conditionality in The Gambia. *Africa* 69(1): 1-22.

SCOFIELD, RUPERT (1997), Village banking: A report from 5 countries. *The Unesco Courier* (January): 32-36.

SCOTT, JAMES C. (1985), *Weapons of the weak: Every day forms of peasant resistance.* New Haven: Yale University Press.

SCOTT, JAMES C. (1998), *Seeing like a state: How certain schemes to improve the human condition have failed.* New Haven and London: Yale University Press.

SEEKINGS, JEREMY (1992), Civic organisations in South African townships. *South African Review* 6: 216-238.

SHAPERA, J. (1956), *Government and politics in tribal societies.* London: Watts.

SHARP, JOHN S. & ANDREW D. SPIEGEL (1985), Vulerability to impoverishment in South African rural areas: The erosion of kinship and neighbourhood as social resources. *Africa* 55(2): 133-152.

SHIPTON, PARKER (1995), How Gambians save: Culture and economic strategy at an ethnic crossroads. In: J.I. Guyer, ed., *Money matters: Instability, values and social payments in the modern history of West African Communities*, pp. 245-276. Portsmouth and London: Heinemann and James Currey.

SIMMEL, GEORG (1990), *The philosophy of money.* London/New York: Routledge.

SINDANE, J. & I. LIEBENBERG (2000), Reconstruction and the reciprocal other: The philosophical practice of ubuntu and democracy in African society. *Politeia* 19(3): 31-46.

SLUKA, JEFFREY A.(1990), Participant observation in violent docial contexts. *Human Organization* 49(2): 114-126.

SLUKA, JEFFREY A. (1995), Reflections on managing danger in fieldwork: Dangerous anthropology in Belfast. In: C. Nordstrom & A.C.G.M. Robben, eds., *Fieldwork under fire: Contemporary studies of violence and survival*, pp. 276-294. Berkeley, Los Angeles, London: University of California Press.

SMELSER, NEIL J. (1998), The rational and the ambivalent in the social sciences; 1997 Presidential Address. *American Sociological Review* 63: 1-16.

SMETS, PEER (2000), ROSCAs as a source of housing finance for the urban poor: An analysis of self-help practices from Hyderabad, India. *Community Development Journal* 35(1): 16-30.

SMETS, PEER (2002), *Housing finance and the urban poor: Building and financing low-income housing in Hyderebad, India.* PhD thesis, Free University, Amsterdam..

SMETS, PEER & ERIK BÄHRE (2004 ), When coercion takes over: The limits of social capital in microfinance schemes. In: H. Lont & O. Hospes, eds., *Livelihood and microfinance: Anthropological and sociological perspectives on savings and debt*, pp. 215-236. Dewlft: Eburon.

SPIEGEL, ANDREW (1987), Dispersing dependants: A response to the exigencies of labour migration in rural Transkei. In: J. Eades, ed., *Migrants, workers, and the social orderASA Monographs.* London and New York: Tavistock Publications.

SZTOMPKA, PIOTR (1999), *Trust: A sociological theory.* Cambridge: Cambridge University Press.

TAUSSIG, MICHAEL (1980), *The devil and commodity fetishism in South America.* Chapel Hill: University of California Press.

TAUSSIG, MICHAEL (1995), The sun gives without receiving: An old story. *Comparative Studies in Society and History* 37(2): 368-398.

TEMPELS, PLACIED P. (1946), *Bantoe-filosofie*. Antwerpen: De Sikkel.

THODEN VAN VELZEN, H.U.E. (1973), Robinson Crusoe and Friday: Strenght and weakness of the big man paradigm. *Man* 8(4): 592-612.

THODEN VAN VELZEN, H.U.E. (1995), Revenants that cannot be shaken: Collective fantasies in a Maroon society. *American Anthropologist* 97(4): 722-732.

THODEN VAN VELZEN, H.U.E. & W. VAN WETERING (1991), *The great father and the danger: Religious cults, material forces, and collective fantasies in the world of the Surinamese Maroons*. Leiden: KITLV Press.

THOMAS, ELMAR (1991), Rotating credit associations in Cape Town. In: E.P.-W.a.C. Rogerson, ed., *South Africa's informal economy*, pp. 290-304. Cape Town: Oxford University Press.

THORNTON, ROBERT & M RAMPHELE (1988), The quest for community. In: E. Boonzaier & J. Sharp, eds., *South African keywords: The uses and abuses of political concepts*, pp. 29-39. Cape Town and Johannesburg: David Philip.

TUSENIUS, R (1998), African and South Africa: Ready for a renaissance. *Management Today* 14(5): 16-21.

VAIL, LEROY (1989), Introduction: Ethnicity in Southern African History. In: L. Vail, ed., *The creation of tribalism in Southern Africa*, pp. 1-21. London: Currey.

VAN DE PORT, MATTIJS (1998), *Gypsies, wars and other instances of the wild: Civilisation and its discontent in a Serbian town*. Amsterdam: Amsterdam University Press.

VAN DE PORT, MATTIJS (1999),'It takes a Serb to know a Serb': Uncovering the roots of obstinate otherness in Serbia. *Critique of Anthropology* 19(1): 7-30.

VAN DER GEEST, SJAAK (1997), Money and respect: The changing value of old age in rural Ghana. *Africa* 67(4): 534-559.

VAN DER LINDEN, JAN (1997), On popular participation in a culture of patronage; patrons and grassroots organization in a sites and services project in Hyderabad, Pakistan. *Environment and Urbanization* 9(1): 81-90.

VAN DER LINDEN, M., ed. 1996), *Social security mutualism: The comparative history of mutual benefit societies*. Bern: Peter Lang.

VAN DER LINDEN, M. & J. SLUIJS, eds. (1996), *Onderlinge hulpfondsen: Historische en etnografische essays*. Amsterdam: IISG.VAN KESSEL, INEKE (2000), *'Beyond our wildest dreams': The United Democratic Front and the transformation of South Africa.* Charlottesville: University Press of Virginia.

VAN KESSEL, INEKE (2001), De agenda van de Afrikaanse renaissance: Modernisering, traditionalisering of afrikanisering? *Internationale Spectator* 55(4): 171-175.

VAN WETERING, INEKE (1987), Informal supportive networks: Quasi-kin groups, religion and social order among Surinam Creoles in the Netherlands. *The Netherlands Journal of Sociology* 23(2): 92-101.

VAN WETERING, INEKE (1999), ROSCAs, ethnicity and strategy: Surinamese Creole women's savings clubs in Amsterdam. In: R. Barot, H. Bradley & S. Fenton, eds., *Ethnicity, gender and social change*, pp. 60-77. Houndsmill: Macmillian.

VEBLEN, T (1899), The theory of the leisure class. In: R. Tilman, ed., *A Veblan treasury: From leisure class to war, peace, and capitalism*, pp. 3-100. London: M.E. Sharp.

VELEZ-IBAÑEZ, CARLOS G. (1983), *Bonds of mutual trust: The cultural system of rotating credit associations among urban Mexicans and Chicanos*. New Brunswick, New Jersey: Rutgers University Press.

VERDERY, KATHERINE (1999), *The political lives of dead bodies, Reburial and postsocialist change*. New York: Colombia University Press.

VERHOEF, GRIETJIE (2001), Informal financial service institutions for survival: African women and stokvels in urban South Africa, 1930-1998. *Enterprise and Society* 2(2): 259-296.

VÖLKER, BEATE & HENK FLAP (1995), The effects of institutional transformation on personal networks: East Germany, four years later. *Netherlands Journal of Social Sciences* 31(2): 87-110.

WACQUANT, LOÏC J.D. (1997), Elias in the dark ghetto. *Amsterdams Sociologisch Tijdschrift* 24(3/4): 340-347

WEBB, NICHOLAS (1989), *Informal credit markets in Cape Town, Guguletu: A Case Study*. B.A. Hons., University of Cape Town.

WEISS, BRAD (1993), 'Buying her grave': Money, movement and Aids in North-West Tanzania. *Africa* 63(1): 19-35.

WILLIAMS, TERRY *et al.* (1992), Personal safety in dangerous places. *Journal of Contemporary Ethnography* 21(3): 343-374.

WILSON, FRANCIS (1972), *Migrant labour*. Johannesburg: South African Council of Churches and SPRO-CAS.

WILSON, FRANCIS & M. RAMPHELE (1994), *Uprooting poverty: The South African challenge*. Cape Town and Johannesburg: David Philip.

WILSON, MONICA & ARCHIE MAFEJE (1963), *Langa: A study of social groups in an African township*. Cape Town, London, New York: Oxford University Press.

WILSON, MONICA *et al.* (1952), *Social structure*. Keiskammahoek Rural Survey iii.

WINNICOTT, D.W. (1991), *Playing and reality*. London and New York: Routledge.

WOLF, ERIC (1982), *Europe and the people without history*. Berkeley, Los Angeles, London: University of California Press.

WOLF, ERIC (1999), *Envisioning power: Ideologies of dominance and crisis*. Los Angeles, London: University of Califorina Press.

WOOLCOCK, MICHAEL (1998), Social capital and economic development: Toward a theoretical synthesis and policy framework. *Theory and Society* 27: 151-208.

ZELIZER, VIVIANA A. (1994), *The social meaning of money*. New York: Basic Books.

# Newspapers

*Cape Times*

1998 Western Cape is crime hot spot: SA winning war on violent crime. In *Cape Times*.

*Mail and Guardian*

1998a Whatever happened to the dream of low-cost housing? In *Mail and Guardian*, pp. 4-5.

1998b UDM wants Cape peace summit. In *Mail and Guardian*.

2001 Rainbow nation or Tower of Babel?, Vol. 2001: *Mail and Guardian online*.

# Index

# AFRIKA-STUDIECENTRUM SERIES

ISSN 1570–9310

1. Konings, P. and Nyamnjoh, F.B. *Negotiating an Anglophone Identity.* A Study of the Politics of Recognition and Representation in Cameroon. 2003. ISBN 90 04 13295 3
2. Wels, H. *Private Wildlife Conservation in Zimbabwe.* Joint Ventures and Reciprocity. 2003. ISBN 90 04 13697 5.
3. Spierenburg, M.J. *Strangers, Spirits and Land Reforms.* Conflicts about Land in Dande, Northern Zimbabwe. 2004. ISBN 90 04 13657 5.
4. Müller, T.R. *The Making of Elite Women.* Revolution and Nation Building in Eritrea. 2005. ISBN 90 04 14287 8.
5. Ntsebeza, L. *Democracy Compromised.* Chiefs and the politics of the land in South Africa. 2005. ISBN 90 04 14482 X.
6. Evers, S., Spierenburg, M. and Wels, H. *Competing Jurisdictions.* Settling land claims in Africa. 2005. ISBN 90 04 14780 2.
7. Foeken, D. "*To Subsidise My Income*". Urban Farming in an East-African Town. 2006. ISBN-13: 978-90-04-15202-1, ISBN-10: 90-04-15202-4.
8. Bähre, E. *Money and Violence.* Financial Self-Help Groups in a South African Township. 2007. ISBN-13: 978 90 04 15726 2, ISBN-10: 90 04 15726 3

www.ingramcontent.com/pod-product-compliance
Lightning Source LLC
Chambersburg PA
CBHW061211240926
51846CB00006B/1181
*9789004157262*